How the Mind Explains Behavior

How the Mind Explains Behavior

Folk Explanations, Meaning, and Social Interaction

Bertram F. Malle

A Bradford Book
The MIT Press
Cambridge, Massachusetts
London, England

MIT Press books may be purchased at special quantity discounts for business or sales promotional use. For information, please email special_sales@mitpress.mit.edu or write to Special Sales Department, The MIT Press, 5 Cambridge Center, Cambridge, MA 02142.

This book was set in Stone Sans and Stone Serif by Graphic Composition, Inc., and was printed and bound in the United States of America.

Library of Congress Cataloging-in-Publication Data

Malle, Bertram F.
 How the mind explains behavior : folk explanations, meaning, and social interaction / Bertram F. Malle.
   p. cm.
"A Bradford book."
Includes bibliographical references and index.
ISBN 0-262-13445-4 (hc : alk. paper)
1. Attribution (Social psychology). I. Title
HM1076.M35 2004

2004044831

10 9 8 7 6 5 4 3 2 1

Contents

Preface

The ideas that found expression here were first inspired by Jerry Bruner's magnificent book *Acts of Meaning* and a seminar held by Fred Dretske and Michael Bratman at Stanford University on action explanation. Thereafter, nothing in the attribution literature meant quite the same for me again.

Along the way, many people provided support, inspiration, and helped keep up my persistence: Laura Carstensen, Delia Cioffi, Herb Clark, Carol Dweck, Alison Gopnik, Al Hastorf, Len Horowitz, Joshua Knobe, Lara London, Tom Lyon, Al Mele, Ronaldo Mendoza, Walter Mischel, Lee Ross, Bernie Weiner, and H. G. Zilian. Al Mele and Dan Ames read the entire manuscript, and Joshua Knobe most of it, and all offered invaluable observations, criticism, and suggestions. Many other people read portions of this book or some of its earlier installments and provided helpful feedback: Craig Anderson, Holly Arrow, Garth Fletcher, Dave Hamilton, Sara Hodges, John McClure, and Mick Rothbart. (I am sorry to those I am forgetting here; they made their mark nonetheless.) Without my collaborators over the years, too, this work would not have been possible: Dare Baldwin, Tom Givón, Bill Ickes, Shua Knobe, Lou Moses, Sarah Nelson, Gale Pearce, and Matt O'Laughlin. The Society of Experimental Social Psychology, the National Science Foundation, and Marilynn Brewer stepped in at opportune times when a boost in confidence was needed.

This book was begun during a sabbatical leave from the University of Oregon in gorgeous New Zealand, in Garth Fletcher's house, surrounded by his generosity. It was continued during visits to Victoria University of Wellington (hosted by John McClure), Macquarie University, Sydney (Max Coltheart), the University of Melbourne (Yoshi Kashima), Flinders University, Adelaide (Neil Brewer), and the Barossa Valley, where I reveled in Lynn and

Ian Leader-Elliott's hospitality. The book was finally completed in beautiful Eugene, just when the Japanese maples leafed out in our garden.

I am grateful to New Zealand artist John Drawbridge, who generously allowed me to use his oil painting *Double Portrait* for the cover of the book. I discovered the beauty of his work in an art exhibition held at the City Gallery of Wellington and have been held captive by it since. Many thanks also to Greg O'Brien who curated the exhibition and contacted John Drawbridge on my behalf.

This book is dedicated to my parents, whose trust, love, and support enabled all this, and to my wife Lara, who has been enormously patient and encouraging during the time of writing and who helps, at all times, with the general task of finding meaning.

Introduction

Every day we are faced with human behavior that is puzzling and that we would like to understand. Why was the fellow in the coffee shop smiling? Why does my longtime friend no longer call? Why did the policemen beat the suspect? Answers to these questions come in the form of behavior explanations, which are a fundamental tool of social cognition and thus part of the cognitive apparatus with which humans make sense of themselves, other people, and the complexities of the social world. Without the ability to construct explanations, human social behavior would be a series of actions and reactions, driven mostly by power and resources. With behavior explanations, social behavior can be highly complex and nuanced yet still comprehensible, allowing for often impressively coordinated interactions that rely on mutual understanding and attunement. Behavior explanations help people find meaning in social interaction—from a flirting glance to a quirky apology, from a friend's well-meaning gibe to a colleague's disguised provocation.

But behavior explanations are not only in the mind, furnishing insight, understanding, and meaning for participants and observers of social interaction. Behavior explanations are also overt verbal actions used for social purposes, and in particular for managing ongoing interactions. When asked why they did something, people verbally explain their behavior and thereby facilitate interpersonal coordination, or they try to save face, justifying a questionable action. Similarly, people offer explanations for others' behavior, sometimes making the agent look good, sometimes not.

Thus, behavior explanations are in the mind when people try to find meaning in the stream of behaviors and events around them, and behavior explanations are social actions when people use them for persuasion, communication, and impression management.

This book attempts to unite these two aspects of explanation within a comprehensive theoretical model that also illuminates why the two aspects exist and why they are intimately tied to each other. In presenting this model, I hope to advance our knowledge and understanding of behavior explanations in general and of the central role they play in both social cognition and social interaction. Equally important, I hope to instill in the reader the kind of awe that I have gained for the sophisticated and subtle patterns of folk behavior explanation. Next to language and self-consciousness, social cognition—and behavior explanation as one of its major tools—is arguably the most astounding advance of human evolution, and it deserves both detailed scientific attention and profound admiration.

But the informed reader may wonder why we need another theory of behavior explanation. Don't we have enough attribution theories already? Indeed, the phenomenon of behavior explanation has been studied under the heading of attribution theory for a long time and by many researchers. However, the "attribution" label refers to a variety of phenomena, including not only authentic explanations but also trait inferences, causal judgments, and responsibility ascriptions. I will argue that theories of the latter phenomena (especially of trait inferences) have repeatedly and mistakenly been applied to the phenomenon of behavior explanations, neglecting both the unique conceptual framework that underlies these explanations and their dual nature as meaning-making and interaction-managing tools. This is then the reason why we need a new theory: Because there hasn't been one offered that genuinely accounts for behavior explanations.

To support this historical claim, I devote chapter 1 to a review of the major theories of attribution and attempt to clarify why behavior explanations have somehow been mistaken for trait inferences or simple causal judgments. Chapter 1 also assembles some of the insights that the attribution tradition and its successors have offered—insights without which no theory of behavior explanations would be possible. Readers from outside social psychology might save this chapter for later, as the actual theoretical contributions starting in chapter 2 are independent of the historical argument. Social psychologists, I hope, will read this chapter with an open mind, as I paint a picture of attribution research that differs significantly from that found in traditional textbooks. I have tried to be historically accurate, using many direct quotes to illustrate what past attribution scholars have really said, but whether this will suffice to change the textbook portrayal of attribution theory remains to be seen.

The theory of behavior explanations I propose characterizes explanations as deeply embedded in people's conceptual framework of mind and behavior (often called *theory of mind*). In fact, it is by virtue of this conceptual framework that humans can explain behavior at all. Thus, in chapter 2, I devote significant attention to the nature, function, and origins of theory of mind and the place of behavior explanations within it. This discussion draws heavily on extant developmental, clinical, philosophical, and evolutionary work but ties these different strands together into an integrated foundation for the study of behavior explanations.

In chapter 3 I turn to the antecedents of behavior explanations—when and for what purposes people form explanations. I explore what people gain when they find "meaning" in a behavior through private (in-the-mind) explanations and when they manage interactions through communicative explanations. I also discuss why people so often wonder about other people's actions but about their own experiences and what implications this pattern might have for the language of human behavior.

The introduction of the actual theory of behavior explanation spans two chapters. Chapter 4 focuses on the conceptual structure of explanations—the concepts of intentionality and mental states that fundamentally shape the way humans see, interpret, and respond to behavior. This conceptual structure gives rise to four distinct modes of explanation and significant features of each mode. Chapter 5 examines the processes involved in the actual construction of explanations, including the choices between multiple modes and features of explanation, the psychological determinants of these choices, and the cognitive processes that underlie the selection of specific explanations in specific contexts.

The theory of behavior explanations is then applied to a number of fascinating questions. Chapter 6 analyzes the significant linguistic, communicative, and interpersonal aspects of behavior explanations—aspects that are often ignored by traditional person–situation models of attribution. In particular, I examine the specific linguistic tools by which behaviors and their explanations get expressed and the broader question of how explanations as communicative acts are used for social, impression-managing purposes.

Chapter 7 takes up the accepted insight that explanations of one's own behavior differ from explanations of other people's behavior. But exactly how

they differ, and why, are questions that are answered very differently by the
folk-conceptual theory of explanation and traditional attribution theory. In
fact, whereas we can find reliable actor–observer asymmetries in explanatory parameters described by the folk-conceptual theory, the seemingly consistent body of research on person–situation differences between actors and
observers may well be based on misinterpretations of the evidence.

Another fascinating question concerns potential differences in the way
people explain individual persons' behaviors and whole groups' behaviors
(chapter 8). The folk-conceptual theory of explanation allows us to develop
a solid prediction about the nature of differences between individual and
group behavior explanations, and the data so far support this prediction.
Moreover, a detailed inspection of how explanations are used in propaganda
supporting or disparaging various groups reveals once more the interplay of
the meaning-finding and impression-managing aspects of explanations.

Chapter 9 begins with a summary of the insights gained, especially about
the multiple functions of behavior explanations and the key role of a theory
of mind therein. I then highlight the relative strengths of folk-conceptual
theory over traditional attribution theory but also enumerate open questions that the folk-conceptual theory currently does not answer. I close with
a number of research applications of this theory, from psychopathology to
intimate relationships to political conflict.

1 History: Past Research on Attribution and Behavior Explanation

Many reviews have been written about the productive and well-known area of attribution theory (e.g., Shaver 1975; Fiske and Taylor 1991; Försterling 2001; D. T. Gilbert 1998; Hastorf Schneider, and Polefka 1970; Kelley and Michela 1980; Ross and Fletcher 1985; Weary, Stanley, and Harvey 1989). Some of these reviews incorporate critical thoughts about the classic theories but, by and large, they represent the "standard view" of attribution theory, both in terms of its history and its substantial claims. A composite sketch of this standard view looks something like this:

1. Heider (1958) argued that people try to identify the dispositional properties that underlie observed behavior and do so by attributing behavior either to external (situational) or internal (dispositional) causes.

2. Jones and Davis (1965) built on Heider and focused on the conditions under which people observe an agent's behavior and either do or do not attribute a correspondent disposition to the agent. Later, other researchers elaborated on Jones and Davis's approach by studying the precise cognitive processes that underlie dispositional attributions.

3. Kelley (1967) theorized in detail about the information processing people engage in when explaining social events. His model describes the rational analysis of patterns of covariation among three elements—a *person* acting toward a *stimulus* in particular *circumstances*—and derives the conditions under which people make attributions to the person or the stimulus.

4. In studying attributions for achievement outcomes, Weiner and colleagues (1972) found that people rely not only on the person–situation dimension of causality but also on the dimensions of stability and controllability, and these three-dimensional causal judgments mediate some of people's emotions and motivations in response to social outcomes.

In the present chapter, I contrast this standard view with quotes and interpretations of the classic attribution works by Heider (1958), Jones and Davis
(1965), and Kelley (1967), complemented to a smaller extent by analyses of
some of the more recent work on explanations. Because there are so many
excellent reviews available on the standard view, I will spend relatively little
time recounting it. My goal is, rather, to point out those aspects of prior attribution theories that are not generally emphasized. In so doing I will point
to what seem to me to be historical misunderstandings and theoretical difficulties that have not been adequately resolved. The subsequent chapters
then introduce a theory of behavior explanations that builds on previous
theories but also tries to remove some of their difficulties and, in particular,
tries to be a genuine theory of behavior explanations, not one of trait inferences, causal judgments, or responsibility ascriptions.

1.1   Attribution as Perception: Heider

Psychological research on attribution began with the work of Fritz Heider,
who developed models of attribution for both object perception and person
perception. His theory of object perception (first described in his 1920 dissertation) is rarely cited today, but it serves as the foundation for his later
theory of person perception, so I will briefly review it (see also Malle and
Ickes 2000).

1.1.1   Object Perception

Heider's early theorizing was an attempt to solve one of the core philosophical problems of phenomenology: the relation between sense qualities
and real objects. That is, Heider asked how it was possible that we take
sense qualities to be qualities of objects, given that sense qualities are "here"
in the mind, whereas object qualities are "out there" in the physical world.
Heider's answer began with the distinction between *things* (physical objects)
and the *media* by which things affect the perceiver (Heider 1920, 1925; see
also 1959). For example, a ticking watch (thing) causes systematic air vibra-
tions around it (medium), which in turn engage the eardrum (another
medium) and lead to perception. Heider argued that media have a considerable degree of variance but are shaped by the relative invariance of things.
The perceptual apparatus reconstructs things from their effects on the me-

dia, and Heider termed this reconstructive process *attribution*. In Heider's theory of object perception, then, attribution generates representations of the relatively invariant qualities of things from the characteristic variances they cause in their media. Perceivers faced with sensory data thus see the perceptual object as "out there" because they attribute the sensory data to their underlying causes in the world (Heider 1920).[1]

1.1.2 Person Perception, Dispositions, and Personal Causality

After his early work on object perception Heider turned to the domain of social interactions, wondering how people perceive each other in interaction and, especially, how they make sense of each other's behavior. Heider proposed that a process of attribution is also involved in *person perception,* but he recognized that person perception is more complex than object perception—due to the manifold observational data available and the manifold causes (e.g., beliefs, desires, emotions, traits) to which these data can be attributed. In addition, it was clear to Heider that persons are targets of perception very different from inanimate objects. Persons are "perceived as action centers and as such can do something to us. They can benefit or harm us intentionally, and we can benefit or harm them. Persons have abilities, wishes and sentiments; they can act purposefully, and can perceive or watch us" (1958, p. 21). Heider repeatedly refers here to the intentionality of persons, which he considered a core assumption in the conceptual framework that underlies social perception. With the help of such concepts as intentionality and the inference of wishes, purposes, sentiments, and other internal states, Heider argued, perceivers bring order to the massive stream of behavioral data.

Even though, in one sense, person perception is like object perception—a process of extracting invariance out of variance—Heider saw crucial differences between the two (and these differences are often glossed over by Heider interpreters). The first difference is that in the social domain, *variance* refers to the agent's behavior and *invariance* refers to the inferred perceptions, intentions, motives, traits, and sentiments, which are all relatively invariant against the stream of ongoing behavior. Subsequent attribution scholars often focused on only one type of invariance, namely traits, because they interpreted Heider's notion of *disposition* as referring to stable personality factors (i.e., traits, attitudes, or abilities).[2] But it was the agent's *motives* that occupied a special role in Heider's model: "The underlying causes of events, *especially the motives of other persons,* are the invariances of the environment that are relevant to [the perceiver]; they give meaning to what he experiences" (1958, p. 81; emphasis added). But even though Heider (1958) occasionally referred to traits and abilities when talking about dispositions (e.g., pp. 30, 80), he considered "motives, intentions, sentiments . . . the core processes which manifest themselves in overt behavior" (p. 34). In the study of social perception, then, Heider's terms *disposition* and *invariance* referred primarily to mental and motivational states, and the practice in social psychology of considering dispositions to be stable traits is quite different from Heider's original theory.

The second crucial difference between person perception and object perception is that when people perform a causal (i.e., "attributional") analysis of human behavior, their judgments of causality follow one of two conceptual models (ibid., chap. 4). The first is a model of *impersonal causality,* applied to unintentional human behaviors (such as sneezing or feeling pain) as well as physical events (such as stones rolling or leaves falling). The second is a model of *personal causality,* applied only to human agents who perform an intentional action (such as cleaning the kitchen or inviting someone to dinner). "Personal causality," Heider wrote, "refers to instances in which *p* causes *x* intentionally. That is to say, the action is purposive" (ibid., p. 100).

1.1.3   Heider and the Person–Situation Distinction

Ensuing attribution research set aside Heider's distinction between personal and impersonal causality and claimed instead that Heider had argued for a distinction between *person* (or internal) causes and *situation* (or external) causes of behavior.[3] That is, when people try to explain behavior, they attempt to find out whether the behavior was caused by factors internal to the person (e.g., mood, motives, personality) or by factors in the external situation (e.g., physical environment, other people). But even though Heider at times referred to these two classes of internal/person and external/situation causes (see below), the distinction he cared far more about was that between personal and impersonal causality, a distinction that refers to two kinds of behaviors (intentional and unintentional) and the different ways people think about them.

There are two problems associated with this misunderstanding that the personal–impersonal distinction is a person–situation distinction. First, not all internal causes fall under personal causality because, "unless intention ties together the cause–effect relations, we do not have a case of true personal causality" (Heider 1958, p. 100). Thus, those internal causes that do *not* involve intentions (e.g., tiredness, moods, emotions) belong to the impersonal class: "[E]ffects involving persons but not intentions . . . are more appropriately represented as cases of impersonal causality" (p. 101). A driving blunder due to tiredness, for example, was subsumed by Heider under impersonal causality but would be considered an internal or person factor within post–Heiderian attribution theory.

Second and far more important is the problem that researchers working with the person–situation distinction began to omit a major element of human social cognition: the distinction between intentional and unintentional behavior. Because it seemed so easy to classify *any* explanation as either referring to the person or the situation, researchers stopped tracking whether the behavior explained was actually intentional or unintentional—but that was exactly what the personal–impersonal distinction was supposed to capture. This omission mattered a great deal because the intentionality distinction plays an essential role in the interpretation and social control of behavior and in the evaluation of morality. The dichotomy between person and situation causes fails to capture all these important roles.

But why has it been believed that Heider proposed a person–situation dichotomy in attribution? One section in particular may have spawned this belief (ibid., 1958, pp. 82–84). There Heider endorsed Lewin's famous equation that characterizes any "action outcome" (the result of an action) as "dependent upon a combination of effective personal force and effective environmental force" (p. 82). As is clear from elaborations of this claim (pp. 83–87), Heider argued that for an action outcome to occur (which is sometimes just the performance of the action itself), there needs to be a concomitance of two elements: the agent's attempt to perform the action (*trying*) and supporting factors (*can*) that lie in the agent (e.g., ability, confidence) or in the environment (e.g., opportunity, luck, favorable conditions). Heider catalogued here the necessary elements that have to join together for an intentional action to succeed in producing its desired outcome—the "conditions of successful action" (p. 110). Consequently, when people point to the presence of these elements, they clarify what enabled the action outcome to be attained (Malle et al. 2000; McClure and Hilton 1997). Such *enabling factor explanations* answer the specific explanatory question of *how it was possible* that an action outcome was attained (see chapter 3 of this book).

The section in question thus expresses Heider's belief that people distinguish between internal and external causal factors *when they explain how action outcomes were attained.* Answers to this question can indeed refer to either person factors (e.g., effort and ability) or situation factors (e.g., task difficulty and luck), but there is no indication in the text that Heider thought people use the internal–external distinction when explaining behavior in general. On the contrary, Heider stated that people explain *why* a person is acting by referring to the "reasons behind the intention" (1958, p. 110; see also pp. 125–129). The contrast between these two types of explanations can be illustrated with the following passage from Daniel Gilbert (1998, p. 96):

If a pitcher who wishes to retire a batter (motivation) throws a burning fastball (action) directly into the wind (environmental influence), then the observer should conclude that the pitcher has a particularly strong arm (ability). If a batter tries to hit that ball (motivation) but fails (action), then the observer should conclude that the batter lacked coordination (ability) or was blinded by the sun (environmental influence).

The observer's reasoning in this passage is entirely focused on accounting for successful or failed outcomes; the question *why* the batter and the pitcher acted as they did is not answered by reference to either arm, wind, or sun. The why-question is in fact already answered by mentioning the pitcher's obvious desire to retire the batter and the batter's wish to hit the ball and get a run. As in virtually all cases of enabling factor explanations, in this case too, the question *why* the agent acted is not at issue (because the answer is obvious); what is at issue is the question *how the outcome was attained* (Malle et al. 2000).

In an interview with Bill Ickes (1976, p. 14), Heider explicitly distinguished between these two types of question, and hence between two types of explanation:

1 the attribution of *outcomes* to causal factors (i.e., enabling factor explanations);[4]

2. the attribution of *intentional actions* to the actor's motives (i.e., reasons for acting).

Heider himself never developed a model of motive attributions (or *reason explanations*), and he in fact felt that these explanations had not been adequately treated by contemporary attribution work (Ickes 1976, p. 14; see also Buss 1978; Fiske and Taylor 1991). What Heider did develop—in the passages and sections of his book that describe action attainment as a function of *trying* and *can*—was the core of a model of outcome attribution, and he felt that this issue was later advanced in Bernard Weiner's work (e.g., Weiner et al. 1972).

It seems likely, then, that scholars who claimed Heider proposed the external–internal dichotomy as the fundamental dimension of explanation in fact mistakenly applied Heider's model of outcome attribution to the domain of motive attribution or action explanation. The following passages from Hastorf et al. (1970) illustrate the confusion between the two types of explanation (indicated in square brackets):

Presumably the outcomes of action are caused by some combination of personal characteristics and environmental forces [outcome attribution]. The person may have done something because he had to do it . . . or because he wanted to do it [action explanation]. (p. 64)

When we infer that the combination of ability and effort was stronger than the external forces, we infer that internal causality was present [outcome attribution]. Only then do we say such things as "he did it because he wanted to" [action explanation]. (p. 89)

In both of these passages, the authors treat two different explanatory questions as if they were one and the same. The judgment whether "he did it because he wanted to" or "because he had to do it" clarifies the agent's motives for acting (by means of a reason explanation). These reasons can be given even before the agent tries to perform the action (because reasons explain the intention, whether or not it gets fulfilled). By contrast, the judgment as to whether ability, effort, or external forces enabled the action outcome clarifies how it was possible that the action outcome was attained (by means of an enabling factor explanation). Enabling explanations can be given only after the agent[5] tried to perform the action—if she succeeded, for example, one might say it was because of her ability.

Because these two explanation types—reason explanations (motive attributions) and enabling factor explanations (outcome attributions)—answer such different questions, it is unfortunate that the attribution literature after

Heider collapsed them into one (cf. Zuckerman 1978). What makes this collapse even more unfortunate is that only enabling factor explanations can be classified into the traditional internal–external (person–situation) scheme, whereas reason explanations make very different conceptual assumptions and have a very different linguistic surface (Malle 1999; Malle et al. 2000). Much confusion in the attribution literature resulted from this collapse, and I will propose an alternative theory in chapters 4 and 5.

1.1.4 Summary

The textbook view of Heider's attribution theory differs from the theoretical position Heider took in his 1958 book. Even though Heider's whole analysis was predicated on the distinction between *personal causality* (intentional events) and *impersonal causality* (unintentional events), he is consistently credited with introducing the person–situation dichotomy in attribution. Heider indeed claimed that people explain outcomes and all unintentional events by reference to causes (which can be located either in the person or the situation); but, more importantly, he claimed that people explain intentional events (cases of personal causality) by reference to reasons. The dichotomy between person and situation causes thus applies to some but not all modes of behavior explanation, with explanations of actions by reasons being the critical exception. Reason explanations, though very frequent in everyday life, were not treated in detail by Heider and, perhaps as a result, were long overlooked by attribution researchers.

1.2 Attribution as Trait Inference: Jones and Davis

Two years after its publication, Heider's (1958) attribution work was lauded in a book review by Harold Kelley (1960). However, attribution theory's launch toward public prominence came several years later, after Edward Jones and Keith Davis (1965) published their acclaimed "theory of correspondent inference."

1.2.1 Action Explanation versus Trait Inference

The first few pages of Jones and Davis's (1965) paper appeared to address just the issue that Heider had left open: exactly how people explain intentional action by means of motives and reasons. The authors wrote that their theory was attempting to account for:

- "a perceiver's inferences about what an actor was trying to achieve by a particular action" (p. 222);
- "the attribution of intentions" (p. 220);
- the process of finding "sufficient reason why the person acted" (p. 220).

These statements appear to usher in a theory of explanations for intentional action. And indeed, Jones and Davis's section I was entitled "The Naive Explanation of Human Action: Explanation by Attributing Intentions." There the authors argued that "the perceiver's explanation comes to a stop when an intention or motive is assigned that has the quality of being reason enough" (p. 220). However, page 220 was the only one Jones and Davis devoted to action explanations. In actuality, their chapter offered an account of the conditions under which perceivers infer traits (such as arrogance or dominance) from single behavioral events.[6] Even though the beginning of the chapter mentioned both inferences of intentions and inferences of dispositions (by which they specifically meant stable traits and attitudes, straying from Heider's broader use of the term), the chapter quickly developed an exclusive focus on traits and attitudes. Likewise, all of the empirical studies Jones and Davis reviewed in support of their theory featured trait ratings as dependent variables. Not surprisingly, then, the paper's summary section stated:

To say that an inference is correspondent, then, is to say that a disposition is being rather directly reflected in behavior, and that this disposition is unusual in its strength or intensity. Operationally, correspondence means ratings toward the extremes of trait dimensions which are given with confidence. (Jones and Davis 1965, p. 264)

Jones and Davis thus sidestepped the social perceiver's task of inferring the agent's reasons for acting and instead provided a theory of inferring traits. As David Hamilton (1998) put it, "correspondent-inference theory was an important theory of how people make dispositional inferences, but not really a theory of how people make causal attributions" (p. 107). Why Jones and Davis moved from a theory of action explanation, promised in their introductory remarks, to a theory of trait inference is not entirely clear, but clues can be found in their decision to entitle the whole chapter "From Acts to Dispositions: The Attribution Process in Person Perception" and in their characterization of traits as that "toward which the perceiver presses in attaching significance to action" (Jones and Davis 1965, p. 222). Jones and Davis regarded trait inferences as the ultimate aim of the "attribution process" and action perception in general, a position that would soon dominate the field (see, e.g., Shaver 1975).

1.2.2 A Saving Effort

Daniel Gilbert (1998) attempted, rather heroically, to extract more out of the Jones and Davis chapter than can be found there at first blush. Specifically, he tried to show that the theory of correspondent inference in fact accounts for people's explanations of action via intentions (even though Gilbert concurs with Jones and Davis that traits are ultimately what perceivers are after). To this end, Gilbert adopted Jones and Davis's uncommonly broad definition of *intentions* as referring to a "constellation of beliefs, desires, plans, and goals" (D. T. Gilbert 1998, p. 105). He also adopted Jones and Davis's two principles that guide diagnostic inferences about an actor's dispositions: the principle of noncommon effects (inferences reveal something about an agent if they rely on an action's effects that are unique to that action, not shared by alternative actions) and the principle of desirability (inferences reveal something about an agent if they rely on those action effects that are not obviously socially desirable). Finally, Gilbert applied the two principles to a simple action ("Why did Frank cross the room and turn on the television?") and argued that these principles would allow the perceiver to infer the actor's "intention," yielding an answer such as "because he wanted to watch the news."

Does this reconstruction salvage Jones and Davis's attempts to account for action explanations? I think not. First, attention to noncommon and undesirable effects will yield only one type of "intention," namely goals (because the principles are concerned only with desired or undesired effects of actions). This leaves out a major element in the explanation of action, namely references to beliefs, such as when Frank turned on the television because "he thought that the news was on." No analysis of act–effects can yield a straightforward belief reason explanation.

Second, the act–effects analysis works alright so long as the action in question is a choice between clearly demarcated options that have a manageable set of effects. But many human actions are not like that, which causes problems for the analysis. For one thing, we have to assume that the perceiver selects the agent's relevant options of acting from sheer infinite possibilities, but correspondent inference theory is silent on how this selection might work. In addition, we have to assume that the perceiver considers each potential action's relevant effects, and here, too, the theory is silent on how this selection from another set of infinite possibilities might work.

Third, Jones and Davis's model of intention inferences (via noncommon and undesirable action effects) will typically yield only an answer to the question of *what* the person was doing, not *why* she was doing it—as the authors themselves point out (1965, pp. 222, 228). Granted, sometimes a redescription of a movement pattern in terms of action verbs (e.g., "He was walking toward the window") will be informative and hint at possible explanations, but it will not itself supply these explanations. That is, it will not answer the question "*Why* was he walking toward the window?" Subsequent models of correspondent inference (Gilbert and Malone 1995; Quattrone 1982; Trope 1986) also did not incorporate people's answers to why-questions. For example, in D. T. Gilbert's (1989) multistage model of attribution, the early process of intention inference is called "action identification" (what is the person doing?) and is not credited with explanatory force. The later stage is called "attributional," but it is concerned with either inferring or not inferring an extraordinary disposition—a process quite distinct from ascribing motives or reasons for why the person acted.

1.2.3 Summary

Jones and Davis (1965) introduced an important issue in social perception by asking under what conditions people infer traits from (single) behaviors. Their theorizing about these correspondent inferences was highly influential, leading to research on the "fundamental attribution error" (Ross 1977), stereotypes (e.g., Gilbert and Hixon 1991; Yzerbyt, Rogier, and Fiske 1998), and the cognitive underpinnings of impression formation (e.g., Gilbert and Malone 1995; Trope 1986). However, even under the most charitable reconstruction, Jones and Davis (or theorists in their wake) have not offered a theory of how ordinary people explain behavior, only how they infer traits from behavior—two processes that are just not the same (Hilton, Smith, and Kin 1995; Hamilton 1998).

1.3 Attribution as Causal Judgment: Kelley

Kelley's (1967) paper, "Attribution theory in social psychology," is generally considered the first systematic and general treatment of lay causal explanations. Kelley's self-ascribed goal in the paper was "to highlight some of the central ideas contained in Heider's theory" (p. 192). Specifically, the two central ideas on which Kelley focused were:

1. In the attribution process "the choice is between external attribution and internal [. . .] attribution" (p. 194).

2. The procedure of arriving at these external or internal attributions is analogous to experimental methodology.[7]

Two issues require discussion here, one historical, the other substantive. The historical one concerns Kelley's claim that the two ideas just listed were indeed central to Heider's theory. The substantive issue concerns the claim that the two ideas together provide a strong foundation for a theory of behavior explanation.

1.3.1   The Historical Issue: Kelley Representing Heider

Evidence for the claim that Heider considered the attribution process a choice between external and internal causes appears strong if we consult secondary literature on attribution, but, as argued earlier, this appearance is based on a misrepresentation of Heider's theory. For Heider, the personal–impersonal distinction was more fundamental than the external–internal distinction because it identified two very different domains of causality. Only when there is no intention causing the event (i.e., in the case of impersonal/unintentional events and outcomes) does the external–internal dichotomy apply. Explanations of intentional action, by contrast, are based on the conceptual framework of personal causality, which involves intentionality and the agent's reasons.

Support for Kelley's second claim, that Heider considered the attribution process analogous to experimental methodology, lies in a quote from the very end of Heider's book (Heider 1958, p. 297), which is itself largely based on the section "Attribution of Desire and Pleasure" (ibid., pp. 146–160). But in that section Heider focuses entirely on the attribution of unintentional events (such as enjoyment); and to such unintentional events, both the external–internal distinction and the strategy of covariation assessment apply. Heider never claimed, however, that all behavioral events are explained that way. In particular, nowhere did he argue that the external–internal distinction and the strategy of covariation assessment provide a model of how people explain intentional action.

1.3.2   The Substantive Issue: Kelley's Theory of Behavior Explanations

Whether or not Kelley correctly represented Heider, the more important question is whether Kelley's theory accounts for people's explanations of behavior. As a starting point, consider the following example Kelley offers to illustrate the attribution process:

Am I to take my enjoyment of a movie as a basis for an attribution to the movie (that it is intrinsically enjoyable) or for an attribution to myself (that I have a specific kind of desire relevant to movies)? The inference as to where to locate the dispositional properties responsible for the effect is made by interpreting the raw data (the enjoyment) in the context of subsidiary information from experiment-like variations of conditions. (Kelley 1967, p. 194)

This example features an actor's wondering about the meaning or explanation of enjoyment—an unintentional event. Indeed, throughout the chapter Kelley applies his attribution analysis to "*effects* such as experiences, sensations, or responses" (p. 196), "impressions" (p. 197), as well as arousal states and evaluative reactions (pp. 231–232). All of these events are unintentional, and the person–situation causal analysis applies quite well to this type of event—but to this type only. Kelley himself, it appears from the text, believed that his model also extended to the case of "inferring a person's intentions from knowledge of the consequences of his actions" (p. 196; see also p. 193), but no theory, empirical data, or examples clarify how this extension might work.[8] Of course, the absence of such clarification is not proof of its impossibility. So let me illustrate some of the difficulties one quickly runs into when using the person–situation dichotomy for intentional actions. Consider the following scenario:

Having just arrived in the department as a new Assistant Professor, Pauline finds in her mailbox a note that says "Let's have lunch tomorrow. Faculty club at 12:30?— *Fred.*" Pauline is a bit surprised. She met Fred W. during her interview, but she wouldn't have expected him to ask her out for lunch.

Pauline now tries to explain Fred's action of leaving the note in her mailbox. (By assumption, Fred's action is intentional, so we rule out the possibility that Fred unwittingly put the note in the wrong mailbox.) What does Kelley's attribution model have to say about this situation? The theory would claim that Pauline's choice is between a person attribution (something about Fred caused the action) and a situation attribution (something about her or the circumstances caused the action). But right away, this is a confusing choice. Surely something about Fred must have been present in order for him to put the note in her mailbox: motives, an intention, a fairly controlled movement—all inescapable implications of Fred's action being intentional. And so it goes with all such actions (Kruglanski 1975). Intentional actions ought to elicit person attributions because people perceive them as caused by the agent's intention and motives (D'Andrade 1987; Heider 1958; Malle and Knobe 1997a). Nonetheless, the situation probably played some role in Fred's choice as well—but the situation as *subjectively represented* by Fred: He wouldn't have put this note in Pauline's mailbox if he hadn't *expected* her to check her mailbox in due time and if he hadn't *thought* about the coordination of time and place for the lunch and had not *hoped* her response to the invitation to be positive.

Consequently, a theory that portrays explainers of intentional actions as making a choice between person and situation attributions is amiss. We need a theoretical instrument that captures the explainer's interpretation of the agent's considerations and deliberations that motivated his action. For if Pauline knew Fred's deliberations, she would at once understand and be able to explain why he wrote the note.

But perhaps we were too quick in dismissing Kelley's approach to the mailbox scenario. Is there not a sense in which the "experimental methodology" Kelley has in mind could prove useful? If so, Pauline would have to ask the three questions about consensus, distinctiveness, and consistency and thus arrive at a plausible explanation of Fred's action. But this will generate few answers if we play it by the book. No other faculty member has so far, on Pauline's first day on the job, left a note in her mailbox (low consensus). What can she conclude from that? Fred may have wanted to welcome her, or go out on a date with her, or discuss some common research ideas with her—there are just too many possibilities. All of these explanations might be labeled "person attributions," because they are possible goals/desires Fred had when leaving the note. But the inference of a person attribution is uninformative in this case. Pauline does not doubt that Fred had some goal; she wonders rather which goal Fred had.

Similar problems arise with other covariation questions. Does Fred perform this kind of action toward other people too? Pauline won't know, but assuming she finds out that this is the first time Fred did it (high distinctiveness), she learns only that his action has something to do with her, but she still does not know *why* he did it. And if Fred has left this kind of note with other people as well (low distinctiveness), Pauline merely learns that Fred shows some habit, which is also of limited use. She would want to know specifically whether his habit is to invite all new faculty members, or only women, or members of her research area, and so on. Systematic collection of such covariation information (if available) may at times prove helpful in constructing explanations of another's actions. But when it does, the explainer will not try to choose between person versus situation attributions but rather infer specific goals, beliefs, and the like, that were—in the explainer's assessment—the reasons for the agent's action.

Over the years, Kelley's covariation model and its refinements were tested empirically and appeared to receive reasonable support (e.g., Cheng and Novick 1990; Försterling 1992; McArthur 1972).[9] However, all that these tests showed was that people can take covariation information into account when it is made available to them; none of the tests showed that people actually seek out covariation information on their own (cf. Ahn et al. 1995). People may seek out covariation information for such unintentional events as headaches or moods and such outcomes as success or failure. But covariation reasoning about person and situation causes is surely not the exclusive process by which people go about explaining behavior, and it is actually quite ineffectual in the case of explaining intentional actions. (For a continued discussion of covariation reasoning, see 5.4.)

1.3.3 Summary

Kelley's (1967) model of attribution contains two core propositions: (a) that attribution is a choice between external and internal causes and (b) that the cognitive procedure by which people arrive at this choice is covariation assessment. Both propositions are problematic. First, the internal–external dimension cannot be the foundation of a theory of behavior explanation because, though it may be an important distinction in the explanation of unintentional events, it simply does not capture people's explanations of intentional action. Second, covariation assessment is not the only method by which people arrive at explanations. In the straightforward causal model that underlies explanations of unintentional events, covariation reasoning may be useful (though not essential; see Ahn et al. 1995; Johnson, Long, and Robinson 2001; Lalljee and Abelson 1983; Read, 1987). But the causal model of intentional action is far more complex as it involves intentions, subjective reasons, and rationality (Malle 1999). Covariation reasoning can, at best, assist in constructing reason explanations of intentional action.

1.4 Subsequent Attribution Research

The three classic works by Heider, Jones and Davis, and Kelley were of course not the only important contributions to the study of behavior explanation. A number of scholars proposed theoretical additions, refinements, and extensions of attribution theory. I discuss these contributions under four headings: expanded causal dimensions, refined trait inference models, reasons and goals, and conversational processes. Despite their partial success, these contributions still left some old questions unanswered and raised several new ones. By the end of this review, then, we will be able to gather a list of desiderata that a theory of behavior explanations needs to satisfy.

1.4.1 Expanded Causal Dimensions

In the early 1970s, Bernard Weiner analyzed the domain of achievements and, in particular, the emotions and motivations people have toward others who succeed or fail. He relied on Heider's early insights and introduced the causal dimension of stability to complement the common one of externality–internality (Weiner et al. 1972). Empirical studies showed that people who failed because of lack of effort (unstable internal) were evaluated more negatively than those who failed because of inability (stable internal). (For a review see Weiner 1986.) Later Weiner also analyzed other outcomes that happen to people, such as illnesses, unemployment, or obesity. To account for the systematic differences in people's emotions and evaluations toward these outcomes, Weiner introduced the dimension of controllability (1995). Accordingly, empirical studies showed that people are more angry at agents who suffer negative outcomes brought about by controllable causes (e.g., an illness because of risky behavior) than agents who suffer negative outcomes brought about by uncontrollable causes (e.g., an illness because of a genetic precondition). Finally, Abramson, Seligman, and Teasdale (1978) analyzed the cognitive processes underlying helplessness and depression and proposed globality as a further dimension of causes. They suggested that attributing negative outcomes to global causes (especially if they are also internal and stable) was associated with higher degrees of helplessness and depression. Empirical research incorporating this dimension was not flawless, however (Deuser and Anderson 1995), and studies showed the various causal dimensions to be so highly correlated as to make distinctions among them very difficult (e.g., Fincham and Bradbury 1992, table 1).

What all these proposals have in common is that they deal primarily with explanations of and emotional responses to *outcomes*, which are unintentional events. It may well be important to distinguish causes of unintentional events along a variety of dimensions (such as internality, stability, etc.), but for a theory of behavior explanation, these causal dimensions are not the whole story, because they do not apply to reason explanations of intentional behavior (Malle 1999). People are very concerned with explaining intentional behaviors (Malle and Knobe 1997b), and the moral and interpersonal implications of intentional behaviors are typically more significant than those of unintentional events. A theory of behavior explanation must therefore account for how people explain intentional behavior.

1.4.2   Refined Trait Inference Models

I described earlier how Jones and Davis's seminal paper from 1965 subtly turned attention away from action explanation and toward trait inferences. This shift had a lasting impact on attribution research, as is still visible in the numerous theoretical models on how and when people infer traits from single behaviors (e.g., Carlston and Skowronski 1994; Gilbert, Pelham, and Krull 1988; Newman and Uleman 1989; Quattrone 1982; Ross, Amabile, and Steinmetz 1977; Trope 1986). These models describe with great sophistication the process sequence from observing a behavior to inferring a correspondent trait (and adjusting or not adjusting this inference by considering situational forces). But it would be a mistake to assume that these trait inference models describe the process sequence of behavior *explanations*. Trait inferences and behavior explanations are plainly different processes, with different cognitive and social functions and different conceptual requirements (Fein 2001; Hamilton 1998; Hilton, Smith, and Kin 1995; Malle 1999). The methodology, too, of traditional trait inference studies does not reveal anything about behavior explanations. In these studies, by and large following a classic paradigm (Jones and Harris 1967), participants are asked to indicate high or low ratings on trait, attitude, or ability scales; they are never asked to explain why the target person acted as she did.

A new trend, however, promises to lift some of these restrictions on trait inference work. Research that began with Read, Jones, and Miller (1990) has shown that many trait inferences are based on reason explanations or motive ascriptions (Ames in press; Kammrath, Mendoza-Denton, and Mischel 2003; Reeder et al. 2002; Shoda and Mischel 1993). For example, when inferring an agent's morality, aggressiveness, or helpfulness from a given action, perceivers consider the agent's motives and reasons for her action and thus appear to construct behavior explanations before (or while) drawing a trait inference from it. The temporal ordering of these processes is not yet solidly established, but the changes in methodology that these studies introduced (presenting intentional stimulus behaviors and asking people to ascribe motives) represent a critical step forward in reconnecting the two strands of attribution—work on behavior explanations and work on trait inferences.

1.4.3   Reasons and Goals

In 1978, Allen R. Buss wrote a controversial paper in which he criticized mainstream attribution theory at a fundamental level. He argued that ordinary people do not explain all behavior with causes (as Kelley had suggested) but rather use *reasons* to explain intentional behavior. Reasons and causes are fundamentally different types of explanation, Buss, maintained and attribution theory created a good deal of confusion by equating the two. Buss's (1978) paper drew rather negative responses (Harvey and Tucker 1979; Kruglanski 1979), perhaps because his argument was flawed in its details or because he rattled a central pillar of attribution theory, which at the time lay at the heart of social psychology. Either way, mainstream attribution theory remained rather unaffected by this critique. Over the next decade or so, other scholars launched similar critiques, arguing that reasons are an autonomous form of explanation (Locke and Pennington 1982; see also Kalish 1998; Lennon 1990; Schueler 1989) and that attribution theories must incorporate reasons and goals into their conceptual repertoire (e.g., Lalljee and Abelson 1983; Read 1987; for a review see McClure 2002). Edward E. Jones, too, in an interview in 1978, admitted that the reason concept had been missed by early attribution work (Harvey, Ickes, and Kidd 1978, p. 379).

But it remained unclear exactly how the emerging conceptions of reasons and goals could be integrated with the traditional conception of causal attribution. Most proposals relied on a two by two scheme with reasons versus causes on one side, and person versus situation on the other (e.g., Buss 1978; White 1991). This proposal raises serious problems, however. First, reasons are always person causes in that they are the agent's mental states that motivated her action (Davidson 1963; Kruglanski 1975; Locke and Pennington 1982). So what does it mean that a reason can be either a person or a situation factor? A satisfactory theory of behavior explanation needs to clarify whether or not reasons can be classified into a person–situation dichotomy and what such a classification would mean.

The second problem with the early conceptions of reasons and causes is that they tell us nothing about what determines when people use one or the other mode of explanation. The intentionality of the behavior must certainly be involved here (Buss 1978; Heider 1958; White 1991), but do people automatically offer reasons for all intentional behaviors? This cannot be true, as the following examples,[10] taken from student conversations, show:

(1-1)   Why did she reveal the guy's name?—**She was just . . . she's like that. She has nothing to hide.**

(1-2)   Why did your roommate cook all her food in the dorm room this year?—**Well, she had all of her food with her and her hot pot and toaster oven.**

In each of these cases, the agent performs an intentional action, but in none of them could we say that the explanation cites the agent's reasons for performing that action. For example, explanation (1-1) does not suggest that the agent thought "I am like that, I have nothing to hide; I should therefore reveal his name." Nonetheless, reference to these character traits somehow helps explain why the agent revealed the name. Similarly, in explanation (1-2), having her food, pot, and toaster with her was not the agent's reason for cooking in the dorm room (it wasn't as though she discovered the equipment and became motivated to cook). Even so, the presence of the cooking equipment explains an important aspect of her behavior. We need a theory that tells us both when people use alternatives to reason explanations and what the nature of these alternatives is.

Another fundamental problem that an adequate theory of behavior explanation needs to resolve is why reasons are used to explain intentional behavior in the first place. It may seem to some as obvious that they are, but what makes intentional behaviors so different that they require a unique mode of explanation?

1.4.4   Conversational Processes

An important expansion of attribution research was achieved by a series of papers on the conversational nature of explanations (Kidd and Amabile 1981; Hilton 1990; Turnbull 1986). In these contributions, explanations are characterized not as cognitive processes in the social perceiver's mind but rather as publicly observable speech acts. More specifically, they are question–answer pairs, with "Why?" being the question and the explanation being the answer. Even though such pairs sometimes occur in people's own minds, more often they occur as an actual conversational exchange between a questioner and an explainer. This conversational analysis comes with the important implication that, in answering a why-question, explainers must take into consideration (a) exactly what the questioner finds puzzling or abnormal (Hilton and Slugoski 1986; Turnbull 1986) and (b) what information the questioner already has available (Slugoski et al. 1993). In a sense, the explainer anticipates what kinds of possible answers the questioner has in mind when asking the question (Bromberger 1965). This process of tailoring an explanation to the audience with whom one is communicating is evident in the following example:

(1-3)   Q: But why did you have to leave [the football game]?

A: Because that was the time when . . . , it was like Saturday and I was coming back on Sunday, right? [she was there just for the weekend]

Q: Yeah, so you just wanted to pack.

A: Yeah, I had to pack, and I had to get ready, so during that night we could go out.

Q: Oh!

A: . . . so I wouldn't have to spend my whole night packing.

Q: Ya, ahah.

At each step of the way, the questioner engages with the explainer, chronicling, as it were, the process of discovering the answer to the why-question—

from hypothesis (Yeah . . .) to surprise over new information (Oh), to eventual understanding (ahah).

The insight that explanations are subject to conversational processes was a minor revolution, because it pulled attributions out of their cognitive isolation and highlighted the fundamentally social nature of explanations (which any new theory of explanation must grapple with). However, research into the conversational features of explanations did not expand on the conceptual apparatus of *person–situation causes,* inherited from Kelley and, still today, defining the textbook attribution model. This conservative stance is all the more surprising in light of the paradoxes that result from forcing conversationally situated explanations into the categories of person and situation causes (Antaki 1994; Monson and Snyder 1976; Ross 1977). Consider the following examples.

(1-4)   I did my senior research paper in high school on homophobia **because it was just interesting.**

(1-5)*   I did my senior research paper in high school on homophobia **because I was just interested in it.** (See note 10.)

According to the classic approach (e.g., Nisbett et al. 1973), (1-4) would be classified as a situation attribution and (1-5), as a person attribution. But this is puzzling because the two explanations do not seem to tell a different causal story; rather, they appear to be just linguistic variations of each other. Traditional attribution theorists can only shrug in light of such cases and insist that, *in general,* the person–situation dichotomy makes sense. The folk-conceptual theory of behavior explanations, as we will see in chapter 4, can easily account for both the linguistic surface difference and the deeper similarity between these two explanations.

Consider another striking example, in which grandmother is about to purchase a car and grandson explains her decision making.

(1-6)   [The car's color] wasn't a problem any more, she decided, **because grandpa was dead, and he was the one that was anal retentive about cars.**

Despite surface appearances, here too we do not have a situation attribution, because grandfather's being dead and having been anal retentive in the past can hardly cause grandmother's decision in the present. So what kind of explanation is this?

Many more such examples can be found of behavior explanations that are sensible but that traditional causal attribution theories, focusing merely on person–situation categories, cannot adequately describe, even less so account for. The more mature models of dispositional attribution or trait inference (Gilbert 1989; Trope 1986) cannot come to our aid here, nor can the models of responsibility attribution (e.g., Shaver 1985; Weiner 1995), because none of them directly deal with *explanations* of behavior. Traditional attribution theories simply do not provide an adequate model of the tools and functions of folk behavior explanations. These explanations, however, are an essential element of social cognition and social interaction. Through behavior explanations, people find meaning in social behavior, form impressions, and influence other people's impressions; through behavior explanations, they blame and praise, coordinate interaction, and negotiate status and identity; and through these explanations, they tie together social events into narratives, bolster choices and preferences, and justify attitudes. In short, explanations are ubiquitous in social thinking and social behavior. There is no question, then, that a comprehensive theory is needed for this important social-cognitive tool.

1.5   Desiderata for a Theory of Behavior Explanation

The preceding review of classic and contemporary attribution theories has pointed to a number of shortcomings and unanswered questions in the extant literature. To resolve these problems and build a comprehensive scientific model of behavior explanation I propose a two-pronged approach. First, we need to recognize that explanations are people's way of finding meaning in both intentional and unintentional behavior. This meaning, however, emerges not in the ascription of person and situation causes but in the application of reasons, causes, and a variety of other modes of explanation, which are embedded in a conceptual framework called the *folk theory of mind and behavior* (chapter 2). By locating behavior explanations in this folk-conceptual framework, we are able to identify the various modes of explanation, their conditions of occurrence, and the cognitive processes underlying them (chapter 4 and 5). In so doing, we can show that the traditional person–situation dichotomy in attribution theory obscures a number of important distinctions (chapters 6 and 8) and that person–situation effects in attribution research—a seemingly impressive body of findings—may be based on serious misinterpretations of the evidence (e.g., chapter 7).

Second, we need to recognize that behavior explanations are a social tool that people use for a variety of social-interactive purposes. In offering explanations in social contexts, people try to manage social interaction—manage, that is, both the audience's impression of a given behavior and any joint future actions that explainer and audience might perform. These social uses of explanation, too, will be guided by people's folk-conceptual framework, because altering impressions of behavior occurs against the backdrop of shared fundamental assumptions about mind and behavior (chapters 3 and 6). Thus, the program of this book is to introduce the elements of people's conceptual framework of mind and behavior in which explanations are embedded and to offer a scientific theory of behavior explanations that recognizes this framework and takes into account both functions of behavior explanations: to find meaning and to manage interactions.

2 Foundation: The Folk Theory of Mind and Behavior

Behavior explanations are a fascinating human activity. In fact, they seem to be *two* fascinating human activities. For one thing, they are models people form in their minds to find order and meaning in puzzling social actions or psychological states. For another, they are themselves social acts that can have a number of functions, such as helping others understand the meaning of a behavior, assigning blame or praise, or presenting a certain image of the agent.

But what holds these two distinct aspects of behavior explanations together? How can one and the same phenomenon be both a cognitive model and a social act with so many different functions? A good part of the answer lies in the conceptual framework within which behavior explanations are embedded—the network of fundamental assumptions people make about human agency, about its relation to the mind, and about its place in the physical world. I refer to this framework as the *folk theory of mind and behavior,* and this chapter describes its major components, functions, and possible origins.

I devote considerable detail to this discussion, because the literature on behavior explanations (especially in social psychology) has had little contact with the rapidly growing literature on theory of mind, even though behavior explanations are fundamentally tied to the folk theory of mind and behavior. Furthermore, many reviews or discussions on theory of mind have been written from a particular theoretical perspective and integrative reviews are rare (but see Moses and Chandler 1992), so in much of chapter 2 I attempt to offer such an integrative review, touching on clinical, developmental, and evolutionary aspects. I believe that anyone who can appreciate the complexity of the folk theory of mind will expect a model of behavior explanation that is no less complex and that clarifies how major concepts such as intentionality, belief, or desire shape explanations of behavior. I therefore close the chapter with a sketch of the features that behavior explanations inherit from the folk theory of mind, thereby previewing the detailed theoretical treatment of explanations in chapters 3 through 5.

Briefly, I should remind the reader of the standard attribution position on the matter of conceptual foundations of behavior explanations. According to textbooks and the majority of research publications, people treat human behavior much like any other event: as an effect that is brought about by causes. When explaining behavior, people allegedly classify these causes into two major categories: person and situation causes. Thus, whenever social perceivers try to explain a behavior, they figure out whether it was primarily caused by the person or by the situation. The way they figure this out, so the standard account goes, is by searching for covariation patterns—information about the co-occurrence of the behavior in question with (a) the given agent versus other agents and (b) the given stimulus or context versus other stimuli or contexts.

Though this standard theory may be valuable in specific domains and under specific conditions (which we will identify in chapters 4 and 5), it does not tell the whole story of behavior explanations. To begin with, standard theory greatly simplifies the conceptual framework in which explanations are embedded. The present approach is committed to an empirical study of ordinary people's assumptions about human agency and mind, which guide their explanations of behavior. It will quickly become clear that these assumptions go far beyond standard attribution concepts of cause–effect and person–situation and represent a sophisticated folk model of mind and behavior.

2.1   What a Folk Theory Is (and Is Not)

2.1.1   Labels

People make a number of fundamental assumptions about human behavior and its relation to the mind. These assumptions are interrelated and form a network that is variably referred to as *commonsense psychology, naïve theory of action, theory of mind,* or *folk psychology* (Bruner 1990; Churchland 1981; Heider 1958; Leslie 1987; Perner 1991; Premack and Woodruff 1978; Wellman 1990). One might expect that these different labels refer to different slices of the phenomenon (Whiten 1994), but currently there is little consensus on what those fine-grained distinctions might be. Thus I will use the term *folk theory of mind and behavior* (and sometimes the short form *theory of mind*) to designate the *conceptual framework that guides people's cognition of behavior and the mind.*

2.1.2   Conceptual Framework

When I characterize the folk theory of mind as a *conceptual framework* I am referring to a network of concepts (such as *agent, intention,* and *reason*) that stand in semantic relation to each other and form a model of the inter-related phenomena in question. These concepts serve as filters and catego-rization devices in that they selectively respond to certain perceptual input and classify that input as, say, an agent, action, or intention. These classifi-cations activate (or in some cases inhibit) other concepts and then trigger or serve certain psychological processes: prediction, explanation, and evalua-tion, among others.

Explaining an intentional action, for example, relies on the perceptual classification of movement patterns as *action* performed by an *agent.* This classification normally triggers an immediate search for other stimulus in-formation that may reveal the agent's *intention* (Dittrich and Lea 1994; Pre-mack and Premack 1995). It also triggers a search for stored knowledge or reasonable assumptions about the agent's *beliefs, desires,* and other mental states pertinent to the action and context. When these presumed mental states can be arranged in a reasoning chain (that the agent herself presum-ably entertained), the action is explained by its reasons (Malle 1999).

In addition to emphasizing what the folk theory of mind and behavior *is* (a conceptual framework) I should also point out what I believe it is not. First, it is not just a set of *beliefs* about how the mind works. As a funda-mental conceptual framework for processing information about human be-ings, the folk theory of mind is prior to (i.e., presupposed by) such midrange belief structures as ideologies, dynamic versus static views of personality, or stereotypes (cf. Hong, Levy, and Chiu 2001). Beliefs, in the ordinary sense of the word, are acquired through experience, including indirect experience such as hearsay. But humans do not learn merely through experience that other people have mental states or that there is a basic difference between intentional and unintentional behavior (Fodor 1992). It even sounds odd to claim that people "believe" that their fellow humans have mental states, for they really couldn't imagine otherwise. Experience may very well be necessary to practice and refine the application of key concepts of mind and behavior, but experience is not what teaches humans about the concepts themselves, at least not in the way that experience teaches humans a vast store of facts about plants, animals, and physical surroundings.

Second, the folk theory of mind is not a set of cultural maxims. Such maxims are rules or obligations that can be intentionally broken, but there really isn't any obvious way in which social perceivers could "break" their assumptions about the mind. Nor do autistic children, who lack much of a theory of mind, break rules or maxims; they simply don't have certain concepts to think about other people's and their own minds (Raffman 1999).

Strictly speaking, theory of mind is not an ability either. The relevant ability is that of representing mental states, and this ability is made possible by a number of factors, among them perceptual sensitivities, inferential processes, imagination—and a sophisticated conceptual framework. So theory of mind is a requisite component of the ability to represent mental states, but it is not identical to it.

I should also emphasize that the folk theory of mind and behavior is a part of human social cognition but is certainly not synonymous with it. Sometimes the two terms, *theory of mind* and *social cognition,* are used synonymously (along with *social intelligence, Machiavellian intelligence,* and the like), but such an equation would be a mistake (Haslam and Fiske forthcoming). Theory of mind as a conceptual framework influences and supports a variety of social-cognitive processes. But these processes are phenomena in their own right, and together with a theory of mind they make up the complex web of social cognition. This web also includes conceptions of relationships, sensitivity to power, formation of categories for groups of people, stereotypes based on easily classifiable features, and an implicit theory of personality. None of these conceptions and processes would be what they are without the framework of mind and behavior, but they are certainly not reducible to that framework.

2.1.3   Correspondence to Reality

The postulate of a folk theory of mind and its foundational role in social cognition and interaction does not come with a guarantee that this theory always leads to accurate representations of what is "out there"—the objective behavior and mental states of other human beings—or even of what is "in here"—one's own mental states. At the same time, it seems highly unlikely that *Homo sapiens* would have evolved this sophisticated conceptual framework without there being a sufficient correspondence between its concepts and the social reality humans try to understand and adapt to.

The emphasis here must be on *sufficient* correspondence between concepts and social reality. We should not, for example, expect correspondence at the level of brain structure, as the folk theory of mind does not imply any claims about neural architecture (Egan 1995; Margolis 1991; Stich and Nichols 1992). Rather, the theory generates "functionalist" claims: It characterizes the phenomena in question by their regular antecedents and consequences as well as by their relations to other phenomena in the same domain. At this functional level, the folk theory of mind corresponds sufficiently well to the reality of human mind and behavior so as to be successful in explanation, prediction, and control of interpersonal behavior. But it has nothing to say about the "constituent nature"—neurological, ontological, or other-logical—of mental states, intentionality, and the like. Nor does it have to. The folk theory of mind is just at the right level of analysis to interpret other people's behavior or to coordinate one's preferences and plans with those of others. In this sense, theory of mind is perhaps like classical physics—highly useful in the macro world but incomplete when applied to microscopic processes.

Whatever its precise accuracy as a model of reality, however, the folk theory of mind has a tremendous impact on social behavior, for without such a conceptual framework people would not grasp the complexity of human action and experience. This impact on social behavior is what cognitive and social scientists try to understand, and in this endeavor it does not really matter whether theory of mind corresponds to reality.

2.1.4 A Theory?

There has been some debate over the question of whether people's framework of mind and behavior truly warrants the *theory* designation (for a review see Davies and Stone 1995). As often happens with such debates, novel observers will find that neither of the extreme positions is particularly compelling. It seems difficult to deny that there exists *some* similarity between the folk theory of mind and a scientific theory. Both relate concepts to each other, include general assumptions, postulate unobservables, and serve explanatory and predictive functions. However, equally hard to deny is the fact that there are important differences between folk theories and scientific theories. One of the critical differences is that people can operate in any given domain without a scientific theory, but they could not successfully operate in the domain of human affairs without a folk theory of mind and behavior. Thus, this folk theory resembles a set of Kantian[1] categories of social cognition: the fundamental concepts by which people grasp social reality. Unlike the concepts of a scientific theory, these folk concepts are not formalized in any way and are implicit—that is, people don't normally apply them consciously (Forguson 1989).

2.1.5   Abstract Laws or Simulation?

Conceiving of the folk theory of mind and behavior as a conceptual framework may help resolve another debate—this one over the specific capacity that underlies people's ascription of mental states (see Carruthers and Smith 1996; Davies and Stone 1995).

On one side of the debate we find scholars who have characterized theory of mind as a set of abstract principles or lawlike knowledge structure—rather like a scientific theory (Gopnik and Wellman 1992, 1994; Gopnik and Meltzoff 1997; see Stich and Ravenscroft 1994 for a discussion). This position, called the "theory theory," emphasizes that the child's inferences, explanations, and predictions of mental states rely on such principles or laws as "the actions of ourselves and others are linked to internal states" (Gopnik and Meltzoff 1997, p. 134), "people act to satisfy their desires" (Mitchell 1997, p. 5), or "If an agent desires x, and sees that x exists, he will do things to get x" (Gopnik and Wellman 1994, p. 265). When social perceivers make inferences about their own and other people's minds, they apply these and other abstract laws to the specific situation. Importantly, there is no difference between ascriptions of mental states to others and to oneself—both are theoretical inferences grounded in an abstract knowledge structure (Gopnik 1993).

On the other side of the debate we find scholars who argue that explanations and predictions of others' behaviors rely on a process of "simulation." That is, social perceivers use their own faculties of perceiving, feeling, and reasoning as models that deliver predictions or explanations about another person's perceiving, feeling, and reasoning (Gordon 1986, 1992; Goldman 1989, 2001). In the simplest case this process is something like *projection*. The social perceiver assumes that "other = self" with respect to mental states such as perceptions, beliefs, or motives, and given that the perceiver has (not necessarily conscious) access to his own mental states, ascribing them to others is a straightforward matter. More sophisticated is the attempt to literally simulate the other person's situation and mind states when one expects that they differ from one's own. Here, too, perceivers use their own faculty of deliberation, reasoning, and decision making to deliver, say, an action explanation or prediction, but this simulation can be corrected for whatever differences perceivers consider between the other person and themselves. A key claim of simulation theory is that mental state ascription isn't based on theoretical inference, either in the first-person case or the third-person case. People don't infer their own mental states, as they are simply available to them; and they don't infer other people's mental states using abstract laws, because they can more easily project or simulate those states.

Each position has its supporting evidence as well as its specific problems, but what the two have in common is that they focus on the psychological mechanisms of mental state ascription more so than on the conceptual framework that underpins it.[2] In fact, this conceptual framework is typically presupposed while researchers debate how social perceivers *use* this framework—either to make inferences on the basis of abstract laws or to run simulations on the basis of first-person data. But neither inferences nor simulations are possible without the fundamental concepts that organize perception, reasoning, simulation, and inference. No abstract law can be acquired or grasped without concepts acting as filters and groupings of perceptual input; and no introspective simulation can mature beyond projection without the classification of one's own and others' mental states into such central categories as belief, desire, and emotion.

If we consider theory of mind fundamentally to be a conceptual framework, we are free to allow a variety of psychological processes to do the job of mental state ascription—inference from knowledge structures, projection, conscious or unconscious simulation, introspection, and perhaps several more. Indeed, the research literature suggests that all these processes play a role in the social cognition of mind and behavior (Ames in press; Blakemore and Decety 2001; Krueger and Clement 1997; Nickerson 1999; Ross, Greene, and House 1977), and often a mixture of them is necessary to solve any given problem. For example, conducting a simulation of a particular person's mental states in a particular context requires a wealth of cultural, situational, and person-specific knowledge, which includes at least some abstract rules and laws (Wilkerson 2001). Similarly, abstract principles such as the desire-belief-intention inference rule must be "filled in" with the other person's presently occurring *contents* of mental states, and this filling-in process may very well rely on projection and simulation (Heal 1996).

In sum, the debate over the nature of mental state inference loses its edge when we heed the distinction between a conceptual framework of mind and behavior on the one hand and the various cognitive processes that make use of this framework on the other. The implication for a theory of folk behavior explanation is clear. When social perceivers offer behavior explanations, they rely (a) on a network of concepts that filter, classify, and organize perceptual input and existing knowledge and (b) on a number of subsequent processes, such as inference and simulation, that deliver an explanatory proposition. We shall see later that folk behavior explanations can be grouped into four different "modes" (causes, reasons, casual histories, and enabling factors), and these modes differ both in the concepts that define them and in the kinds of processes that are recruited to produce them. Indeed, the multifaceted nature of folk behavior explanations may be one of the best arguments for a pluralistic interpretation of theory of mind, embedding both simulation and abstract inference within a mentalistic conceptual framework (Malle 2001b).

2.2 Function and Dysfunction of Theory of Mind

I suggested earlier that people would not successfully operate in the domain of human affairs without a folk theory of mind and behavior. Evidence to support this claim is not quite as direct as one would like, because no humans completely lack a theory of mind. But we do have both anecdotal and systematic evidence suggesting that a folk theory of mind frames and enables complex perception and cognition of human behavior in a way that is all but indispensable. I begin by describing a few cognitive and interpersonal achievements that would not be possible without concepts of mind, and then I examine what happens when at least part of a theory of mind is missing.

2.2.1 Achievements of a Theory of Mind
Consider first the case of a perceiver who notices another person pull out her wallet in front of a cashier. Without a conceptual framework of mind and behavior the perceiver would not understand what the large moving organ-

ism's encounter with the smaller object means. He would also be rather ineffective at predicting the other large moving organism's likely response. With a framework of mind and behavior, however, perceivers can parse this complex scene into fundamental categories of reaching, grasping, and exchanging (Baird and Baldwin 2001; Woodward, Somerville, and Guajardo 2001), and after acquiring the pertinent cultural knowledge, they elaborate their interpretation into the script of paying (Schank and Abelson 1977). People's theory of mind thus frames and interprets perceptions of human behavior in a particular way—as perceptions of agents who can act intentionally and who have feelings, desires, and beliefs that guide their actions (Wellman 1990; Perner 1991).

Suppose now you are in the market for an office chair and actually found one you approve of. However, you aren't quite convinced that you will still like it after sitting on it for a whole day, typing away at your computer. So you ask the salesperson whether you could take the chair home with you to try it out for a day or two. The salesperson agrees but asks to take an imprint of your credit card. Why would you agree to that? You reason that he wants some kind of security because he fears that, without it, there is a chance you might not return the chair. You further realize that he thinks just having your address wouldn't suffice (it might be fake, suing you would be a hassle, etc.) but that he assumes a credit card imprint would do because if you don't return the chair, he can charge the purchase price to your card. So the transaction makes sense in light of the salesperson's goals. You also realize that it fulfills your own goals, because you get to try out the chair without giving up any cash (which, you notice, you don't have on you) and you still have the option of not buying the chair. Furthermore, even though the imprint is blank right now, you can be sure that the salesperson won't go mad and charge ten thousand dollars to your account with the imprint, because he must know he would lose his job and could get sued for fraud, and even if he did go mad, you know that the credit card company would release you from paying the ten thousand dollars. Finally, you know that the salesperson knows all that, and presumably knows, too, that you are aware of it. So you jointly realize that this is a fair transaction and go ahead with it.

No doubt, without a theory of mind you would be quite lost in this case. In fact, it is not entirely clear whether, without a theory of mind, there would even be such things as office chairs and credit cards. But granted there are, nobody would agree to this transaction (and others like it) absent a theory of mind. Neither you nor the salesperson could rely on conditioning from past experience with the other person (because there is no past experience), nor could you rely on reciprocal altruism, because there is no guarantee for a future transaction. Plain and simple, you need to understand minds (others' as well as your own) to engage in social transactions and exchanges.

Even more obvious, but no less powerful, is the role of theory of mind in communicative action (Gibbs 1998; Sperber and Wilson 2002). Take a speech act such as *promising*, which would be impossible to accomplish without significant considerations of one's own commitment to action, expressed as a public announcement perceived by the other person as that commitment for future action (Astington 1988; Searle 1969). And even such seemingly innocuous communicative behaviors as initiating a conversation or taking turns require an appreciation of the other person's attention and intentions at that moment (Clark and Brennan 1991; Schober 1998). More generally, linguistic behavior is infused with speakers' subtle adjustments to what they assume the listener already knows, doesn't want to hear, or tries to find out, and these adjustments are found at all levels of language—phonetic, morphemic, syntactic, semantic, and pragmatic (Clark 1996; Givón 1997; Krauss and Fussell 1991).

Finally, and most fundamentally, to communicate something to another person (an "addressee") is an intention to bring about, with the things one says, a certain mind state in the addressee that involves her recognition of that intention.[3] This sounds complicated, yet we do it all the time. For every utterance spoken, the addressee must make multiple inferences—about the intended audience of the speaker's utterance, the referents and meaning of the speaker's words, and the type of social act intended (assertion, question, advice, teasing, etc.). The process of inferring what the speaker "has in mind" is so automated that we don't have to track it consciously—unless it begins to break down (Grice 1975). When we ask, for instance, "What do you mean by that?," we signal that we heard the speaker's words but did not recognize the intention behind them, did not recognize in which mind state the speaker wanted us to be on hearing those words.

2.2.2 Theory of Mind Deficits
In addition to showing some of the achievements made possible by a theory of mind, we can also look at the striking cases in which some parts of that

framework are missing. Most widely known in this respect are autistic individuals who have enormous difficulty dealing with other people's mental states (Baron-Cohen 2000; Frith 2000; Leslie 1992). Autistic people are not completely unaware of other minds, but their conceptual understanding of the mental world is severely limited, and as a result they are baffled by the complexity of mind–behavior connections. Often they respond merely to surface behaviors or are not responsive to social interaction at all, because many of their interaction partners' intentions, thoughts, and sentiments elude them.

The autistic person's problem, however, does not seem to be one of *perception* of relevant inputs, but primarily one of lacking an *interpretive frame*, resulting in social perception that is strangely raw and mechanical. One autistic person reports[4]:

I know people's faces down to the acne scars on the left corners of their chins and what their eyes do when they speak, and how the hairs of their eyebrows curl, and how their hairlines curve around the tops of their foreheads. [. . .] The best I can do is start picking up bits of data during my encounter with them because there's not much else I can do. It's pretty tiring, though, and explains something of why social situations are so draining for me. [. . . .] That said, I'm not sure what kind of information about them I'm attempting to process. (Blackburn et al. 2000)

What seems to be missing, as another autistic person remarks, is an "automatic processing of 'people information.'" The data come in, but they cannot be interpreted using concepts of agency and mind. Temple Grandin observes in one of her illuminating books about living with autism: "I do not read subtle emotional cues. I have had to learn by trial and error what certain gestures and facial expressions meant" (Grandin 1995, p. 135).

How can one survive in social interactions if emotional cues and social meaning are so elusive? As one discussant put it, "autistic people who are very intelligent may learn to model other people in a more analytical way." Temple Grandin states that "it was years before I realized that other people are guided by their emotions during most social interactions. For me, the proper behavior during all social interactions had to be learned by intellect" (ibid., p. 87). This mechanical, analytical mode of processing, however, is very tiresome and slow: "Given time I may be able to analyze someone in various ways, and seem to get good results, but may not pick up on certain aspects of an interaction until I am obsessing over it hours or days later" (Blackburn et al. 2000). Temple Grandin again:

I had to think about every social interaction. When other students swooned over the Beatles, I called their reaction an ISP—interesting sociological phenomenon. I was a scientist trying to figure out the ways of the natives. (Grandin 1995, p. 132)

Thus, many autistic persons in principle seem able to pick up the available social information (facial expressions, body movements, etc.), but they lack the *network of concepts* that would allow them to interpret with ease and swiftness the meaning of this information.[5] As a result, faces, looks, and gestures are merely physical events for autistic persons, and the distinction between persons and objects is largely overlooked. To illustrate, Simon Baron-Cohen (1992) describes the case of Jane, who at one point sat at a lunch table with several people and suddenly climbed onto the table, using other bodies as support, knocking over people's food or stepping into it, all in pursuit of grabbing a piece of cake at the other end of the table. "The idea that she could have used words, or gestures, or even eye-contact, to request a piece of cake did not seem to have even entered her mind," writes Baron-Cohen (1992, p. 13).

Neither before nor after the table incident did Jane engage in any kind of impression management (e.g., "Excuse me," "Oops," "I am sorry") or any behavior explanations (e.g., "I just could not resist this gorgeous piece of cake . . ."). Because she is oblivious to other people's thoughts and feelings, the need for managing people's impressions and reactions would never occur to her. This obliviousness to others' impressions not only spoils ongoing interactions but also stands in the way of generally grasping social conventions such as politeness, etiquette, and other rules of conduct. These conventions protect and manage the impressions and reactions of other people, and if one doesn't understand what is there to be protected, conventions make little sense. The only way to fit in with conventional social life is to learn rules by heart and create, as Ms. Grandin does, a library of *if-then* scenarios, all the while remaining hopelessly confused when even small details in an interaction pattern are novel and unlike any pattern previously encountered, learned, and catalogued. In a sense, mastering social interaction for autistic persons is like acquiring syntax without semantics—learning the grammar of a language without understanding the meaning of its words.

A telling example of obliviousness to social conventions can be found in Oliver Sacks's (1995) description of meeting Temple Grandin for the first time. He arrived at her office, hungry, thirsty, and exhausted after a long day of travel, and was hoping that Ms. Grandin would offer him coffee or something like it. Not aware of any of her visitor's bodily and mental states, Ms. Grandin immediately started talking about her work and, "with a certain unstoppable impetus and fixity," continued on for a long time, until Sacks finally broke convention (among strangers) and asked directly for a cup of coffee. Lacking the ability to infer other people's thoughts and feelings in context, Temple Grandin can act appropriately only if she can recall a rule from her "video library" of how people behave in different circumstances. "She would play these [videos] over and over again and learn, by degrees, to correlate what she saw, so that she could then predict how people in similar circumstances might act" (Sacks 1995, p. 260).

But of course it is impossible to memorize predictive rules for every possible situation. Robert Gordon (1992) argued that the impossibility of having comprehensive rules of this sort is significant evidence for the (at least partial) involvement of "simulation processes" in mental state inference. Had Temple Grandin even briefly simulated what it might be like for Oliver Sacks in that situation, she may have offered him some water, coffee, or a snack. Lacking this spontaneous ability to simulate the other mind, she must rely on the catalogue of behavioral rules she has acquired from numerous past interactions. But all too often she will lack a rule, or the appropriate rule is simply not triggered by the slightly novel interaction in which she finds herself.

The deficit of theory of mind in autism is striking, but equally striking is the circumscribed nature of this deficit. Mental concepts appear to be the only concepts that are reliably missing among autistic people (Baron-Cohen, Leslie, and Frith 1985); and their deficit can therefore not be attributed to some sort of general concept acquisition problem. Rather, autistic individuals specifically lack large portions of the conceptual framework of mind and behavior. Currently we do not know exactly what prevents autistic children from acquiring mental state concepts, but the following likely candidates have been identified:

1. dysfunctions in important cognitive precursors to theory of mind, such as joint attention (Dawson et al. 2002; Mundy and Sigman 1989; Mundy and Neal 2001), imitation (Hobson and Lee 1999; Rogers 1999), and responsiveness to faces (e.g., Klin et al. 2002);

2. the resulting reduction of preverbal and verbal interaction with adults, canceling the benefits of adults' and the child's communicative reference to

mental states (Bruner and Feldman 1994; Dunn, Brown, and Beardsall 1991; Hughes and Dunn 1998; Peterson and Siegal 2000); and

3. dysfunctions in introspection or executive control of one's own mental states (Carlson and Moses 2001; Frith and Happé 1999; Hughes 1998).

2.3   The Developing Framework of Mind and Behavior

If the folk theory of mind is a conceptual framework, what concepts does it include and how are they networked together? Work by Thomas Shultz and his colleagues (1980, 1988; Shultz and Wells 1985) highlighted the importance of a concept of intentionality in the developing interpretation of behavior (first recognized by Piaget 1932). Roy D'Andrade (1987) outlined a folk model of the mind that comprises a small number of mental state types (perceptions, beliefs, feelings, desires, intentions) that differ in their causal origin (outside or inside the mind), their controllability, and their typical relations to each other (e.g., feelings explain desires, which explain intentions, but not the other way around). Developmental models by Josef Perner (1991) and Henry Wellman (1990) provided a detailed look at fundamental concepts of mental states, especially the representational concepts of belief and desire and their possible origins in the grasping of perception and emotion (see also Gopnik and Meltzoff 1997). Alan Leslie (1994) and Simon Baron-Cohen (1995) discussed what they consider core modules of a developing theory of mind but that one could also interpret as core concepts. The following sketch of the folk theory of mind and behavior draws on all this innovative work (and on the expanding theory of mind literature in general; e.g., Malle, Moses, and Baldwin 2001b; Zelazo, Astington, and Olson 1999) but also tries to integrate the concepts of *mind* with the concepts of *behavior*. The sketch is set up as a number of conceptual distinctions and their interconnections.

The first distinction is that between *agents* and all other entities in the physical world. Soon after birth, infants show a capacity to imitate human facial movements (Meltzoff and Moore 1977, 1989), but they don't imitate simlar movements displayed by an object (Legerstee 1991). At three months they can distinguish human motion from random, nonbiological motion (Bertenthal 1993), and by nine months they show first evidence of perceptual sensitivity to self-propelled movement and goal-directed action (Gergely et al. 1995; Premack 1990; Wellman and Philips 2001; Woodward,

Sommerville, and Guajardo 2001). By one year of age, infants begin to view the goals of others in a more abstract manner, dissociating the individual actions within a sequence from the ultimate goal (Sommerville 2002). Though this goal concept is not mentalistic (that is, no understanding of the mental world is necessary to have the concept), the appreciation of goal objects to which actions are directed is an important first step toward distinguishing intentional from unintentional behavior.

Another important step is the recognition of agents' gaze (Corkum and Moore 1998; Johnson, Slaughter, and Carey 1998; Phillips, Wellman, and Spelke 2002), which offers a reliable clue for goal direction and also supports the infant's capacity to engage in joint attention—something that cannot occur with objects, only *with* people *toward* objects. By focusing their attention on significant objects and coordinating this attention with another person's attention on the same objects, children learn to coordinate joint action and interaction. Moreover, the objects of joint attention are anchors in the world akin to meeting places, and we might say that a "meeting of the minds" occurs first in the external world. These objects or anchors are also reference points from which important deviations can be registered ("now we are both attending, now we are not"), and these deviations can help explain behavior ("when we are not jointly attending, our responses are different"). In fact, it seems possible that in its earliest stages, joint attention is an expansion of the individual mind (*"we* attend to *X"*). Only later, discrepancies in the data base are noticed—for example, memory of attending alone is different from memory of attending *with* another person and different from memory of attending *to* that person. As a result, children begin to differentiate reliably between their own contribution and the other person's contribution to joint attention and joint action.

With their focused interest in agents, infants get a lot of practice in perceiving intentional action. They may at first have a concept of intentionality that is confounded with the concept of agency (intentional actions are just what agents do). But already at nine months infants not only differentiate between human hand movements and mechanical movements, but they seem to differentiate between human hand movements that are goal directed and those that are not (Woodward 1998, 1999). Thus, goal-directedness is not only a feature that discriminates agents from nonagents but also goes some way toward distinguishing particular agent behaviors (intentional ones) from others (unintentional ones). What helps in this task of distinguishing intentional from unintentional behavior is infants' ability to detect a meaningful structure in continuous behavior streams—a structure that corresponds to the actual pattern of intentions the agent executes. Baldwin, Baird, Saylor, and Clark (2001) showed that infants as young as ten to eleven months are more sensitive to interruptions of a behavior stream in the middle of an executed intention than to interruptions at the end of an executed intention, suggesting that they process the complete arc of an intentional action as a natural unit.

Early in the second year of life, children show compelling evidence of classifying intentional and unintentional behaviors into distinct categories (Carpenter, Akhtar, and Tomasello 1998; Phillips, Wellman, and Spelke 2002). This distinction relies at first on several perceptual and functional features. Accidental behaviors are those that look uncoordinated, are not directed at significant objects, and are associated with adults' characteristic expressions of negative affect in face and voice (e.g., "uh-oh"). Intentional behaviors are those that look coordinated, are directed at significant objects, and are associated with adults' expressions of positive affect in face and voice (e.g., "there!"). By eighteen months, the processing of action has become so sophisticated that children can imitate and complete action sequences even if another person performed those actions incompletely or unsuccessfully (Meltzoff 1995). Thus, children at this age seem to infer the goal or intention inherent in an initiated action and can then themselves execute this intention. What may underlie such an inference process is a sort of self–other matching mechanism that links representations of other-performed actions with plans for self-performed actions (Grèzes and Decety 2001; Meltzoff and Brooks 2001). Thus, when observing the adult's action pattern, the child's representation of planning that same action becomes activated and is then available for execution.

Both the agency concept and the intentionality concept are initially based on the infant's sensitivity to characteristic features of human behavior, but because these features are in reality associated with certain classes of mental events (e.g., direction of action ≈ goals; action boundaries ≈ intentions; facial expressions ≈ emotions), children learn to deal with minds while they are processing behavior (Baird and Baldwin 2001). During the preschool years, genuinely mentalistic concepts finally emerge, beginning with the understanding of desires (by age two) and beliefs (by age three), concepts that are also reliably used in children's talk about the mind (Brown 1973) and explanations of behavior (Bartsch and Wellman 1989).

At the age of three, however, children still have difficulty realizing that different people can have different beliefs, and especially that another person might believe something that they themselves do not believe. Believing, at that age, is understood more as copying reality than as representing reality, and perspective taking—or the awareness of others' mental states as different from one's own—is still very difficult. This all changes with another watershed of theory of mind development around the age of four (Perner 1991; Wellman 1990), when children acquire a full-fledged belief concept that makes them see beliefs as fallible representations (not copies) of reality, permitting a distinction between what the child believes and what other people believe (cf. Wimmer and Perner 1983). Aided perhaps by numerous clashes between their own and other people's desires, beliefs, and intentions, children in the preschool years thus learn that different people represent the world in different ways and therefore frequently want, see, and know different things.

With the arrival of genuinely mentalistic concepts, the distinction between intentional and unintentional behaviors is understood in a novel and refined way, namely, as based on characteristic mental states, primarily intention, desire, and belief. Early on, the concepts of desire and intention seem to be confounded (Astington 2001; Moses 2001), but with the solidification of the belief concept, children recognize that intentions prepare for action in light of desires and beliefs whereas desires can stand on their own and do not necessarily lead to action.

When reaching its mature stage (perhaps not before puberty; Kugelmass and Breznitz 1968), the intentionality concept consists of five components that must typically all be seen as present for an action to be considered intentional: that agent had a *desire* for an outcome, a *belief* that the action would lead to that outcome, an *intention* to perform the action, the *skill* to perform the action, and *awareness* of fulfilling the intention while performing the action (Malle and Knobe 1997a; for possible limitations see Knobe 2003a,b). I should emphasize that the actual cognitive process of assessing intentionality often relies on heuristics (e.g., assuming intentionality unless counterevidence is available) rather than on a five-step decision process. Moreover, even after infancy, perceptual discrimination based on behavioral indicators (e.g., facial expressions, motion pattern) features prominently in judgments of intentionality. The full five-component concept, however, sets the boundaries for any judgment of intentionality and provides the conditions that settle disputes about an action's intentionality (Malle and Nelson 2003).

With the intentionality concept becoming "mentalized," the idea of self-propelledness turns into a more refined notion of *choice* (Kalish 1998), a conceptual advance that is probably aided by the child's refined capacity for self-regulation (Mischel, Ebbesen, and Raskoff-Zeiss 1972; Russell 1996). Choice captures both the process of forming an intention (or deciding) and its behavioral implementation in an act of trying. In the adult folk theory, choice is seen as the key force in human behavior. Choice is not normally assumed to be present in other objects and events (an assumption from which the philosophical tension derives between freedom of the will and determinism), though choice is sometimes projected onto other events, as in the anthropomorphizing of natural and technological phenomena.

In contrast to the generative power of choice and intentional action, unintentional events are perceived as mere results of other events—in the physical world (e.g., a branch breaks under the weight of the snow), in the social world (e.g., a child cries because it got separated from its mother), or in the psychological world (e.g., a nightmare is induced by high fever).

Besides the intentional–unintentional distinction, people also make a mind–body or *observable–unobservable* distinction, whose origin lies in the first mental concepts emerging during the preschool years. Perhaps facilitated by increasing self-awareness and introspective abilities, children begin to recognize the correspondence but also discrimination between publicly observable signs and unobservable mental states.[6] These mental states (which are frequently unintentional; see chapter 3) can have important influences on the agent's actions and interactions with others, so increasingly fine distinctions are made among such event classes as bodily states, sensations, emotions, and thoughts.

The developing social perceiver does not stop at recognizing certain behaviors as performed intentionally. He also wants to know what the agent's specific intention or ultimate goal is, and what specific emotions she feels when failing or succeeding in her action. Such contentful mental state inferences require a grasp of the complex interplay between behavioral and situational cues, cultural norms, and the agent's idiosyncratic attributes (such as preferences and attitudes). From this database, and (sometimes, at least) from the perceiver's own simulation of what he would feel, think, or do in the given circumstances, specific ascriptions can emerge of the agent's beliefs, desires, and emotions in the given context. A full appreciation of these contentful mental states also involves an understanding of *equifinality* (Heider 1958)—the idea that intentional agents can fulfill a goal in multiple ways and that, if they fail one way, they will reason about it and try to pursue it another way.

In addition to the core distinctions of agency, intentionality, observability, and their subsumed concepts of beliefs, desire, intention, emotion, and so on, the conceptual network of mind and behavior has various extensions. Many of them are concepts that are abstractions from mental events, such as *attitude* and *value*, processes of attention and thinking as part of a stream of consciousness (Flavell 1999), and the notion of *personality traits*, potentially derived from patterns of behavior assumed to be caused by characteristic mental states (Ames et al. 2001). These concepts are used to grasp more temporally stable individual differences among agents and form the basis of person schemas (Kelly 1955) as well as stereotypes (Stangor and Lange 1994).

Besides developing a conceptual framework, humans also have to learn to *use* this framework—in inference, reasoning, imagination, and so on. Many important social phenomena, such as empathy, perspective taking, sympathy, introspection, self-disclosure, emotional intelligence, and social intelligence critically rely on the folk theory of mind, linking a variety of psychological processes with the conceptual network. Little research has explored these linkages between processes and concepts. Interesting cultural variations should be found there (cf. Lillard 1998; Wellman 1998) as well as variations across the life span and across different family experiences.

2.4 Evolutionary Origins

Let me now look far back—back to the origins of a theory of mind in human evolutionary history. This exploration will help put theory of mind in its broadest social context and highlight what a fundamental achievement it is for humans to reason about mental states. With a full appreciation of this achievement and its social origins we can then better understand the specific nature of behavior explanations as a core capacity in people's arsenal of finding meaning and managing social interaction.

In contrast to the increasingly detailed picture of theory of mind ontogeny, we obviously know much less about the evolutionary path of this powerful social-cognitive tool. A sketch of some reasonable answers, however, is possible, and I will organize it around three questions:

1. What were the selective advantages that favored an emerging capacity to represent the mind?

2. Whence did the capacity emerge? That is, what were the cognitive precursors of a full-fledged theory of mind?

3. When did the capacity emerge?

2.4.1 Selective Advantages

The representation of mental states influences both self-regulation (when one represents one's own mind) and social interaction (when one represents other people's minds). Even though both of these sets of functions are candidates for selective advantages, the literature has overwhelmingly focused on social interaction as the evolutionary advantage of a theory of mind. Within this focus, there are two main models about the social functions favoring the emergence of theory of mind. The first focuses on *social competition;* the second focuses on *social coordination.*

The first model is perhaps the more radical of the two, subscribing to a *Machiavellian hypothesis*—that mental state inferences primarily support the manipulation of other people for selfish gain, rely mainly on deception and counterdeception, and are part of an arsenal of manipulative tactics in a competitive social game (Cummins 1998; Humphrey 1976; Krebs and Dawkins 1984; Byrne and Whiten 1988).

Cummins (1998), for example, places the emergence of a theory of mind into the context of a dominance hierarchy. Such a hierarchy provides fertile ground for the development of deception, Cummins argues, as lower-ranking individuals would benefit from a capacity to deceive higher-ranking individuals in order to access a greater share of resources (such as food or mating partners). Higher-ranking individuals, on their part, would benefit from a capacity to detect deception and cheating (p. 37):

The struggle for survival in chimpanzee societies is best characterized as a struggle between dominance and the outwitting of dominance, between recognizing your opponent's intentions and hiding your own. *The evolution of mind emerges from this scene as a strategic arms race in which the weaponry is ever-increasing mental capacity to represent and manipulate internal representations of the minds of others.* (Italics in the original)

As a modern example of such a struggle, Cummins cites sibling rivalry, in which younger siblings are apt to develop faster than normal their potential to represent the older sibling's mental states. And indeed, studies suggest that, on average, children with older siblings pass the false-belief test (the litmus test for theory of mind) at an earlier age than do children without older siblings (e.g., Jenkins and Astington 1996; Ruffman et al. 1998). However, on closer inspection we find that the data do not support the rivalry hypothesis. Some findings show no relationship of theory of mind indicators with the number of older siblings (Arranz et al. 2002); some show a relationship with the number of *any* siblings, even younger ones (Peterson 2001); and some show a relationship with the number of adult kin or peers generally available for interaction (Lewis et al. 1996). In addition, explanations offered for these correlations involve factors that don't fit the dominance theory very well, such as pretend play (Watson 1999), mental state language (Ruffman et al. 1998), parental encouragement to reflect on other people's feelings (Ruffman, Perner, and Parkin 1999), and general interaction opportunities (Peterson 2001). Thus, the overall results suggest a general benefit of "interaction practice" for the development of mental state inference, quite independent of dominance lines.[7]

There are other, more general problems with competitive Machiavellian models. The "arms race" argument implies that modern humans should be highly adept at both deceiving and detecting deception; but the evidence does not speak for human excellence in detecting deception (Malone and DePaulo 2001). Humans of different cultures may be apt to spot and shun "social cheaters" (those who broke or are about to break a social contract; Sugiyama, Tooby, and Cosmides 2002), but such detection does not rely on a theory of mind but on the registration of unfair input–output ratios or failed contributions.[8] Moreover, any cheater responsiveness would actually suggest that selfish and exploitative social behavior is not productive in the long run, especially not as a community-wide pattern.

A further problem with competitive Machiavellian models is that they don't account at all for some of the most powerful tools of human evolution: imitation, teaching, communication, and the growth of organized social groups—all phenomena that rely on trust and cooperation, not on selfishness and competition (Givón and Young 1994). As a corollary, competition models overlook the fact that theory of mind develops in the first four years of life, at a time when children do not primarily compete with their parents or refine their talents of deceiving and detecting deception. Children of this age show enormous trust, attachment, and vulnerability vis-à-vis their parents as well as select other adults who are their teachers, protectors, and partners in growing up.

In contrast to the relatively dark Machiavellian portrait of humans as engaged in social competition, *coordination models* paint the functional story of theory of mind in brighter colors. What they emphasize is that humans track other people's thoughts, goals, and emotions to coordinate ongoing interaction (Bogdan 2000; Goody 1995; Malle 2002a; Strum, Forster, and Hutchins 1997). As Asch (1952) put it, "We interact with each other . . . via emotions and thoughts that are capable of taking into account the emotions and thoughts of others" (p. 142).

We can break down the benefits of a theory of mind for coordinating interaction into at least three elements. First, mental state inferences serve the completion of communal actions, such as group hunting, building shelter, or migrating into new territories. In such joint actions of multiple individuals, sophisticated prior planning, division of labor, and the dynamic updating of one another's mental states during execution are critical for success. Interestingly, recent computer simulations by John Orbell and his colleagues suggest that mindreading capacities may provide a necessary precondition for cooperation to evolve in an ecology akin to prisoner dilemma games (Orbell et al. in press).

Second, the ability to empathize with others' emotions or to correctly guess their desires and beliefs is especially important for hominid child rearing, because human newborns (at least since *Homo erectus*, two million years ago) are far less developed and therefore need more care, protection, and teaching than any other primates. Without a theory of mind, then, human ancestors might not have been able to raise adaptively fit offspring.

Finally, mental state inference is a key ingredient in the most powerful of cooperative cultural processes: teaching and communication (e.g., Mameli 2001; Origgi and Sperber 2000; Rogoff et al. 2003; Sperber 2000). Whenever social learning, linguistic communication, and direct instruction arose during human evolution, the capacity to represent and adjust to others' mental states must have been in place at that time (Malle 2002a).

For a long time, coordination models have not been promoted as strongly as their Machiavellian alternatives. Recent work, however, is beginning to document the strengths of this hypothesis (Bogdan 2000; Donald 1991; Dunbar 1996; Orbell et al. in press; Tomasello 1998a; Whiten 1999). Theory of mind, then, appears to be adaptive primarily for its power to facilitate and refine social coordination in communal action, child rearing, and cultural processes.

Coordination models are also far more successful at integrating the capacity to explain behavior within a theory of mind. Whereas it would largely suffice to *predict* behavior in a world of competition, a world that is oriented toward coordination demands the flexibility of behavior explanation. When communal action breaks down, for instance, explanations help pinpoint possible causes and so offer ways to renew that action. In child rearing too, caretakers will be able to learn from interactions with their offspring if they can find meaning in behavior; likewise, children learn from interactions with caretakers if they can explain their actions. Finally, all sorts of cultural processes are aided by behavior explanations: social teaching and learning, persuasion and other social influence, as well as communication and its many imperfections that demand interpretive and corrective processes. In short, any specific evolutionary story about the emergence of behavior explanations is far better told within a model of coordination than within one of competition.

2.4.2 Precursors to an Evolving Theory of Mind

Most scholars assume that the phylogenetic emergence of a theory of mind was a gradual process. The goal then becomes to identify precursors of the fully fledged capacity. A precursor must be primitive enough to operate without mental state concepts or inferences, but it must be sophisticated enough to provide a true launching pad for such concepts and inferences. Without attempting to be exhaustive I focus on five candidate precursors (for background reading see Baron-Cohen 1995; Gopnik and Meltzoff 1997; Leslie 1994; Premack 1990; Tomasello and Call 1999).

The first is the capacity for imitation, which involves the linking of a representation of another's behavior to the organism's own motor program for that same behavior (Blakemore and Decety 2001). What makes imitation an important precursor of mental state inference is that the linkage of others' behavior with one's own behavior can be expanded into a linkage of mental states accompanying one's own behavior with (thus inferred) mental events accompanying others' behavior (Meltzoff and Brooks 2001). This expanded linkage, which we may call empathy, can rely on two different mechanisms.

One mechanism is a noninferential form of empathy, in which the other person's affect-expressing behaviors (e.g., crying) are imitatively mirrored in the perceiver's behavior, which in turn triggers (in reverse direction) an affective state in the perceiver similar to that in the other person (Levenson and Ruef 1997). To the extent that perceivers can, in this way, "reconstruct" in themselves the mental states that the other person is in, behavioral imitation becomes mental imitation. We might say that the perceiver "resonates" with the other's affect (Gallese and Goldman 1998)—a capacity that may be especially important in child rearing.

An alternative mechanism that supports the expanded linkage between one's own and other people's mental states may be a primitive form of introspection (far from full-blown self-consciousness). Here, the perceiver registers his own mental states that accompany certain behaviors and replicates or simulates these mental states when observing another person perform the respective behaviors (Goldman 2001; Gordon 1992).

In either case, to move from behavioral imitation to mental imitation requires some ability to distinctly register and/or reconstruct one's experiences. This primitive introspective ability should therefore be considered the second precursor of mental state inference.[9]

Third, of critical importance is the grasp of a person's *directedness* to an object. An organism that understands directedness observes the reliable orientation of certain body parts (e.g., eyes, hands) toward certain objects and, from these observations, makes predictions about subsequent behavior. The directedness concept thus precedes the more sophisticated mental concepts of attention and goal (Wellman and Phillips 2001).

The understanding of directedness relies on the prior ability to appropriately parse the behavior stream into intention-relevant units (Baird and Baldwin 2001), which is the fourth precursor. These units may at first be derived from a spatial frequency analysis of movement (e.g., fast versus slow, small versus large, start versus stop), with no understanding of the units' meaning. With increasing appreciation of person–object directedness (and aided by repeat viewing), certain movement patterns, such as approach and grasp or look and turn, will become distinct and—with the help of imitative and introspective capacities—meaningful beyond observable pattern recognition.

A final precursor is the capacity for joint attention, which is the recognition that self and another person are both directed at the same object. This recognition relies in all likelihood on eye detection and gaze following (Baron-Cohen 1995; Butterworth 1991) and requires, similar to imitation, a sort of matching between self and other ("I am directed at O and she is directed at O"). The behavior of declarative pointing ("Look, a butterfly") becomes a powerful means to instigate joint attention, and emotions simultaneously triggered by the object of attention become shared emotions, furthering the practice for empathy.

The emergence of these precursors may well have taken a few million years (MacWhinney 2002). But once several of them were in place, they built on each other and enabled new capacities to evolve. I have already pointed to the supportive role that introspection plays in refining imitation and to the necessary role of grasping directedness for the development of joint attention. Beyond that, joint attention and introspection help differentiate the concept of directedness into subclasses that may launch distinct mental state concepts: pre-action approach (→ goals), pre-action avoidance (→ fear), post-action success expression (→ joy), and post-action failure expression (→ anger). This differentiated grasp of directedness in turn refines imitation, because the perceiver now becomes sensitive to (and can imitate) more abstract agent–object relations, not only mere physical movement patterns. An appreciation of joint attention and imitation finally facilitates simple forms of teaching, sharing, and other socially coordinated actions.

2.4.3   When Did Theory of Mind Emerge?

One approach to narrow down the time frame for the emergence of a theory of mind is to look at successively older milestones in human evolution and ask whether they could have possibly been accomplished without a theory of mind. The first such milestone is *Homo sapiens*'s painting of imaginary figures in the caves of Lascaux, about twenty thoursand years ago. To paint such figures, one needs to represent one's own symbolic act of painting, one's representation of a (never before seen) creature, and most likely also the responses of community members. Lewis Binford (1981) also credits *Homo* of this age with fully mastering organized hunting, which certainly

requires multiple representations of one's own and others' plans, perceptions, thoughts, and intentions, all embedded in a joint goal.

A next, older milestone is the great migration period, starting at least one
hundred thousand years ago, when *Homo sapiens* left Africa and expanded
into Asia, Europe, Australia, and finally the Americas (Cavalli-Sforza 2000).
The level of coordination, planning, mutual trust, and joint action in preparing for and executing an extended migration is inconceivable without a
theory of mind. Moreover, the migration to Australia, and probably to south-
east Asia, required the use of boats, whose construction, use, and maintenance required social planning and understanding as well as teaching and
learning of technology (e.g., maritime navigation principles). Cavalli-Sforza
also suggests that human language acquired its modern complexity around
one hundred thousand years ago, which would have been a tremendous
tool to use during migration over many generations. What exactly "modern complexity" means is a bit unclear, but it can perhaps be defined as
the simultaneous presence of syntactic power to represent complex facts
and communicative power to socially transmit these representations to offspring and community members, leading to a hitherto unknown efficiency
of teaching and learning. Clearly, these characteristics of language, and the
conditions of acquiring it, presuppose an advanced theory of mind.

According to the archaeological record, there was an even earlier migration period, when *Homo erectus* expanded from Africa into Asia about one to
two million years ago (Cavalli-Sforza 2000). If at this time, too, migration involved social coordination, then theory of mind could be more than a million years old, and with it the social organization in which mentalizing was
learned, practiced, and put to cooperative use.

One critical archaeological finding strengthens this hypothesis (Leakey
1994). Skull measurements of the Turkana boy (a young *Homo erectus* from
about 1.5 million years ago) suggest that *erectus* infants were born with
brains about a third of the adult size. Apparently, baby brains could not be
any larger given the constraints on the diameter of the female pelvis open-
ing that would still support flexible locomotion. The infants' low maturity
and helplessness (unparalleled among primates) required more care and
social protection, but it also opened the door for more social learning. The
infant's brain growth (adding 200% of its starting volume) must have occurred in the context of social and emotional interactions and in exposure
to sophisticated behavior patterns, the learning of which literally became

part of the child's anatomy. We might also speculate (with Mameli 2001) that adults treated infants as more capable than they really were, expressing expectations that pushed learning forward in each successive generation. This is a purely cultural evolution process, but one with enormous power. Just consider similar phenomena today, when parents expect their children to learn, do, and become so much more than genetically indistinguishable children one hundred to two hundred years ago. In this way education is highly progressive: Each generation that was expected to learn more than the previous one expects the next generation to learn even more.

Homo erectus still had much to learn. There is no archaeological record older than 1.4 million years of organized tool manufacturing using complex template replications (often taken as a sign of joint planning and teaching); no record of rituals, personal decoration, or burying; and little evidence of sustained and sophisticated social organization (Mithen 1996). Over the next million years, the *Homo* species experienced a last increase in brain volume (from about 900cc to 1350cc), but it may have been the anatomical integration and cultural exploitation of the isolated abilities already available in *Homo erectus* that made the biggest difference (Calvin 1996; Mithen 1996). Similarly, the moderately advanced theory of mind in *erectus* may have acquired some refinement over this time period, but it was arguably the coalescence of theory of mind, language, and cognitive simulation—all in the context of growing and complexifying social organization—that spawned modern intelligence, social and otherwise (Smith 1996; Devlin 2000; Dunbar 1993; Malle 2002a).

The current archaeological record is sparse for the time between two and six million years ago, so it is difficult to say when the precursors of *Homo erectus*'s theory of mind emerged. Initial research on theory of mind was sparked by the hypothesis that the great apes[10] share with humans the capacity to represent mental states (Premack and Woodruff 1978; see also Byrne and White 1988). If so, theory of mind would be at least six million years old, which is the time when humans split off from the evolutionary line shared with apes. Increasingly over the last decade, however, theories and evidence have shifted toward the position that genuine theory of mind capacities can only be found in humans and must therefore have evolved some time after the hominid split off six million years ago (Baron-Cohen 1999; Malle 2002a; Povinelli 1996, 2001; Tomasello 1998b). The evidence currently available is incomplete and thus makes any position on this issue tentative. However, the data appear to favor the claim that apes, smart as they are in many respects, do not have genuine mindreading capacities.

2.4.3 Ape Theory of Mind?

For the reader who would like to see the support for this (tentative) conclusion, I offer a brief excursion in to the extant literature on ape theory of mind. To begin with, the evidence supporting the claim that apes are able to make mental state inferences consists primarily of field observations, anecdotes, and single-case studies (e.g., Byrne and Whiten 1988; Gómez 1996; Premack and Woodruff 1978; Savage-Rumbaugh 1984). By contrast, the evidence against mindreading capacities in apes consists primarily of controlled experiments and some field studies (Povinelli and Eddy 1996a; Tomasello and Call 1997).

When comparing these findings, one might argue that apes show more evidence of mental state inference capacities in the wild than in the laboratory. But that would not be correct. It isn't the case that the same tests are run in the wild and in the lab and that apes pass them in one context but not in the other. It also isn't the case that the laboratory somehow inhibits intelligent behavior, for some of the most remarkable achievements in ape symbolic communication, imitation, and attention have occurred in laboratory contexts (e.g., Povinelli, Nelson, and Boysen 1990; Savage-Rumbaugh and Lewin 1994; for a review, see Tomasello and Call 1997). Rather, the social behaviors that seem to suggest mindreading capacities in the wild are subject to a number of alternative explanations not involving mental state inference. Under laboratory conditions, by comparison, proper controls can be put in place that could isolate genuine mindreading, and in those contexts apes do not show compelling evidence of grasping mental states.

Apes do display, however, two capacities that make them socially competent without having to employ mental state inferences: refined behavior reading and intelligent learning. Behavior reading is the ability to monitor other organisms' movements, orientations, gazes, and action directions without considering mental states (Povinelli 2001; Tomasello and Call 1997). Intelligent learners rely on associative and operant learning but are sensitive to complex stimulus configurations and, with enough trials, can detect statistical relationships between their behaviors and certain outcomes.

Until recently, the predominant belief was that apes recognize and manipulate mental states whereas monkeys are merely excellent behavior readers (e.g., Cheney and Seyfarth 1990; Mitchell 1997; Mithen 1996; Whiten 1996). However, Povinelli (2001) examined the primate literature on theory of mind and concluded that apes, too, derive their social intelligence from a refined behavior reading system. Apes' behavior reading is more sophisticated and flexible than the monkeys' system but does not include a recognition that the mind is the underlying source of observed behavior (see also Tomsello and Call 1997).

As one example of this limitation, Povinelli and Eddy (1996a) found that, despite their refined practice of locking onto eyes and following gaze, chimpanzees showed no grasp of the mental nature of seeing. In study after study, the apes failed to appreciate the fact that eyes that are covered (e.g., by a bucket or blindfolds) cannot process visual information. Eyes, as well as body posture, are carefully processed as indicators of subsequent events and can therefore become discriminative stimuli; but eyes are not understood as an entrance to the mind.

When we apply this model of behavior reading and learning to anecdotes that are highly suggestive of primate theory of mind (e.g., Byrne and Whiten 1988), we see that the postulate of mindreading is not necessary to account for these findings. For example, chimp A holds a banana behind his back until a competitor is out of sight and then eats the banana on his own. Or consider chimp E, who tries to mate with a female in the vicinity of a higher-status male and covers his erect penis in a way that prevents the higher-status male from seeing it. Behaviors like these are often interpreted as demonstrating deception and *thereby* demonstrate representations of the other's seeing, wanting, and believing.

There is little doubt that these behaviors are functionally deceptive; but what cognitive mechanism underlies them is far less clear (Hauser 1996). It isn't difficult to see that the behaviors may well be enabled by behavior reading capacities and intelligent learning. Chimp A can accomplish the banana deception by (a) monitoring conspecific B's body orientation and field of gaze vis-à-vis A, (b) being sensitive to a class of B's orientations that in the past have led to loss of resources, and (c) learning that positioning the banana behind her back is met with the reward of keeping it. Similarly, chimp E's deception requires only orientation monitoring and learning that positioning his hand over his penis a certain way leads to positive outcomes.

Just as we don't ascribe mentalizing capacities to animals that play dead, feign injury, or change their appearance on sighting a predator, we should be cautious to ascribe mentalizing capacities to the deceptive behaviors we see in wild apes. Sophisticated as they are, these behaviors may rely merely on good behavior reading skills and intelligent learning.

The same caution applies to laboratory findings. For example, Sarah, the chimp tested by Premack and Woodruff (1978), needed fifty learning trials to reliably accomplish a deceptive pointing gesture (misleading a trainer into turning over one cup that did not contain food so that Sarah could keep the food under the other cup to herself). This large number of trials suggests both that imperative gestures (pointing to the cup that has the food that Sarah wants) are deeply ingrained in apes and that extended learning, not mental understanding, explains Sarah's eventual display of the deceptive pointing gesture.

Similarly, Povinelli and colleagues (1992) trained chimps to take one of two roles in a mutually dependent interaction sequence with a human. In the sequence, the "informant" pointed to a tray that, from his perspective, visibly contained food. Then the "operator," who could not see the contents of the trays, followed the pointing and made the selected tray available (using some mechanical device). Finally, both informant and operator shared the culinary reward. Three out of four chimps were easily able to switch roles—that is, they were able to be a proper operator after only having been trained as informant or a proper informant after only having been trained as an operator. One might be inclined to interpret this finding as demonstrating chimpanzees' ability to read their partner's intentions and then replicate that intention after switching to his role (Mitchell 1997). However, an alternative account emphasizes the chimpanzees' ability to parse and represent action sequences and to be sensitive to the mutual dependence of these actions in gaining a reward. It appears that the chimps translated an other-action into a self-action, reminiscent of the claims made about "mirror neurons" (Rizzolotti et al. 2002) and suggestive of at least a simple form of imitation. By itself, however, this accomplishment does not provide strong evidence for mental state inferences.

When we turn away from theory of mind capacities proper and examine some of the precursors of theory of mind, it is obvious that great apes can parse action into intention-relevant units (e.g., when responding to communicative actions; Savage-Rumbaugh et al. 1993), and they are capable of understanding the directedness of actions at objects and individuals (e.g., when interacting in mutual dependence; Povinelli, Nelson, and Boysen 1992). But we also find significant limitations of apes' precursor abilities. Unenculturated chimpanzees show no reliable skills of joint attention and social referencing (Tomasello 1998b). That is, they do not point to or show objects to each other (Premack 1988), and they do not use others' faces as indicators for how they should feel about a new object. Apes' imitative learning abilities are also limited (Hauser 1996; Smith 1996; Tomasello 1996; Whiten 1999), though this assessment is difficult to make given the many different subforms of imitation (Russon et al. 1998; Whiten and Ham 1992). Apes' action programs can be "primed" by others' actions, which increases the likelihood that they will perform a similar action; but spontaneous copying of others' behaviors is rare. Also, it seems quite clear that active adult-to-child teaching is virtually nonexistent among apes (Boesch 1991, 1993), though once again, it depends on what we expect from genuine teaching. At last some apes have put their young into opportunities that facilitate individual learning; but they hardly ever *demonstrate* to their young a sequence of actions (Russon 1997). We might suspect that apes can exhibit simple forms of imitation and teaching, especially after human enculturation (Call and Tomasello 1996). However, we certainly don't see a complete set of theory of mind precursors in our closest primate relatives.

Perhaps the future will bring empirical evidence that could convince skeptics to attribute genuine mental state inference abilities—or at least precursors of theory of mind—to the great apes. For now, I conclude that a theory of mind emerged after the hominid split-off some time between six million and two million years ago. This is, unfortunately, a large time window and one for which we currently have the sparsest archaeological evidence (Leakey 1994). In consolation, we can be fairly confident that future research in archaeology as well as primatology will teach us much more about the evolutionary history of theory of mind.

2.5 Summary

I have gone to some detail in describing the components, functions, and origins of the folk theory of mind, and I did so for multiple reasons. First, this folk-conceptual framework is an essential element of human social cognition but has been repeatedly overlooked in social psychological treatments of social cognition (e.g., Augoustinos and Walker 1995; Fiske and Taylor 1991; Kunda 1999). For that reason alone it deserves serious attention.

Second, read side by side, the developmental, clinical, and evolutionary literatures illustrate the complexity of the folk theory of mind and thereby prepare the reader for a similar complexity that characterizes behavior explanations. In addition, interesting questions for research arise from this multifaceted picture of theory of mind. For example, autistic individuals should show impoverished explanations of behavior to the extent that they lack mental and intentional concepts. The specific deficits in their explanations may conversely reveal the elements of a theory of mind that they have mastered and those they have not. As another example, if chimpanzees do have at least some elements of a theory of mind, then they should be able to use this capacity to explain behavior. Measuring explanations without language is of course a challenge, but at the same time it represents an attractive opportunity to isolate the functions of explanation that are independent of language.

Third, and most important, if the folk theory of mind guides all thinking about human behavior, then behavior explanations, too, must be under this guidance. What consequences does such a guidance have for explanations? Put differently, what is it that uniquely characterizes those explanations that rely on a theory of mind? This question was not addressed by traditional attribution research, and by answering it the theory proposed in this book deviates most markedly from traditional approaches. Chapters 4 through 6 lay out the answer in detail. The following précis highlights some of its elements by sketching the place of behavior explanations within a theory of mind.

2.6 Précis: Behavior Explanations within a Theory of Mind

One possible characterization of behavior explanations within a theory of mind is that they make reference to *mental causes* (whereas explanations of physical events do not). This is the position taken by several developmental researchers who have traced the origin and advancement of behavior explanations throughout the preschool years. According to this position, children as young as three systematically use "psychological" or mental state explanations for human behavior (e.g., Wellman, Hickling, and Schult 1997). Such psychological explanations comprise statements that refer to the agent's beliefs and desires but also to moods and lack of knowledge (Schult and Wellman 1997; Bartsch and Wellman 1995, chap. 6).

The mental cause position is certainly correct in several respects. Humans not only recognize causality among physical events, and better than the great apes do (Povinelli 2000), but they also recognize causality among mental and behavioral events. Moreover, they can depict these causal relations in sophisticated language. Mental causes set psychological explanations apart from physical explanations, which is one achievement of a theory of mind (Wellman, Hickling, and Schult 1997; Schult and Wellman 1997). However, a theory of mind confers more than that on explanations.

A pure mental cause model confounds two types of psychological causation that are distinct in people's folk theory of mind (Buss 1978; Heider 1958; Malle 1999; Searle 1983). The first is a version of straightforward "mechanical" causation—one that explains unintentional events by referring to mental causes (such as moods, emotions, or wants) in the same mechanical way that physical causes explain physical events. The second is *intentional causation,* which refers to representational mental states (such as beliefs and desires) as the *reasons* of an agent's intentional action. Within mechanical causation, mere causes explain unintentional behavior. Within intentional causation, the agent's reasons explain intentional action in a way that presumes some amount of deliberation, rationality, and choice on the part of the agent.

As a result of conflating the two mechanisms of causation, current developmental studies on explanation do not tell us whether three-year-old children who give "psychological explanations" appreciate the difference between mental states as reasons (e.g., "She bought milk because she wanted to make a cake") and mental states as causes (e.g., "She was nervous because she really wanted to win the game"). This is a particularly intriguing question since three-year-olds do seem to distinguish between intentional and unintentional behavior, and we must now wonder whether they have a distinct concept of intentional causation.

The class of behavior explanations that is uniquely guided by the human theory of mind is thus defined not by the type of cause (e.g., mental versus physical) but by the presumed mechanism of causation (i.e., intentional versus mechanical). This uniqueness is anchored in the folk concept of intentionality. The concept not only identifies certain mental causes that characteristically bring about intentional behaviors (i.e., beliefs, desires, intentions), but it tells us more about the causal mechanism that is uniquely involved in producing intentional action—that of reasoning and choice. Thus, a theory of behavior explanation must put special emphasis on accurately describing and accounting for reason explanations of intentional action, because they are what uniquely characterizes behavior explanations as embedded in a folk theory of mind.

The following chapters lay out in detail how the conceptual framework of mind is one essential determinant of the natural phenomenon of behavior explanations. I begin with basic questions in chapter 3: Why do people form behavior explanations, under what conditions, and which kinds of behaviors do they explain? Then I move to the specific concepts and tools that make up *how* people explain behavior (chapter 4). Finally, I examine the psychological processes that underlie people's construction of behavior explanations (chapter 5).

3   Origins: Why and When People Explain Behavior

I once read this intriguing message on the Internet:

A woman was asked "*Why did you stay with your abusive husband?*" She asked in return: "Why does everyone ask that? Why don't they ask, *Why did he do that?*"

This exchange harbors many insights. One is that the woman, in her retort, did not just want an explanation for why everyone asks the one question rather than the other; she also *criticized* the act of asking one question rather the other. In general, explanations (i.e., answers to why-questions) have multiple functions and multiple motives. This chapter explores what those motives are—what the *point* is of explaining behavior.

Asking why people explain behavior is a quaintly self-conscious question, because in answering it we of course provide a behavior explanation. And just as in folk explanations of behavior, in our scientific explanation, too, we must distinguish between different ways of answering this why-question. Any given time people explain a behavior, we might say "They want to know," "They want to make the other person understand," or "They are trying to avoid blame." Many reasons such as these exist that account for why people explain specific behaviors in specific situations. As psychologists, however, we are also interested in the "causal histories" that underlie those reasons—the background factors that generate the many specific reasons across situations.

I contend that there are two such causal histories, or broad motivations, for explaining behavior: finding meaning and managing social interaction. These two causal histories correspond to the two forms in which explanations exist in the world: as cognitive representations and as communicative acts. This duality of explanations will recur many times in this book; for now I focus on the motivational origin of each form.

3.1 Finding Meaning

Meaning is an elusive term. There is the meaning of a word, the meaning of someone's utterance, the meaning of a behavior, and, larger yet, the meaning of life, the universe, and everything (see Adams 1982, for an explication of the latter). The meaning of a behavior is what concerns us most here, but the meaning of words and utterances show some parallels with the meaning of behaviors. In all three cases, meaning points to the place of an element within a larger whole. The meaning of a word can typically be understood only within a network of other terms; the meaning of an utterance can only be understood within the context in which it was expressed; and the meaning of an action can only be understood in the context of other actions and their relationship to the world. In addition, there is an important hierarchical relation: To understand the meaning of words, one must understand the meaning of utterances, and to understand the meaning of utterances, one must understand the meaning of actions. Developmentally, a child learns to understand actions first, then the meaning of (short) utterances, and finally the specific, lexical meaning of words, even in isolation. In evolution, too, a language that contains words with isolated, lexical meaning is quite sophisticated and must have emerged from a language in which whole speech acts and gestures have meaning ("Go!" "Give me this"), and such a language had to be preceded by the grasp of actions as meaningful events—events that are directed at something, done for some purpose (Malle 2002a; Wray 2000).

When people search for meaning, they strive for an understanding of one thing in its relationship to other things. Searching for meaning restores the coherence within a "knowledge structure," a network of representations. People search for meaning when a link is missing in their representation of reality or when various elements in this representation contradict each other. In Moravcsik's (1998) terms, this is a situation in which something is *problematic*. "The problematic," he writes, "involves seeing something strange in light of some [. . .] structures and beliefs that we have already" (p. 158). Finding meaning is then to reconcile the strange element with these structures, thereby making the network of representations complete and coherent (Kruglanski 1989; Read, Druian, and Miller 1989; Read and Miller 1998; Thagard 1989). This coherence is achieved by linking the strange element to some part of the structure. In the case of actions the linkage can vary—the meaning of a behavior could be information about how it arose, to what it points in the future, or what other events it resembles.

The search and creation of meaning may be a uniquely human capacity. Indeed, Jerome Bruner (1990) emphasized that "the central concept of a human psychology is *meaning* and the processes and transactions involved in the construction of meanings" (p. 33). Some animals can be surprised, perhaps confused. But humans can actively manage their surprise or confusion by seeking clarifying information, reasoning about the facts at hand, recalling similar pasts, and simulating possible futures. This ability to detect gaps in one's understanding and to reinstate understanding by constructing explanations is obviously a powerful tool for succeeding in novel environments and for manipulating environments in line with one's own purposes (Craik 1943; Gopnik 2000).

People's persistent attempts to create meaning—and the pains they experience when lacking meaning—have been widely recognized and documented. Robert Jervis (1976) pointed out that "to admit that a phenomenon cannot be explained . . . is both psychologically uncomfortable and intellectually unsatisfying" (p. 319). Alison Gopnik (2000) remarked that explanations have the "character of a motivational or drive system" and that not having an explanation can be an "unsettling, disturbing, and arousing experience, one that seems to compel us to some sort of resolution" (p. 311). Harold Garfinkel (1967) and other "ethnomethodologists" illustrated the distress and dismay that people experience when fundamental rules of conduct (e.g., listening, politeness, and turn taking in conversation) are breached and, hence, the meaning of an interaction suddenly is cast in doubt. In fact, for most cases in which expectations are violated, even ones less significant than involving basic social conduct, people will wonder why and try to come up with an explanation (Clary and Tesser 1983; Hastie 1984; Weiner 1985b).

The phenomenon of dissonance reduction can also be taken as an attempt to render one's actions meaningful (Stone 2001). If I acted in a way that was unusual or surprising (and especially if it was somewhat socially undesirable), I have a hard time admitting to myself that I don't know why I acted this way. As a result, I will try to come up with a sensible reason for why I acted, hence I *rationalize* my action. Not every causal narrative will be equally "meaningful," but having no narrative is apparently distressing.

Victims of traumatic events can experience a state of meaninglessness when fundamental assumptions about their life, social justice, or human nature have been shattered (Frankl 1962; Janoff-Bulman 1992; Taylor 1983; Zimbardo 1999), and they can more successfully overcome this trauma by means of constructing explanations (Orbuch et al. 1994). In deteriorating relationships, too, and especially after a divorce, people try to construct a meaningful web of explanations (Harvey, Orbuch, and Weber 1992; Weiss 1975). All these challenges might be subsumed under the category of threats to the self, which certainly seem to trigger a search for meaning and explanation (Liu and Steele 1986).

As one of the three major factors common to all counseling and psychotherapy techniques, Day (2004), following Frank and Frank (1991), identifies a "rationale, conceptual scheme, or myth that provides a plausible explanation for the client's symptoms and prescribes a ritual or procedure for resolving them; the client and therapist both must accept the rationale, scheme, or myth" (p. 8). In the medical domain, too, finding meaning plays a critical role in the success of treatments. Daniel Moerman (2002) presents fascinating evidence for numerous ways in which patients' health improves even when no active physical treatment is applied. This phenomenon is usually referred to as the "placebo effect," but Moerman argues convincingly that it is more than just a nuisance effect of expectancies and conditioning. Rather, it is a "meaning response." Patients get better when they have a label for what is wrong with them; when they see their doctor convinced that a certain treatment will help them; when they take a pill or undergo a surgical intervention that they believe changes their disturbed internal state; or when they take part in some other ritual (e.g., talking, dancing, praying) that promises to restore health. In each case, patients are pained not only by the illness itself but by an incomplete and inconsistent model of their state of being (the illness is the "problematic" or "strange" element in Moravcsik's terms). With the help of the treatment, they are able to restore some coherence by adding a new "link"—the purported causal force of the intervention.

Finally, one could consider society's handling of mental illness as a form of restoring collective meaning. By classifying mental deviations into a scheme of illnesses, characteristic symptoms, and degrees of abnormality, strange and inexplicable actions become somewhat more meaningful (both to observers and to the agents themselves). But not only the medical model of mental illness reflects this need for meaning. Even its major opponents explain "away" the behavioral or psychological deviance by considering mental illness as a social labeling process (Horwitz 2002; Szasz 1961) or as rational impression management (Braginsky and Braginsky 1971; Fontana 1971; Schlenker 1980, chap. 10). Such attempts to leave no deviant patterns unexplained can lead to quite stunning assertions; to wit, that mental patients seek institutionalization primarily when life outside becomes unpleasant, such as during the winter months (Braginsky, Braginsky, and Ring 1969) or that mental patients actually desire to remain in their institutions (Krim 1968).

In all of the above cases, people face challenges to their understanding and wonder why the challenging events occurred. Conversely, reaching an understanding of the events places the events in a larger network of assumptions and beliefs, generating the pleasure of "cognitive consonance" and promising to reinstate control, predictability, self-integrity, and conceptual coherence.

Finding meaning for behavior is probably related to the more general human tendency to find significance in virtually any stimulus patterns— constellations of clouds, stars, or tea leaves, patterns of objects falling, planets moving, or weather changing. One might expect, then, that finding meaning in nature by means of explanations is a general phenomenon of which behavior explanations are a specific instance.

However, I suggest the opposite view, that most of the other attempts to find meaning are modeled after meaning in the human behavior domain. Early science was usually anthropomorphic in the sense that it postulated humanlike forces in the natural world, and religion and spirituality frequently include agents (gods, angels, and the like) who have knowledge, plans, emotions, and perform actions. Even in describing and explaining computer processes or the behavior of subatomic particles, experts and lay people alike use language that is heavily colored by the folk theory of mind and behavior (e.g., Herbsleb 1999; Huhns and Singh 1998).

Despite the wide range of situations that can pose a question of meaning, the domain of human behavior is particularly prone to cause surprise and confusion and hence to trigger a search for meaning. That is because behavior is inherently more complex and variable than other natural processes (excepting, perhaps, random processes) and because people who live in social communities are highly dependent on each other's actions and experiences—or rather, on an understanding of each other's actions and experiences. Some scholars have even argued that, in human history, the challenges of social communities that grew in size and complexity sparked the evolution not only of *social* cognition, including behavior explanations and predictions, but also of cognition in general, including language, reasoning, and creative thinking (e.g., Bogdan 2000). The conceptual and cognitive apparatus that helps people construct meaning for human behavior may well be fundamental to cognition and, at the very least, cannot be reduced to general cognitive capacities such as covariation detection or memory for temporal and physical contiguity (*pace* Cheng and Novick 1990; Försterling 1992; Glymour 2000).

3.1.1 Explanatory Meaning and What It Facilitates

Meaning brings intrinsic pleasure and its absence, displeasure. But, surely, the complex explanation apparatus has not evolved merely to bring humans more pleasure. Its adaptive value must lie in cognitive operations or social conduct that would be difficult or impossible to sustain without this apparatus. There are at least three classes of such conduct that are critically facilitated by explanations. They are social prediction, self-regulation, and behavior management.

One can predict some behaviors merely by observing a repeated pattern, without being able to explain why that pattern holds. However, for most human behavior, these actuarial predictions will not get us very far. Explanations aim at identifying the factors that generated the behavior, such as reasons, emotions, specific situational factors, or traits. Identifying some of these factors greatly improves one's ability to predict the resulting behavioral event.

Self-regulation, too, is aided by explanatory meaning. Self-regulation is a hallmark of human psychology—people can decide not to act on their immediate desires, delay short-term gratification in favor of long-term benefits, distract themselves, direct their emotions and moods, and even alter (with practice) their physiological responses. All of these regulatory actions are of course imperfect—how often do we succumb to short-term gains or fail to regulate our moods?—but with explanatory knowledge they can be improved. If I know, for example, that my food lust can be better held in check when I take time to prepare an elaborate meal rather than just popping a TV dinner into the microwave, I can both regulate looming weight gain and enjoy the benefits of excellent food.

Finally, even though one can occasionally manage (i.e., influence, prevent, encourage) other people's behavior without knowing what drives it, having such knowledge permits behavior management that is far more effective and reliable. Take the example of a school counselor faced with a young student who cannot sit still in class and is unable to study for any significant amount of time. If the counselor learns that the student's grandfather is dying, subsequent attempts to change the student's unruly behavior will take a very different route than if the counselor had no such knowledge (and might resort to a crude attention deficit disorder diagnosis).

But we may not want go as far as to assume that prediction and control (of self and other) are the *point* of explanations. If prediction by itself were so important, humans would have evolved a capacity to formulate regression equations (which they have not; Nisbett and Ross 1980). And if control by itself were so important, people would not need to be aware of the mediating cognitive event of understanding—they could simply act on the tacit knowledge of how to regulate and manage themselves and their environment (like many animals do). There is an added benefit of representing— of being actually aware of—the understanding gained through explanations. By knowing why events happen, by understanding the mechanisms by which events unfold, people can simulate counterfactual as well as future events under a variety of possible circumstances (Craik 1943). Moreover, explanations also enter into people's evaluations of others—blame, for example, often depends on the presumed cause of or justification for a transgression. Finally, people can regulate the very process of finding meaning, increasing the search intensity when being a detective (professionally or in everyday social life) and decreasing it when having to perform under pressure, such as a soldier in combat, or an athlete in competition.

3.2   Managing Interactions

Finding meaning through behavior explanations, we have seen, is both rewarding in itself and beneficial for a number of other social goals. Simply representing meaning in one's mind, however, is insufficient in many social settings where managing people's thoughts and actions is of primary importance (which is arguably the case in all of social interaction; Goffman 1959; Leary 1995; Schlenker 1980). Explanations have to be formulated in language to effectively change an audience's impressions, move their emotions, or direct their actions. Clarifying one's goals, excusing one's actions, or presenting someone else's motives as virtuous all require communicating one's explanation to an audience. The social-interactive functions that are served by communicative explanations constitute the second major motivation for behavior explanations.

When behavior explanations are expressed in communication, their function lies in the meaning they achieve for one's *communication partner*. Thus, communicative explanations are an attempt to create meaning in another person, much like private explanations are an attempt to create meaning in oneself. In many cases, the ultimate aim is *shared meaning* among the interaction partners—a common representation of reality about which they can jointly reason and on which they can jointly act (Higgins 1992).

But communicative explanations also allow the explainer to influence the other person's beliefs, impressions, and ultimately actions (Antaki 1994; Forsyth 1980; Scott and Lyman 1968; Schlenker 1980). By influencing the mind or behavior of one's interaction partners, communicative explanations are one way of *managing social interaction*. This function becomes readily apparent when we consider cases in which actors behaved in an undesirable way and use explanations to adjust their communication partner's impression of them. For example, a research assistant explained his absence in lab and class this way:

(3-1) I apologize for not being in contact with you lately. I have been out of town for the last week. I had some personal family matters that I had to attend to and that could not be helped. I had to miss class because of this as well. I am working on the project and should have a lot to give you this week.

The function of managing interactions may at first glance seem like a specific version of the broader notion that explanations help the person control his or her environment (Heider 1958). But according to this broad control notion, it is the *knowledge* contained in explanations (the cognitive model of how the world works) that helps explainers control the environment, whereas in the case of interaction management, it is the *social speech act* of offering an explanation that helps explainers gain control. Explanations that control the environment actually have to be true; explanations that manage interaction only have to be compelling. If they are, communicative explanations can successfully create a feeling of understanding in one's audience, manage a joint plan, or justify a dubitable action.

Explanations that manage interaction must be verbally expressed. Compared to meaning-finding explanations, interaction-managing explanations therefore develop later during childhood, and presumably evolved more recently in human history, because they require fairly sophisticated language capacity. But because both in development and evolution new challenges are preferably met with existing tools, verbal explanations that manage interactions are in all likelihood constructed according to the same principles and conceptual assumptions as are explanations that find meaning. Precisely because communicative explanations try to create and shape meaning in one's interaction partners, these explanations have to look and operate just like the kinds of explanations that the interaction partners would construct if they tried to explain the relevant events to themselves.

Table 3.1 summarizes the discussion so far. The general motivation of finding meaning gives rise to private explanations, which occur in the mind and whose specific goals center on the explainer's gain in understanding and control. The general motivation of managing interactions gives rise to communicative explanations, which occur in conversation and whose

Table 3.1
Comparison between two major motivations for behavior explanations

	Finding Meaning	Managing Interaction
Explanation Class	Private explanations	Communicative explanations
Context	In private thought	In conversation
Specific Goals	• satisfy one's own curiosity	• satisfy others' curiosity
	• allay one's confusion	• lessen their confusion
	• predict or manipulate reality	• manage their impressions
		• manipulate their behavior
		• combat disagreements
		• coordinate joint plans or actions
Conceptual Framework	Folk theory of mind and behavior	Folk theory of mind and behavior

specific goals include the audience's gain in understanding, the explainer's control over it, and the coordination of joint activities. Significantly, both private and communicative explanations are framed by the same assumptions people have about mind and behavior. So even though the two classes of explanation differ in their functions and social-cognitive roles, they rely on the same conceptual framework—the folk theory of mind and behavior (see chapter 2).

Now that we have a reasonable notion of *why* people construct explanations, the next question is *when*, or under what specific circumstances, people construct explanations.

3.3   When Do People Explain Behavior? A Theory of Wondering Why

In discussing the specific conditions that lead to behavior explanations, I consider first the case of private explanations (those given to oneself facing a why-question) and then move on to communicative explanations.

3.3.1   Wondering Why in Private Thought

When do people ask why-questions in a search for meaning? The previous section has provided us with one condition: when there is lack of understanding. But there are at least two more conditions. One appears trivial but is nonetheless powerful: People try to explain only events that they are aware of. There are plenty of events and behaviors going on at any moment that I don't understand and for which I might want an explanation if only I were aware of them; but fortunately I am not, or else I would do nothing but seek explanations.

In addition to event awareness and lack of understanding, there is one more condition of wondering why, and it further qualifies the notion that lack of understanding always triggers explanations. Unexplained events are bothersome only if a person cares about them. Unless people care about something they don't understand, they will not wonder why. (This shows once more that the intrinsic meaning-providing function of explanations is tightly connected with other, more extrinsic functions such as coordination or control.) However, the threshold for finding *human behavior* relevant appears to be quite low—that is, people seem to care about other people's behaviors almost by default. How else would we account for the pleasures of people-watching, wondering about their history and goals, and speculating about their relationships?

These are then the three conditions for wondering why (Malle and Knobe 1997b).[1]

• *Awareness.* To wonder why an event occurred, people must be aware of the event—that is, notice, observe, or think about it.

• *Lack of understanding.* Once people are aware of an event, they wonder why it occurred only if they do not already have an explanation—that is, they must be in a state of nonunderstanding (or have a "knowledge gap"; Bromberger 1965; Hilton and Slugoski 1986; Hilton 1990). Nonunderstanding is subjective—for people to wonder why, they must *believe* they lack an explanation (even if in fact they do have one), and if people believe they do have an explanation (even if in fact they do not), they will not wonder why.

• *Relevance.* Once people are aware of an event and think they do not understand why it occurred, they have to care about the event and their own lack of understanding it. They will care, and be motivated to wonder why, if their lack of understanding challenges a current or enduring goal, assumption, or principle (e.g., Jones and Thibaut 1958; Kruglanski 1989; Heider 1958).

This theory of wondering why accounts for the consistent finding in the literature that negative events are likely to elicit wonderings (e.g., Bohner et al. 1988; Wong and Weiner 1981). That is because negative events are more likely than positive events to satisfy all three conditions of wondering. Negative events typically satisfy the condition of awareness as people quickly and strongly attend to negative events (Pratto and John 1991; Taylor 1991). Negative events also tend to create nonunderstanding because they contradict people's general expectation that good things will happen (Boucher and Osgood 1969; Taylor 1991). And negative events are typically relevant because they challenge a variety of people's needs—for control, prediction, self-integrity, or cognitive and affective balance (Heider 1958; Steele 1988; Taylor 1991).

The theory of wondering why also accounts for the finding that unexpected or surprising events are likely to elicit wonderings (e.g., Pyszczynski and Greenberg 1981), because they are more likely than expected events to satisfy the conditions of wondering why. Unexpected events typically satisfy the condition of awareness because they are noticed and processed longer (e.g., Belmore 1987; see Fiske and Taylor 1991, for a review); they create nonunderstanding because, by definition, they contradict prior knowledge; and they are relevant because they challenge assumptions and make prediction or control more difficult.

3.3.2 Wondering Why in Communication

How does this theory of wondering why apply to communicative explanations? Such explanations are motivated by attempts to manage one's interaction partner's thoughts and actions, such as when an explainer specifically tries to create meaning in his interaction partner. People will communicate such behavior explanations when they assume that their partner wonders why a particular behavioral event occurred.

It stands to reason that explainers will obey the same three conditions of wondering why that we have just analyzed for private explanations. That is, people explain an event to another person when they think that this person is aware of the event, does not understand it, and cares about understanding it. The explainer will recognize the need for an explanation most readily when the interaction partner directly expresses her nonunderstanding by asking a why-question. However, our studies of explanations in conversation (Malle and Knobe 1997b; Malle and Pearce 2001) suggest that the frequency of explicit why-questions is rather low. More often speakers *anticipate* that their conversation partner will wonder about an event and spontaneously, or even preemptively, offer an explanation. At times, speakers may respond to a frown or a confused look on their partner's face, but often they will just monitor their own speech and identify a potential need for clarification. In one of our studies, we recorded conversations among friends and strangers and found that only 15 out of 451 explanation episodes (3%) were elicited by the partner's explicit why-questions (Malle, Knobe, and Nelson 2004, study 3).

Communicated behavior explanations are also used for more self-interested interaction management, in which the explainer attempts to adjust, or at times manipulate, the other person's beliefs or actions. Often this management will amount to shaping the audience's impression of the particular behavior explained, and in the most typical case the agent will explain her own action in order to make it look better in the eyes of her audience. But occasionally explainers try to manage the audience's impressions of another agent's behavior, such as when the press speaker accounts for the president's most recent decisions. The impression that the explainer tries to create will normally be a favorable one, but it can be unfavorable as well (e.g., when the opposition accounts for the president's most recent decisions).

A final point to make is that social power modulates the offering of communicative explanations. Those lower in the power hierarchy will be inclined to preemptively offer behavior explanations but not expect the same from those above them. Conversely, those higher up in the hierarchy are in a position to ask why-questions but are not normally themselves answerable to others' why-questions. George W. Bush (in a recent interview with Bob Woodward) put it this way:

I am the commander, see. I do not need to explain why I say things. That's the interesting thing about being the president. Maybe somebody needs to explain to me why they need to say something, but I don't feel like I owe anybody an explanation. (CBS 2002)

3.4   Which Behavioral Events People Explain

Now that we have clarified why and when people explain behavioral events, we have one last question to consider: what kinds of behavioral events do people explain? This question was never posed within the classic attribution framework, because all behavioral events were considered alike (i.e., effects brought about by internal or external causes). But within the folk theory of mind and behavior we find distinct behavioral event types, and so we need to ask which of these event types people select to explain.

There are at least two folk distinctions that are of critical importance for people's selection of events to explain (Malle and Knobe 1997b). People distinguish between events that are *intentional* (e.g., writing a letter) and those that are *unintentional* (e.g., knocking over a glass), and they distinguish between events that are *publicly observable* (e.g., interrupting someone) and those that are *unobservable* (e.g., feeling wistful). By crossing these distinctions, four event types result (see figure 3.1), which can be labeled as follows: (a) *actions* (observable and intentional; e.g., asking for a favor, greeting), (b) *mere behaviors* (observable and unintentional; e.g., shivering, crying), (c) *intentional thoughts* (unobservable and intentional; e.g., searching for things to say, imagining a weekend in the mountains), and (d) *experiences* (unobservable and unintentional; e.g., being nervous, feeling angry).

	Intentional	Unintentional
Observable	actions	mere behaviors
Unobservable	intentional thoughts	experiences

Figure 3.1
Folk classification of behavioral events.

Which of these behavioral event types people explain depends on three variables:

1. The conditions of wondering why (awareness, nonunderstanding, and relevance);

2. The perspective from which the behavior is explained (from the *actor* perspective, people explain their own behavior; from the *observer* perspective, they explain other people's behavior); and

3. The explanation context (in private thought or in conversation).

Bearing in mind these variables we can derive three central predictions (Malle and Knobe 1997b), described next.

3.4.1   Prediction 1: Unobservable versus Observable Events

The first prediction is that, in private contexts, actors explain more unobservable than observable events, whereas observers explain more observable than unobservable events. This prediction derives from the awareness condition: Actors have relatively less awareness of their own publicly observable events (e.g., facial expressions, gestures, postures) than of their own unobservable events (e.g., sensations, thoughts, feelings), whereas observers have less awareness of other people's unobservable events (their mental states) than of their observable events (actions, expressions, etc.). Evidence for such an asymmetry in awareness comes, for example, from Sheldon and Johnson (1993) who asked people to estimate which of several objects they usually think about when speaking with another person. The two most frequently chosen objects of awareness were people's own thoughts and feelings and the other person's appearance. Other studies show that actors find it difficult to accurately track their own observable behaviors (Gosling et al.

1998) and that observers find it difficult to reliably infer others' mental states (Ickes 1993). Moreover, according to data from our own lab (Malle and Pearce 2001), what people remember about themselves in an interaction tends to be unobservable events whereas what they remember about their interaction partner tends to be observable events.[2]

This asymmetry in awareness, then, should lead to an asymmetry in the events people try to explain. We found support for our prediction in two ways (Malle and Knobe 1997b). First, we examined wonderings (*attempts* to explain), both from undergraduate students who kept daily protocols of spontaneous why-questions and from the characters of three twentieth-century novels. These why-questions were coded for the perspective from which they were posed (actor, observer) and for the type of event they targeted (observable–unobservable; intentional–unintentional). As predicted, actors wondered about more unobservable events (67%) than observable events (33%), whereas observers wondered about more observable events (74%) than unobservable events (26%). The identical pattern of results emerged when we examined not just wonderings but explanations people actually produced. Two studies examined explanations from memory protocols and diaries, both meant to capture private contexts. As predicted, actors explained to themselves more unobservable events (70%) than observable events (30%) whereas observers explained to themselves more observable events (74%) than unobservable events (26%).

3.4.2 Prediction 2: Unintentional versus Intentional Events

The second prediction is that actors explain more unintentional than intentional events whereas observers explain more intentional than unintentional events. This prediction derives from the conditions of non-understanding and relevance as follows. Actors are rarely in a state of nonunderstanding with respect to their intentional behaviors because they typically know, or at least believe they know, why they performed those behaviors. Unintentional events, such as pain, sweating, or intrusive thoughts, are more puzzling to actors because they did not plan them, so they need to understand why these events occurred and how they can correct their unwelcome occurrence. Observers, on the other hand, will find intentional and unintentional events equally difficult to understand, but they will typically find intentional events to be more relevant, because they are socially consequential and highly diagnostic of a person's desires, beliefs, abilities, and character (Jones and Davis 1965; Malle and Knobe 1997a).

This prediction was confirmed in the same studies as reported above. When we examined why-questions in thought protocols and twentieth-century novels, actors wondered about more unintentional events (73%) than intentional events (27%) whereas observers wondered about more intentional events (67%) than unintentional events (33%). Similarly, in private explanations culled from memory protocols and diaries, actors explained more unintentional events (74%) than intentional events (26%) whereas observers explained more intentional events (65%) than unintentional events (35%).

3.4.3 Prediction 3: Communicative Explanations

The third prediction concerns communicative explanations, in which the actor answers not his own wondering but his conversation partner's wondering. What is at stake here is not the explainer's attempt to find meaning for himself but rather his attempt to manage the interaction partner's understanding and ensuing behavior. The conversation partner to whom an explanation is offered holds of course the observer role with respect to the actor's behavioral events. Therefore, if communicative explanations answer one's conversation partner's wonderings, the actor should explain the kinds of behavioral events that are normally explained from the observer perspective. Indeed, in two studies (analyzing memory protocols and continuous conversations) actors explained those events that their partners qua observers would tend to be interested in—that is, more observable events (60%) than unobservable events (40%), and more intentional events (61%) than unintentional events (39%). I should reiterate that these explanations were only very rarely answers to explicit why-questions; in the vast majority of cases, the explainer anticipated a possible wondering on the part of the interaction partner and spontaneously offered a behavior explanation.

The contrasting pattern of actors' private versus communicative explanations attests to the dual function of explanations. If needed as instruments to find meaning, explanations are constructed in private thought as answers to one's own wondering (most frequently, about unintentional and unobservable events). If needed as instruments to manage interaction, explanations are constructed in conversation as answers to an interaction partner's real or anticipated wondering (most frequently, about intentional and observable events).

3.4.4 General Distribution of Behavioral Events

In addition to these predicted actor–observer patterns of explanation, we also discovered one noteworthy pattern that holds consistently across both perspectives (Malle and Knobe 1997b). The large majority of behavioral events that people describe, wonder about, or explain are *actions* (intentional, observable events) and *experiences* (unintentional, unobservable events), whereas only a small number comprises mere behaviors or intentional thoughts. Why is that?

The prevalence of actions and experiences may be the result of the very actor–observer asymmetries in attention and wondering that my colleagues and I have documented (Malle and Knobe 1997b; Malle and Pearce 2001). From the actor perspective, there are two factors that facilitate attending to, describing, and explaining *experiences:* because they are unintentional (i.e., not well understood) and because they are unobservable (i.e., easily accessible for actors). From the observer perspective, there are two factors that facilitate attending to, describing, and explaining *actions:* because they are intentional (i.e., highly relevant for social interaction) and because they are observable (i.e., publicly accessible). In contrast, there is always one factor that hinders people's attention to mere behaviors (for actors, because they are publicly observable and often difficult to spot on oneself; for observers, because they are unintentional and therefore less relevant). Likewise, there is always one factor that hinders people's attention to intentional thoughts (for actors, because they are intentional and normally well understood; for observers, because they are unobservable). Whichever perspective people find themselves in, more factors on average facilitate a focus on actions or experiences than on the other event types.

This account, however, captures only part of the phenomenon. It fails to clarify why, *within* observable events, actors still care more about actions than about mere behaviors (even though the latter should be favored because of their unintentionality) and why, within unobservable events, observers still care more about experiences than about intentional thoughts (even though the latter should be favored because of their intentionality). To explain this specific pattern, we may posit that, owing to the constant switching between actor and observer perspectives in social interaction, the importance people place as observers on actions habitually carries over to their role of actor and that, correspondingly, the importance people place as actors on experiences habitually carries over to their role of observer.

Alternatively, actions and experiences may, objectively, be the most frequent events in social contexts. Actions are the fundamental currency of social interaction, and given the personal significance and relevance of social actions, people naturally have immediate mental responses to them, which come in the form of perceptions, emotions, and other experiences. This possibility of actions and experiences occurring more frequently in social contexts also has a fascinating parallel in the distribution of verbs (at least in English) across the four types of behavioral events. Specifically, for *interpersonal transactions* (in which one person affects another), there are far more verbs denoting actions and experiences than verbs denoting mere behaviors or intentional thoughts (Malle 2002c). I encourage the reader to take a piece of paper and write down verbs of interpersonal transactions for each of the four behavioral event classes (perhaps setting a time limit of one minute for each):

intentional/observable	unintentional/observable
actions,	*behaviors,*
intentional/unobservable	unintentional/unobservable
thoughts,	*experiences.*

When I do this, I easily generate a long list of actions that a person A performed vis-à-vis a person B (e.g., A greeted, killed, helped, betrayed, flattered, promoted, criticized, called . . . B). Likewise, I easily generate a long list of experiences that B had vis-à-vis A (e.g., B noticed, heard, saw, dreaded, trusted, envied . . . A). But it is quite difficult for me to generate mere behaviors that actually occur between A and B (perhaps A stumbled over, ran into B?) and still more difficult to generate intentional thoughts between A and B (perhaps A attended to, listened to B?). If we assume that language reflects important facts about the world in which linguistic creatures live, this asymmetric distribution of verbs lends support to the claim that, at least in social contexts, actions and experiences are more frequent than other event types.

3.5   Summary

In this chapter I tried to clarify why people explain behavior, when they do it, and which behavioral events they explain. I suggested that two broad motivations elicit behavior explanation: a search for meaning and an attempt to manage ongoing social interaction. Lack of meaning and understanding, in its many forms, is disquieting, so finding meaning is an intrinsic value of explanations. In addition, explanations facilitate (and have possibly evolved to facilitate) other social-cognitive tasks, including prediction, self-regulation, and interaction management. Such management is best achieved when explanations are expressed verbally and create meaning in one's interaction partners or, more broadly, influence their feelings, thoughts, and actions.

Moving from broad motivations to more specific cognitive conditions, I introduced a theory of wondering why that identifies the conditions under which people ask why-questions and offer explanations (Malle and Knobe 1997b). These conditions are awareness, nonunderstanding, and relevance of this nonunderstanding. The theory accounts for past findings on the increase of explanations in the face of negative and unexpected events and makes new predictions about the prevalence of different types of behavior explanations. In particular, the theory predicts the distribution of *which* behavioral events people explain, in their distinct roles as actors and observers and in both private and communicative contexts.

In the next two chapters I introduce theoretical principles that account for *how* people explain behavior. I begin by laying out the conceptual assumptions people make when explaining behavior (chapter 4) and then move to the specific processes that guide the construction of explanations and the choices among various explanatory tools (chapter 5).

4 Conceptual Structure: A Theory of Behavior Explanations I

Theories of lay behavior explanation typically postulate a single kind of explanation: that of citing causes. These causes are then distinguished along some well-known dimensions, and the dimensions favored among researchers include dispositional versus situation causes (Jones and Davis 1965), internal versus external causes (Kelley 1967), and stable versus unstable causes (Weiner et al. 1972).

Over the years, however, a consistent minority of researchers have offered theoretical arguments for an alternative position, contending that people use various types of explanation and that some of these explanations do not follow the "mechanical" logic of causes. The first within this minority was Heider (1958) himself. Even though most of the attribution literature portrayed Heider's contribution as a purely causal model, he in fact drew a major distinction between explanations based on "impersonal causality" (mechanical causes for unintentional behaviors and physical events) and explanations based on "personal causality" (motives or reasons for intentional actions). In addition, but less explicitly, Heider distinguished between motive explanations on the one hand and enabling explanations on the other. For example, we might explain a person's rowing across the river either by saying that he wanted to have a good time (motive explanation) or by saying that he is in good physical condition (enabling explanation).

Some authors took seriously Heider's personal–impersonal distinction and, following pertinent philosophical literature, renamed it the distinction between reasons and causes (Buss 1978; Locke and Pennington 1982). The mainstream attribution literature, however, rejected the theoretical arguments for these two types of explanation (Kruglanski 1979; Harvey and Tucker 1979) and continued to disregard Heider's crucial personal–impersonal distinction.

A significant move toward recognizing the unique nature of reason explanations came with goal-based theories of explanation (Abelson and Lalljee 1988; Read 1987; Schank and Abelson 1977). These theories recognize that humans see each other as active agents who influence the environment and other people by means of plans, goals, and intentional actions. People therefore explain a good deal of human behavior with reference to the constructs of goals and plans, which are integrated into a broad knowledge structure of human behavior. Goal-based theories did not clarify precisely how traditional cause explanations differ from goal-based explanations (and why), nor were they quite right in their claim that all reason explanations refer to goals. Despite these limitations, however, goal-based theories should have altered the course of attribution research. Sadly, they did not. Textbooks and handbooks continued to promote the classic views about causes, the disposition–situation dichotomy, and the covariation model— not because the goal-based theories were flawed, but because the simple attribution models were too well established and no integrative theory was offered that located both causal attributions and goals within a larger theoretical framework of behavior explanation.

In an important recent line of work, John McClure, Denis Hilton, and their colleagues took another stab at reforming established attribution theory. They adopted and refined Heider's (1958) distinction between motive explanations and enabling explanations and identified some of the conditions under which each explanation type is preferred (McClure and Hilton 1997, 1998). This work poses important questions that a comprehensive theory of behavior explanation has to answer: Are goal explanations the same as motive and reason explanations? Why is there a separate mode of enabling explanations for intentional but not for unintentional behaviors? And how do traditional causal explanations fit into this picture of motives and enabling factors?

In summary, the previous literature on lay behavior explanation can be sorted into two camps. The first is inhabited by *monists,* who believe that there is only one kind of explanation, namely causes (differing in some number of attributes, such as internality, stability, etc.). The other camp houses *pluralists,* who believe in multiple modes of explanation. Specific proposals differ in the kinds of explanation modes they consider, such as causes, reasons, motives, goals, enabling factors, or preconditions. My own position is decidedly pluralist, and the theoretical model I am offering tries to organize and systematize the various explanation modes that have been proposed in the past and to integrate them with the traditional notion of causal explanations.

4.1 Three Layers of Theory

The folk-conceptual theory of behavior explanation consists of three distinct layers. At the core lie postulates about the conceptual assumptions and distinctions people make about human behavior and its explanation (e.g., the concepts of intentionality, reasons, and the distinctions among modes of explanation). Second, the theory postulates psychological processes that guide the actual construction of explanations, such as information resources and impression management. Third, the theory has a language-specific layer in which it postulates certain linguistic structures (e.g., within contemporary English) that express people's conceptual assumptions about behavior and its explanation. On the basis of these structures, the theory can then predict the specific social functions served by communicated behavior explanations (e.g., the distancing function of marked belief reasons).

In principle, the three layers are independently falsifiable, but they build on each other in that layers 2 and 3 rely on the conceptual postulates of layer 1. The unique contributions of the folk-conceptual theory are most readily visible within layers 1 and 3, which contain postulates not found in previous theories of explanation and attribution. Layer 2 partially synthesizes psychological processes that previous explanation theories have postulated. But according to the folk-conceptual theory, these psychological processes operate on very different "conceptual objects" (e.g., the mode of reasons), yielding unique predictions about the impact of these processes.

In this chapter I focus on layer 1, the folk-conceptual framework that underlies behavior explanations. Chapter 5 introduces layer 2 (the psychological processes that guide the construction of explanations), and chapter 6 takes up linguistic issues of layer 3.

4.2 Conceptual Structure

In chapter 3, I argued that communicated (interaction-managing) explanations are cut from the same cloth as private (meaning-finding) explanations. From the same *conceptual* cloth, that is. Even though we have seen that private and communicative explanations differ in their functions and in the kinds of behavioral events they tend to focus on, their conceptual structure—the concepts and assumptions that underlie explanations—is the same. This isomorphism makes good sense. When children learn to construct private explanations, they probably learn a great deal from the structure of their caretakers' *communicated* explanations (cf. Bartsch and Wellman 1995), just as children learn about theory of mind in part from their parents' talk about mental states (Dunn, Brown, and Beardsall 1991). Also, when people communicate explanations to their interaction partners, these explanations must correspond to the private explanations that the interaction partners would have come up with had they known more about the behavior at issue.

This isomorphism between private and communicative explanations allows us to formulate a number of postulates about the conceptual structure of behavior explanations that hold both for explanations that find meaning and for explanations that manage social interaction. I first list these postulates as brief statements and then discuss each of them in detail.

4.2.1   Six Postulates about Folk Behavior Explanations

(P1)   People distinguish between intentional and unintentional behavioral events.

(P2)   For behavioral events considered intentional, people use one of three modes of explanation: reason explanations, causal history of reason explanations, or enabling factor explanations.

(P3)   Reason explanations are those behavior explanations that cite agents' reasons for intending to act or for acting intentionally. Reasons are conceptualized as agents' mental states in light of which and on the grounds of which they formed an intention to act.

(P4)   Causal history of reason explanations cite factors that lay in the background of an action's reasons and typically brought them about, thereby helping explain the background of the action. Causal history factors are not themselves reasons, so the agent does not form an intention in light of or on the grounds of causal history factors.

(P5)   Enabling factor explanations do not clarify why the agent intended to act but rather how it was possible that the intention was turned into a successfully performed action. These explanations presuppose the agent's reasons and intention and cite factors that enabled the action to be performed as intended.

(P6)   For behavioral events considered unintentional, people use only one mode of explanation—cause explanations. These explanations cite "mechanical" causes—that is, factors that brought about the unintentional event without the involvement of subjective reasoning or rationality.

4.2.2   Intentional and Unintentional Behavior

The first postulate is that people distinguish between intentional and unintentional behavior. This may not appear to be a terribly controversial claim, but, surprisingly, its implications have been greatly underappreciated in attribution research. In what follows I will try to make clear why the claim is correct and, in subsequent sections, why it is so central to a theory of behavior explanation.

Do people really agree in their judgments of intentionality? In our first study on the topic of intentionality (Malle and Knobe 1997a, study 1), we asked participants to read descriptions of twenty behaviors and to rate them for their intentionality, using an eight-point scale ranging from "not at all" (0) to "completely" (7) intentional. Sample behaviors, along with their mean intentionality ratings, are: "Anne is sweating" ($M = 1.4$), "Anne was worrying about the test results" ($M = 3.7$), "Anne applauded the musicians" ($M = 5.8$), "Anne invited Sue to have lunch with her" ($M = 6.4$). One half of the participants received a working definition of intentionality before they rated the twenty behaviors. The assumption was that if people used their own folk concept to rate the behaviors, then there should be high agreement among participants with or without an experimenter-provided definition. Agreement was high in the whole sample. Any two people's intentionality ratings showed an average intercorrelation of $r(20) = .64$, and any one person showed an average correlation of $r(20) = .80$ with the remaining group, resulting in an inter-rater reliability of $\alpha = .99$. More important, the experimenter-provided definition had absolutely no effect on average agreement, so it appeared that people share a folk concept of intentionality that they spontaneously use when asked to judge behaviors.

The high agreement we found, however, should not be interpreted as demonstrating that intentionality judgments are easy or that people always arrive at the same judgment. What the substantial correlations among intentionality ratings show is that people collectively see certain behaviors as intentional (high ratings), others as unintentional (low ratings), and yet others as ambiguous (midrange ratings). Obviously, ambiguous behaviors are difficult to judge, and a rating in the middle of the scale of intentionality offers a compromise that a forced choice ("Is this behavior intentional or not?") would not allow. In fact, in an unpublished follow-up study on the same twenty behaviors we presented people with forced-choice options (intentional versus unintentional), and the results showed that thirteen of the twenty behaviors yielded strong agreement among participants (fewer than 10% or more than 80% said it was intentional), whereas seven of the behaviors yielded a fair amount of disagreement (between 27% and 63% said it was intentional). The rating data in our original study demonstrated that people agree in their identification of these behaviors as ambiguous, but because of the behaviors' ambiguity, people don't agree on a forced-choice intentionality classification for them (which might approximate a random choice). Thus, people who share the same concept need not arrive at the same judgment for every given object; they just agree on judging the intentionality of those objects that are fairly unambiguous and agree on finding the remaining ones difficult to judge.

So what is this concept of intentionality? A series of descriptive and experimental studies suggested that the folk concept of intentionality consists of five components or conditions (Malle and Knobe 1997a; see also Mele 2001). An action is judged intentional when the agent had a *desire* for an outcome, a *belief* that the action would lead to that outcome, an *intention* to perform the action, the *skill* to perform the action, and *awareness* of fulfilling the intention while performing the action (figure 4.1).

People will of course not always test all five conditions before they make intentionality judgments. In many instances of everyday life, the process of assessing intentionality will rely on prior assumptions, cues, and heuristics. One particularly vivid case of an apparent shortcut was recently documented by Joshua Knobe (2003a,b). In his studies, people are asked to make intentionality judgments about either blameworthy or neutral behaviors for which the presence of one critical intentionality component was manipulated (e.g., intention, skill). The standard prediction would be that only

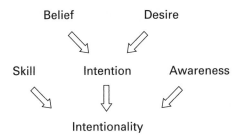

Figure 4.1
The folk concept of intentionality (after Malle and Knobe 1997a).

those behaviors are judged intentional that were performed with the component present. However, blameworthy behaviors were often judged intentional even if skill or intention was missing. This finding sets a potential boundary condition to the five-component model of intentionality, but it remains to be seen whether intentionality judgments would obey the usual conditions if respondents clearly were to separate blame from intentionality (Malle and Nelson 2003; Mele 2001). Surely the agents themselves who perform behaviors without skill or intention would make judgments conforming to the five-component model of intentionality. Knobe's findings may thus demonstrate not a cognitive or conceptual limitation, but a motivational limitation. Whatever the eventual verdict on this issue, the full folk concept of intentionality provides the overarching frame within which disputes and disagreements over intentionality are resolved. If people were to criticize Knobe's respondents for being biased in their intentionality judgment, for example, they would do so by reference to the very components of intentionality that were apparently overlooked.

Knobe's (2003a,b) results do support the general claim that the concept of intentionality is closely related to the assignment of responsibility and blame (e.g., Shaver 1985; Weiner 1995). An agent is more likely to be held responsible or to be blamed when she performed a given negative action intentionally. And even for unintentional behaviors and outcomes, the concept of intentionality is at work. Responsibility is still assigned when the outcome is considered to have been preventable by the agent (i.e., controllable; Weiner 1995) and when it was his or her duty to prevent it (Hamilton 1978). Both preventability and duty entail intentionality, because assigning duties to a person presumes that the person can intentionally fulfill them and preventability presumes that the agent could have intentionally averted the outcome (Malle, Moses, and Baldwin 2001a).

Perhaps the most important function of the intentionality concept is to divide behavioral events into two groups that are processed in different ways by cognitive tools such as attention, explanation, and prediction. Heider (1958) was the first social psychologist to emphasize that people assume two different models of causality for intentional and unintentional behavior (see chapter 1). And because of these different assumptions, people give very different explanations for intentional and unintentional behavior. This insight leads directly to the next postulate.

4.2.3   Three Modes of Explaining Intentional Behavior

According to the second postulate, people use one of three modes of explanation for intentional behavior: reason explanations, causal history of reason explanations, or enabling factor explanations. This claim can be broken down into two parts—first, that intentional behavior is explained by reasons (rather than generic causes, as attribution theory would suggest), and, second, that there are two other explanation modes besides reasons that people use when accounting for intentional behavior—causal history of reason (CHR) explanations and enabling factor explanations.

Reason explanations are a unique class of explanation and have long been so considered by numerous philosophers, sociologists, and at least some psychologists (Burke 1945; Buss 1978, 1979; Davidson 1963; Donellan 1967; Lennon 1990; Locke and Pennington 1982; McClure 2002; Mele 1992; Read 1987; Schueler 1989; Searle 2001). What is relevant for our purposes is what makes reason explanations unique within the folk theory of mind and behavior. Consider the following two explanations.

(4-1)*   Anne studied for the test all day **because she wanted to do well.**

(4-2)   Anne was worrying about the test results **because she wanted to do well.**

These two explanations are linguistically identical; nonetheless, there seems to be something very different going on in the two cases. When reading (4-1), English speakers beyond the age of four will understand that Anne studied *in order to* do well, that she *chose* to study, that she studied *for the reason* stated, namely, that she wanted to do well. These are familiar but far from trivial inferences. They characterize Anne as a thinking, reasoning, planning agent, as someone who chooses what to do in light of what she wants and believes will happen. None of these inferences hold in (4-2). There, Anne's worrying is simply caused by her desire to do well; no reasoning, no planning, no choice is involved.

Obviously, the first behavior (studying all day) is intentional whereas the second (worrying) is unintentional. Empirical studies, theoretical arguments, and everyday experience show one thing very clearly: Reason explanations (those that imply deliberating, planning, choosing in light of one's beliefs and desires) are applied only to intentional behaviors and never to unintentional ones (e.g., Malle 1999). The folk concept of intentionality tells us why: because intentional behaviors, but not unintentional behaviors, require the presence of an intention (or choice), which is itself based on beliefs and desires.

Given that reason explanations are used only for intentional behavior, are all intentional behaviors explained by reasons? No. Social perceivers at times explain an action by pointing to factors that lay in the background of the agent's reasons, such as in her upbringing, personality, culture, or in the immediate context—factors that can be subsumed under the label *causal history of reason explanations* (Malle 1994, 1999). Whereas reasons capture what the agent herself weighed and considered when deciding to act, causal history explanations capture the various causal factors that led up to the agent's reasons (see fig. 4.2).

In addition, there is a third mode of explaining intentional action that clarifies how it was possible that the agent's intention was fulfilled, citing factors that enabled her to actually perform the action as intended. This explanation mode thus accounts for the link between intention and action

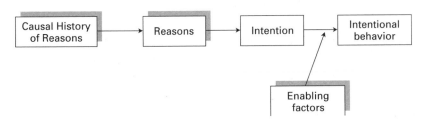

Figure 4.2
Domains of explanation (with shadow) within the folk concept of intentionality.

(see fig. 4.2) and can be called *enabling factor explanations* (Malle 1999; Malle et al. 2000; McClure and Hilton 1997, 1998; Charpa 2001).

The three explanation modes occupy three distinct domains of the folk concept of intentionality, from which they obviously derive. Reasons directly explain what motivated and grounded the agent's forming of an *intention*, whereas causal history of reason explanations clarify the origin of those *reasons* (and hence the background to the intention formation). Finally, enabling factors explain how it was possible that the intention (however motivated) was turned into a successful action.

Postulates three through five provide more detailed claims about each of these explanation modes and are discussed next.

4.2.4 Reason Explanations

When citing reasons, the explainer isn't merely referring to some causal factor that influenced the action in question. Rather, he is picking out what he considers significant steps in the agent's own decision-making process—the process that the agent presumably underwent when deciding to act. These significant steps are the beliefs and desires *in light of which* and *on the grounds of which* the agent formed her intention to act.

The phrase *in light of* signifies the explainer's assumption that the agent actually considered the content of the cited desires or beliefs when deciding to act; that the agent was aware of them and, through this awareness, decided to act a certain way. I have called this assumption the explainer's *subjectivity assumption,* according to which explainers assume that agents are aware of the contents of their reasons (Malle 1999). If Anne invited Ben to dinner in light of the publication of his novel, she did it because she was aware that his novel was published (and, presumably, she wanted to celebrate this event with a dinner). If Mia forgoes chocolate in light of a religious holiday, she does it because she is aware of the holiday (and, presumably, wants to practice her faith).

To test the validity of this subjectivity assumption we (Malle et al. 2000) asked explainers how they felt about reason explanations in which the agent's awareness of the reason's content was explicitly denied (e.g., "Anne invited Ben for dinner because he had helped her paint her room, even though she was not aware that he had helped her paint her room."). The vast majority of people either found such explanations meaningless or they regarded them as something like background causes, not reasons. Thus, in people's folk explanations of behavior, reasons are *conscious reasons* (Malle 1999).

But awareness of the contents of certain beliefs and desires when deciding to act does not by itself turn those states into reasons. If the explainer considers them the agent's reasons he must also assume that the agent decided to act *on the grounds of* those beliefs and desires. That is, the explainer assumes that the agent weighed certain beliefs and desires, typically in combination with other mental states, and regarded the beliefs and desires in question compelling arguments for forming an intention to act. The agent thus decided to act, as we say, *on those grounds*.

Consider the exchange "Why did Leila rush off?"—"She didn't want to be late for class." Here the explainer indicates that, for Leila, the desire not to be late, in the context of some other implicit considerations (class is important, the conversation she was in could be ended quickly, etc.), was grounds for her to rush off. The ways in which mental states are weighed and combined in reason explanations seem to follow certain rules of rationality, and that is why this feature of reason explanations is suitably called the *rationality assumption* (Davidson 1982; Føllesdal 1982; Malle 1999; Mele 1992; Searle 2001). This orderly combining of beliefs and desires is particularly salient in reason explanations that people give of their own actions, thus highlighting their rationality:

(4-3) Why did you go running?—**Um, because I wanted to get in better shape, and . . . I figured that I can do that by going running every day.**

An explainer thus treats mental states as reasons if he feels they meet both the subjectivity assumption and the rationality assumption. Or to use the fitting phrases—if he feels that the agent acted *in light* of and *on the grounds* of the content of those mental states.[1]

Reason explanations have at least two features that are conceptually interesting and psychologically significant (Malle et al. 2000; Malle, Knobe, and Nelson 2004). The first is what type of mental state the explainer cites as a reason; and the second is whether this mental state is linguistically marked.

Reason Types Among the mental states that function as reasons, beliefs and desires are most common, and there is a third class that we might call *valuings*[2] (F.Ex 1998, see appendix; Malle 2001b).

Desire reasons reveal the action's desired outcome, often called *goal, aim, end,* or *purpose.* Consequently, desire reasons provide the most direct answers to the questions "For what purpose?" and "What for?" A desire represents an unrealized state (in the agent or the world) that the agent tries to realize through acting. Other reasons are therefore often directed, as it were, by the desire reason, which is the paradigmatic motive of intentional action.

By citing a desire reason the explainer implicitly ascribes an endorsing or value judgment to the agent (Schueler 2001). For example, "Why did she turn up the volume?"—"To make her brother mad." The statement implies that, from the explainer's viewpoint, the agent endorses the goal of making her brother mad, and so the explainer would be surprised if the agent, in honesty, denied having this goal. (This implication does not hold for a desire state that is offered as a causal history of reason explanation: "He told me some pretty intimate things."—Why?—"He was looking for some sympathy." Here the explainer would not be surprised if the agent denied having this goal.)

Belief reasons encompass a broad range of knowledge, hunches, and assessments that the agent has about the outcome, the action, their causal relation, and relevant circumstances. Beliefs are aimed at representing reality (Adler 2002) and thus are not apt by themselves to instigate action. But they are essential in identifying attainable outcomes and selecting appropriate actions with which to pursue those outcomes. Beliefs also help the agent consider the consequences of considered actions, track changes in the aimed-at outcome, and navigate around obstacles. Beliefs can finally represent other people's wishes and reactions and are therefore crucial in coordinating one's actions with others.

Valuings directly indicate the positive or negative affect toward the action or its outcome. As a group, valuings are quite differentiated, including such states as fear, liking, interest, hating, enjoyment, disappointment, trusting, and missing. Valuings can be directed at objects, events, or states, be they concurrent (e.g., enjoy, appreciate, miss), future directed (e.g., looking forward to, being afraid), or timeless (e.g., she likes the thrill of speed; he enjoys football).

The literature on reason explanations typically mentions only beliefs and desires as candidate mental states that function as reasons (e.g., Bartsch and Wellman 1995; Dretske 1988; Searle 1983). One might therefore suspect that valuings can be subsumed under either desires or beliefs. But subsuming valuings under beliefs quickly runs into problems because beliefs, as representations of reality, can be true or false whereas valuings cannot. It makes little sense to ask whether someone has a "false" valuing. However, many valuings *imply* a belief on the agent's part: When I appreciate it snowing I do believe that it is snowing. But the reverse is not true: I may believe that it is snowing without appreciating it. So whatever the valuing adds over and above the belief, the added element is not itself a belief. It is more like an attitude, an affective stance toward a represented event or state.

So might this affective stance be subsumed under desires? Some valuings resist this subsumption because they are directed at something already existing (e.g., "The applause was extended, because people truly appreciated the magnificent performance") whereas desires are always directed at an object or event not yet available to the agent. On the other hand, some valuings represent, like desires, an object or event that currently does not exist and would please (or displease) the agent if it came into existence—for example, hoping for snow, being afraid of the neighbor's dog.

As a group, then, valuings resist being subsumed under either beliefs or desires. That was also what my research collaborators and I found when we originally began to code naturally occurring behavior explanations. We therefore decided to treat valuings as a separate category of reasons to improve coding precision for both desires and beliefs but also to assess whether the three reason types have psychologically distinct functions. In fact, this approach allowed us to track whether valuings "behaved like" beliefs or desires, leaving the possibility open for a functional subsumption. We will see later that actors provide more belief reasons than observers do (chapter 7) and that belief reasons are used to make the agent appear rational and justified whereas desires are sometimes used to put a better spin on an undesirable action, pointing to a more noble aim the agent might have had (chapter 6). Valuings, by contrast, followed neither one of these functional patterns, and so far we have not identified unique psychological functions of valuings in explanations of behavior. This pattern of results further justifies keeping valuings separate from beliefs and desires so as to not dilute evidence of their unique psychological functions. However, it also suggests that the major role of valuings might lie outside of explanations—a possible topic of future research.

Reason Contents   A second important conceptual feature of reasons is that they are representational states—that is, mental states that have a content, are directed at something. The content that they are directed at is *what* the person likes, believes, or desires (Malle 1999). These specific contents are what allow a reason explanation to render an action intelligible, because the reason contents are to reflect what the agent specifically had in mind when initiating her action. Note, however, that nothing in the folk theory of mind provides the specific reason contents for specific actions. The folk theory implies only that intentional actions be generally explained by beliefs and desires; filling in the specific contents is the explainer's difficult task in constructing explanations (see chapter 5).

Even though reason contents are essential for explanations of intentional action, their psychological study has been difficult. Reason content, one might expect, should carry the force of the famous person–situation dichotomy, because the contents of mental states can readily be about the person, about the situation, and so on. However, in numerous studies we classified reason contents into the traditional person and situation categories but failed to predict psychologically interesting variables. For example, we wondered whether people would offer more reasons with situation content as actors than as observers, but they did not (Malle, Knobe, and Nelson 2004). We also examined whether people would offer more reasons with person content for individuals than for groups (cf. Susskind et al. 1999), but they did not. It is of course possible that other classifications of reason content fare better than the person–situation dichotomy. For example, impression management attempts might result in more socially desirable versus undesirable reason contents.

Regardless of whether a classification of specific reason contents can be found that renders them psychologically significant, the notion of reason content is of great theoretical significance. By distinguishing between reasons as mental states and the content of those reasons, we are able to clarify some puzzling inconsistencies within traditional attribution research (Malle et al. 2000). Before I turn to this clarification, however, a third feature of reasons must be introduced.

Mental State Markers   Reason explanations are expressed in two ways. Explainers can directly mention the reason content in light of which they think the agent acted (e.g., "A stranger asked me what time it was 'cause

I had a watch on") or they can use a mental state verb to mark the agent's subjective mental state that functioned as the agent's reason (e.g., "A stranger asked me what time it was 'cause *she saw* that I had a watch on"). By using marked reasons, explainers indicate explicitly both the type of mental state the reason is (e.g., "She saw/thought/ assumed . . ." → *belief;* "He wanted/longed for . . ." → *desire*) and the specific content of that reason, whereas without markers, only the reason content is mentioned (see table 4.1). The addition or omission of mental state markers thus cleanly separates the two ingredients of reasons—the reason type (belief, desire, or valuing), and the reason content.

Because the presence of mental state markers clearly depicts the conceptual structure of reasons as *mental state + representational content,* marked reasons are the canonical form of reason explanations and examples of reasons in the literature are virtually always marked. However, mental state markers are a linguistic device, not a necessary feature of reasons, because they do not have to be present for people to correctly interpret a given explanation as a reason (Malle et al. 2000). For example, in response to the question "Why did he quit his job?," the answer "His boss was sabotaging him" is a reason explanation that refers to a belief even though no belief marker is visible. This omission of mental state markers usually does not create problems

Table 4.1
Reasons in their marked and unmarked form

Behavior	Reason type	Marked form	Unmarked form
Why did she refuse dessert?	Belief	*She thinks* she's been gaining weight	She's been gaining weight.
Why did he go to the coffee shop?	Desire	*He wanted* to have a real Italian espresso	To have a real Italian espresso.
Why did they sell their car?	Belief	*they felt* it was too small for the family	It was too small for the family.
Why did you get there at 5:30 A.M.?	Desire	*I didn't want* to wait in line	So that I wouldn't have to wait in line.
Why did she stay until after 10?	Valuing[1]	*She liked* the show	The show was fun.

[1] Among valuings, unmarked forms are extremely rare. Moreover, the unmarked forms cannot be created by omitting the mental state verb (as with most beliefs and desires); instead, unmarked valuings are expressed by an evaluative claim about the content of the reason (e.g., "it's fun").

in communication because people rely on the *subjectivity assumption* both when offering reason explanations and when interpreting them.

In analogy to linguistic terminology, we might say that an unmarked reason explanation contains an invisible "trace" of the ascribed mental state, and this trace allows people to interpret an utterance like "His boss was sabotaging him" as "[his belief:] 'My boss is sabotaging me.'" To experimentally demonstrate this trace (i.e., the implied mental state ascription), we presented people with actions and unmarked reason explanations but denied the relevant mental state ascription. For example, "He quit his job because his boss was sabotaging him, but he wasn't aware that his boss was sabotaging him." Evidence for the implied mental state ascription lies in people's surprise, their feeling that this whole sentence makes little sense, and their attempt to reinterpret the explanation as one that is not a reason (Malle et al. 2000, studies 1–2).

Interestingly, unmarked desire reasons make it easier on explainers and their audience than unmarked beliefs, because the trace in desire reasons isn't really invisible. As table 4.1 shows, unmarked desires still show grammatical indications of being desires—primarily with the phrases "(in order) to" or "so that." We will see later that the visibility of the desire trace disqualifies desire reasons from certain psychological functions (chapter 6).

A final conceptual point about mental state markers requires a brief excursion into philosophy, which suggests that the use of mental state markers in the first-person case may reveal some important facts about consciousness. In a subtle and thoughtful discussion of the relation between speech acts and conscious thought, David Rosenthal (forthcoming) argues that for a person's mental state *M* to be conscious the person has to have a higher-order thought that *I am in M* (though this higher-order thought typically is not itself conscious). To support this thesis, Rosenthal examines the special case of beliefs, introducing the distinction between *reports* of one's beliefs ("I think it's raining") and *expressions* of one's beliefs ("It's raining"). Even though reports and expressions are semantically distinct (they have different truth conditions), they obey the same "performance conditions." That is, if in any circumstance it would be appropriate to say one, it would also be appropriate to say the other. This performance-conditional equivalence of "I think that *p*" and "*p*" is a matter of well-entrenched linguistic habit, automatic and second nature. Now, Rosenthal argues, because being able to *report* one's belief requires that belief to be conscious (one couldn't otherwise report it), and because a conscious belief about p is accompanied by a suitable higher-order thought, and because, finally, reporting one's belief ("I think that p") is performance equivalent to expressing that belief ("p"), it follows that the belief expression "p" is always a conscious thought, accompanied by the (nonconscious) higher-order thought "I think that p." Precisely because the expressing speech act "It's raining" is performance equivalent with the reporting speech act "I think it's raining," the two are made conscious by the same corresponding higher-order thought. The important conclusion is that expressions of beliefs—which, in our terminology, are *unmarked beliefs*—are conscious by virtue of their performance equivalence with their higher-order cousins, expressions of marked beliefs (and the same holds for desires, preferences, and other representational states).

Rosenthal also points out several important limitations to his conclusion, one of which is of particular interest here. According to Rosenthal, the above-argued link between language and consciousness holds only for first-person (actor) expressions of mental states, not for third-person (observer) expressions. Marked belief ascriptions such as "She believes that it's raining" are not performance equivalent with the corresponding unmarked case "It's raining." These unmarked third-person cases, when uttered on their own, cannot be used for reporting, only for expressing the *first-person* belief that it's raining. What is remarkable about beliefs used as *reasons*, however, is that even an unmarked third-person ascription ("He is taking the umbrella because it's raining") is typically understood as a belief reason ascription to *the agent*, not just as an expression of the explainer's own belief that it's raining. What we see here is that the folk-conceptual assumptions surrounding reason explanations (subjectivity and rationality) are so powerful that they make the audience interpret certain linguistic forms in ways that, outside of explanations, would never occur.

Before moving on to the other postulates of the present theory of explanation, I will now use the model of reasons just presented to resolve a puzzling finding in attribution research.

4.2.5 Reasons and the Puzzle of Person–Situation Attributions

During the heyday of attribution theory in the 1970s, a puzzle was repeatedly put before attribution researchers that was never resolved within the boundaries of the traditional theory. Monson and Snyder (1976) and Ross

(1977) were the first to pose the problem. Lee Ross (1977, p. 176) compared two explanations: "Jack bought the house because **it was secluded**" (traditionally classified as a situation attribution) and "Jill bought the house because **she wanted privacy**" (traditionally classified as a person attribution). The puzzle for Ross was that these two attributional classifications seemed to be based on subtle differences in linguistic surface, not on fundamental differences in the underlying causal factors. Monson and Snyder (1976), too, argued that the two "reflect differences in language rather than thought" (p. 90). Such a situation should be disconcerting to attribution researchers because they took the person–situation dichotomy to be a fundamental distinction in the *causes* people assign to behavior, not in the linguistic surface of explanations. In fact, however, studies in which free-response explanations were coded into the person–situation scheme were typically based on such linguistic differences in explanation rather than conceptual or causal ones (for evidence, see Malle 1999, study 4; Malle 2002c; Malle et al. 2000, study 4).

Attribution theory could not solve this puzzle because it arose in the context of reason explanations, which were not recognized as distinct from simple cause explanations. Whereas the person–situation dichotomy could be readily applied to causes of unintentional behaviors (e.g., a headache, stumbling, enjoyment), there is no meaningful way to apply that same dichotomy to reason explanations. Consider again "Jack bought the house **because it was secluded**" (classified as a situation cause). This explanation does not describe the seclusion as a situation cause remotely acting on Jack and making him buy the house. Rather, the explanation refers to Jack's (unmarked) belief that the house was secluded, which was his reason for buying it. This belief is of course, qua mental state, a "person factor"; only the *content* of this belief refers to the situation. The same point holds for many other unmarked reasons, such as Antaki's (1994) example of "I went to Spain for my holiday **because it's hot.**" The heat in Spain does not cause the agent from afar to go there; rather, the agent *believes* that it is hot in Spain, and that is her reason for going there.

Thus, the puzzle was grounded in the fact that attribution theory applied the person–situation classification to the linguistic surface structure of reason explanations, even though this surface does not reflect "causes" but rather the operation of three unique parameters: reason type, mental state markers, and reason content. As a result, an unmarked belief reason with situation content may look like a situation cause (e.g., ". . . because it was se-cluded") but the same belief reason with a mental state marker suddenly looks like a person cause ("because she thought/learned/knew that it was secluded"). In this case, the person–situation classification merely captures linguistic patterns that reflect the presence or absence of mental state markers. In other cases, the person–situation classification may follow dif-ferences in reason content (e.g., ". . . because it's hot" versus ". . . so he can lie in the sun") or differences in reason type—because desire reasons, com-pared to belief reasons, more often have person content and more often carry mental state markers (Malle 1999). But whatever reason feature the person–situation coding reflects, none of these features has anything to do with attributional categories of *causes*. In fact, the puzzle first formulated by Ross (1977) stems from the very misapplication of the notion of person–situation causes to reason explanations. Once we apply a more adequate theoretical model to these explanations, the puzzle disappears as we can an-alyze each reason in terms of its linguistic and conceptual features, includ-ing mental state markers, reason types, and reason content.

The person–situation dichotomy has been very popular (in spite of puzzles, doubts, and criticisms) in part because it was a simple distinction that could be easily applied to any explanation. But this simplicity was de-ceptive. It concealed the undesirable fact that in some cases (e.g., cause ex-planations), the person–situation distinction was applied to the difference between actual causes whereas in other cases (i.e., reason explanations) it was applied merely to the linguistic surface of reason expressions. Instead of tolerating such an ambiguous theoretical distinction and reducing reason explanations to their linguistic surface so as to subsume them under this dis-tinction, we must recognize the unique conceptual structure of reason ex-planations and carefully analyze their specific features, such as reason types and mental state markers. By extricating reason explanations from the grip of the person–situation dichotomy we can study the cognitive and prag-matic functions of these features and begin to account for the full complex-ity of behavior explanations.

There is much more to say about reason explanations in subsequent chap-ters, but for now I turn to the remaining postulates of the folk-conceptual theory of explanation, which concern the three modes of explanation that exist besides reasons.

4.2.6 Causal History of Reason Explanations

Despite the tight connection between intentional behavior and reason explanations, some scholars have suspected that not all explanations for intentional behavior cite reasons (e.g., Andrews 2002; Gordon 2001; Hirschberg 1978; Locke and Pennington 1982; Milligan 1980). Consider the following examples of explanations for intentional actions by Kristin Andrews (2002):

(4-4) One might think she hired Smith because **he was the best candidate for the job** [reason], though her action was considerably affected by **her unacknowledged racism** [nonreason].

(4-5) Suppose I ask, "Why did Kurt kill himself?" You might answer, "**His wife had just left him**" [reason] or perhaps "**He had just come out of drug rehab**" [nonreason].

Let me first apply the two defining criteria of reason explanations (subjectivity and rationality) to establish that the explanations in question truly are not reasons. In the first example, the personnel officer was apparently affected by her unacknowledged racism in a way that neither involved awareness of her racism nor a consideration on her part to take racism as grounds for acting. In short, the officer did not think, "I have some unacknowledged racism; I should hire Smith." (By contrast, the preceding reason explanation in this same example implies quite clearly that she believed Smith to be the best candidate for the job and took this fact to be grounds for hiring him.)

The second example suggests that Kurt was in some general sense aware of having just come out of drug rehab, but he was unlikely to have that particular fact on his mind when he decided to kill himself, and he certainly did not regard coming out of drug rehab as grounds for killing himself—on the face of it, it might be grounds for celebrating. (By contrast, he might very well have consciously thought of the fact that his wife just left him and regarded that despairing fact as grounds for committing suicide.)

Clearly, people are providing informative explanations here, but the explanations are not reasons. Nor are they cause explanations, because the behavior is undoubtedly intentional. So what are they? I have called them *causal history of reason explanations* (Malle 1994, 1999), because they refer to the background, context, or origin of the agent's reasons without explicitly mentioning these reasons. Causal history explanations may *imply* certain reasons, or rule out others (see Hirschberg 1978), but they do not explicitly mention them. Instead, what they mention are factors that, in the eyes of the explainer, brought about whatever reasons the agent had. Causal history of reason (CHR) explanations are thus one step removed from the agent's deliberations and choice and rather point to the background of those deliberations and hence to the background of the action at issue.

CHRs in Agent and Situation   It is important to emphasize that causal history explanations, just like reasons, can refer in their content both to factors in the agent and factors in the immediate or broader "situation," including such varied things as the physical context, other people's expectations, and cultural norms. Examples (4-4) and (4-5) focused on causal history factors that reside in the agent. The examples below refer to factors outside the agent.

(4-6)   Why was Nina using drugs?—**She was at a party.**

(4-7)*   Why does Ian work so much?—**Things are expensive around here.**

(4-8)   Why do Japanese businessmen work so much?—**It's part of their culture.**

Thus, the reason–CHR distinction has nothing to do with the classic person–situation dichotomy. What distinguishes CHRs from reasons is that the explainer does not make the subjectivity and rationality assumptions when offering causal histories. In addition, the two explanation modes are used for different cognitive and communicative purposes (as described shortly). Beyond this, causal history factors can be classified along the person–situation dimension, if so desired, but our research thus far suggests that this classification has no predictive significance (Malle, Knobe, and Nelson 2004; O'Laughlin and Malle 2002). The reason–CHR distinction itself, by contrast, does have such significance (see chapters 6 through 8).

CHRs and Reasons: A Folk Distinction   Another point to emphasize is that the distinction between reasons and causal history explanations is not just a theoretician's division. It is a folk-conceptual distinction that people themselves make in their formulations and interpretations of explanations, as we found in numerous studies (Malle, Knobe, and Nelson 2004; Nelson and Malle 2004; O'Laughlin and Malle 2002). Specifically, when people are

directly asked to identify "conscious reasons"[3] among a group of explanations that include both reasons and causal histories, they reliably identify
those explanations that expert coders had a priori designated as reasons
and reliably reject those that had been designated as causal histories (Malle
1999; Malle et al. 2000). A sample of such reliably classified reasons and
causal histories is displayed in table 4.2 (from Malle 1999, table 2).

Putting this contrast into a lighter frame, table 4.3 considers the infamous
question of "Why did the chicken cross the road?" and samples some of the
(alleged) explanations that deep thinkers have provided, grouped into reason explanations and CHR explanations.[4]

CHRs and Reasons in Combination Even though CHR explanations and
reasons are clearly distinct, they are not incompatible. Not only do some
causal histories imply reasons (or at least narrow down the class of reasons
likely for the given action); causal histories and reasons sometimes co-occur.

This co-occurrence can be found in about 23 percent of explanations
for intentional behavior. Consider the following explanatory statements,
which appear to provide a comprehensive picture of the action's motives
and origins.

(4-9)   Why did the alum climb up the [rival fraternity's] flagpole and
snap it?—Um, I think he did it because **he's just stupid and really dumb**
[CHR], and **he was actually drunk that night** [CHR] and decided to

Table 4.2
Reason explanations and causal history of reason (CHR) explanations for the same
behaviors

Behavior	Reason explanation	CHR explanation
By choice, Ian worked 14 hours a day last month	To make more money	He is driven to achieve
	A project was due	That's the cultural norm
Nancy chose not to vote in the last election	None of the candidates appealed to her	She is lazy
	She didn't want to support the system	She doesn't realize that every vote counts
Brian used heavy drugs last Sunday at the party	He was curious what it would feel like	He is a junkie
	He thought it would be cool	He grew up in a drug-dealing home

do it because it was . . . the fraternity was ΣAE, **and he didn't like them** [reason].

(4-10)   Why does your present roommate keep a lot of stuff?—**She's a hoarder** [CHR], big time; plus **her parents moved away** [CHR], so **she has to keep a lot of it** [reason].

Are CHRs Really in the History of Reasons?   The concept of causal history of reason explanations comes with the assumption that the cited factors are in fact interpreted as the causal *history* of *reasons*. What supports this assumption? One, we can systematically rule out alternative folk interpretations of CHR explanations; and two, there are some empirical indications of the correctness of this assumption. Let me consider these points in turn.

In contrast to enabling factors, which do not explain intentions but only actions, CHR factors (i.e., such factors as the ones cited in examples 4-4 to 4-10) explain intentions as well as they explain actions. Just replace any action description in examples (4-4) to (4-10) with an intention description, and the corresponding causal history explanation will still be perfectly adequate. To explain intentions, consequently, CHR factors must be regarded as preceding intentions. But this constraint can be met in two ways: CHR factors can directly antecede intentions but come *after* reasons (mediating, as it were, between reasons and intentions), or they can antecede reasons (and, thereby, also precede intentions). However, the notion that CHR factors (of which the agent is often unaware) could directly cause intentions contradicts the folk concept of intention (Malle and Knobe 2001). According to this concept, intentions are based on a reasoning process that rationally

Table 4.3
Reasons and causal histories for why the chicken crossed the road

Reason explanations
Captain James T. Kirk: To boldly go where no chicken has gone before.
Plato: For the greater good.
Ernest Hemingway: To die. In the rain.

Causal history of reason explanations
Aristotle: It is the nature of chickens to cross roads.
Hippocrates: Because of an excess of phlegm in its pancreas.
Darwin: Chickens, over great periods of time, have been naturally selected in such a way that they are now genetically disposed to cross roads.

combines those beliefs and desires that the agent considered. Intentions can therefore not be directly generated by CHR factors, because these factors are by definition not considered by the agent. Any causal effect of such factors would have to operate on reasons. Thus, the only option compatible with all known constraints of the folk theory of action is that factors such as the ones cited in (4-4) to (4-10) antecede and cause reasons and are therefore justifiably called *causal history of reason* explanations.

In our database of naturally occurring explanations, we also have some clear-cut cases whose grammatical structure indicates that the CHR factor is regarded as causing reasons (besides helping explain the action). Consider, for example, the high school student who explains why her teacher invited her along on a field trip:

(4-11)   I think that he invited me along **because he thought that it'd be interesting to me** [reason], **'cause he knows the type of stuff that I would think would be interesting** [causal history].

Here, the first *because* introduces the agent's belief reason whereas the second *because* (a causal history explanation) clarifies the origin of this reason in the agent's general knowledge.

Conditions of Occurrence   Reasons and CHR factors do not occur with the same frequency. For 61% of behaviors explained, people offer reasons alone, for 16% they offer CHRs alone, and for 23% we see a combination of the two modes.[5] With 84% of behavior explanations offering at least one reason, the reason mode is the clear default for explanations of intentional behavior. There are three conditions, however, that moderate this dominance and increase the occurrence of causal history explanations: limited information resources, pragmatic goals, and the clarification of behavior trends.

I use the term *information resources* to refer to the explainer's ability to recall, infer, or otherwise acquire information relevant to a particular mode of explanation. When people try to explain intentional behavior, they normally attempt to provide a reason explanation first, which requires access to mental state information. If such information is not (and cannot be made) available, the explainer will provide CHR explanations instead—provided, of course, the explainer has at least some relevant causal history information available (O'Laughlin and Malle 2002). For example, a student explained why a couple of his friends laughed at a beggar's expense:

(4-12)   I cannot explain why they did it other than **they were intoxicated** [CHR].

The person in the following example tries to explain why a young man had killed his parents; but lacking any knowledge of the killer's reasons, the explanation consists solely of causal history factors.

(4-13)   I have no clue why he killed his parents. I just think that, **being thirteen** [CHR], **you don't really know the consequences of something you do** [CHR] and **he seemed like he had a lot of issues** [CHR].

Pragmatic goals represent the second condition of increased CHR use. Whereas information resources influence both private and communicative explanations, pragmatic goals operate primarily in communicative explanations. Two such goals are of particular interest here: impression management and audience design.

Impression management refers to the explainer's attempt to influence an audience's perception and evaluation of either the agent or the explainer (both are the same person in the case of actor explanations). In particular, most behavior explanations paint the agent in a certain light, and different explanation modes alter the color of this light. The exact color shades are somewhat subtle, and I will return to them in a more detailed discussion in chapter 6. But the kind of picture that causal history explanations paint is not too difficult to predict: Whereas reasons delineate the agent's subjective deliberations leading up to the action, causal history factors can make the explanation sound more "objective"; and whereas reasons highlight the agent's freedom to choose a certain course of action, causal history factors suggest more the picture of powerful forces impinging on the person's behavior.

In contrast to the somewhat self-interested nature of impression management (Schlenker and Weigold 1992), a second pragmatic goal operates primarily in the service of coordination and communicative success. *Audience design* generally refers to adjustments in communicated messages in light of assumptions about what the audience already knows and what it is still interested in learning (Fussell and Krauss 1992; Horton and Gerrig 2002). Thus, explainers gauge what the audience wants to find out with respect to a particular behavior—for example, the particular reasons the agent had for acting or some general background information. Obviously, if the explainer guesses the latter, causal history explanations will increase. Such a guess may be particularly appropriate if one's audience comprises behaviorists, psychoanalysts, or sociologists, many of whom believe that the "right" explanation of a human action lies, not in the agent's subjective mental states, but in the objective causal factors that preceded those states, be they reinforcement schedules, unconscious drives, or social structures.

Audience design also encourages explainers to skip reasons when they believe them to be obvious (and probably assume that the audience must be wanting to know about something nonobvious). In the following example, it seems obvious that the neighbors complained about a party's noise level because they were bothered by it, so the explainer takes one step back in his explanation and offers a causal history:

(4-14)   Why did somebody complain about the noise level?—I think they complained about the noise level, personally, just because **the insulation in the apartments aren't very good** [CHR], and **usually there's really no noise coming from my apartment at all** [CHR].

Finally, the third condition that increases the rate of causal history explanations holds when an explainer has to account for *behavior trends*—either a series of behaviors performed by one person ("Why does he start fights all the time?") or one kind of behavior independently performed by a number of people ("Why are so many people willing to go into debt?").

Each specific behavior within the trend might be explained by distinct reasons; what causal history explanations could provide is the "common denominator" in the background of all those reasons. When an explainer thus puzzles over a particular behavior trend, the pull will be strong to find causal history explanations that underlay the entire set of behaviors rather than be bogged down by searching for individual reasons that applied to specific behaviors within the trend. We can see here considerations of parsimony at work, which hold both for private explanations and, as a conversational maxim, for communicative explanations (Grice 1975; Hilton 1990). Parsimony is one of the expectations an audience has of the explainer's utterances and thus one of the demands the explainer has to fulfill when constructing suitable communicative explanations. In the case of single behaviors, a reason will often be the most parsimonious and informative mode of explanation, but in the case of behavior trends, causal histories may take reasons' place of being the most parsimonious and informative account because they meet the cognitive economy demands shared by speaker and audience.

The following examples illustrate such explanations for behavior trends—(4-15) providing CHR explanations of an individual agent's repeated actions, (4-16) providing CHR explanations of actions performed by a whole group of people:

(4-15) Why I had not interacted warmly or frequently (as of late) with my ex-beau: **I have been very busy** and **have not had much time in the dorm.**

(4-16) A variety of Japanese businessmen worked seventy hours per week last year. *Why?* **Japan has a brutal work ethic.**

4.2.7 Enabling Factor Explanations

An agent might have reasons to act a certain way, and so she forms an intention. But whether the action occurs may depend on factors beyond the agent's intention and reasons—requiring, for example, skill and facilitating circumstances. A social perceiver may point to these "enabling factors"—factors that helped transform the intention into action—and thereby explain the *successful performance* of an action rather than its motives. For example, if asked "How come Ellen got all her work done?" a student might say, "Because she has one of those new calculators." Ellen's possessing a new calculator does not explain why she was trying to get her work done (her motives). Rather, given that she was trying to get it done, the calculator made it possible for her to accomplish what she was trying to do.

Table 4.4 illustrates a few such *enabling factor explanations*, all given for difficult or unlikely actions that were nevertheless successfully performed (from Malle et al. 2000; McClure and Hilton 1997, 1998; McClure et al. 2001).

In our empirical research, we found that reason explanations and enabling factors occur in diametrically opposing contexts (in one study, their frequencies correlated at $r = -.98$; Malle et al. 2000). By contrast, reasons and CHR explanations tend to co-occur. This pattern suggests that enabling factor explanations answer a question very different from that answered by reasons and causal history explanations. Most social behaviors are easy to perform, so only the question about the agent's motivation comes up, which is best answered with reason or causal history explanations. If, however, a behavior is difficult (i.e., it meets obstacles or requires substantial resources to be

Table 4.4
Enabling factor explanations for difficult actions

Behavior	Explanation
How come John aced the exam?	He's a stats whiz.
Finally I got him to ask me out . . .	. . . because I just asked him "Are you gonna give me your phone number or not?"
Phoebe worked all through the night . . .	. . . because she had a lot of coffee.
Mary is so poor, how come she bought a new car?	She inherited some money.

performed), the question about the action's successful completion comes up and is best answered with enabling factor explanations. Accordingly, enabling factors occur about seven to eight times more frequently with difficult behaviors than with easy behaviors (Malle et al. 2000; see also McClure and Hilton 1997).

Because enabling factor explanations clarify performance rather than motivation, they should increase in response to the question "How was this possible?" relative to the motivational question of "Why?" or "What for?" Indeed, we found that enabling factor explanations occurred four to twelve times more frequently in response to a "How possible?" question than in response to any other explanatory question (Malle et al. 2000). The most common explanatory questions ("Why?" and "How come?") only occasionally elicit enabling factors, and the question "For what reason?" all but eliminates them. Thus, the two main conditions under which enabling factor explanations occur are (a) when the action was particularly difficult but nevertheless succeeded[6] and (b) when the conversation partner asks for, or is likely interested in, the factors that enabled such an action.

To sum up, intentional behavior is primarily explained by *reasons,* which people conceptualize as the mental states the agent considered grounds for acting and in light of which she formed her intention to act ("Why did Martha give in?"—"Because she wanted to end the argument"). Sometimes people also offer *causal history of reason explanations,* the factors that brought about the agent's reasons and thus provide the background for those reasons ("Why did Martha give in?"—"Because she is a pushover." Finally, under specific circumstances people cite *enabling factor explanations,* which take the intention and the agent's reasons for granted and instead explain how it was possible that the agent turned an intention into action ("She hit her free throws because she had practiced them all week").

4.2.8 Cause Explanations of Unintentional Behavior

Whereas people can explain intentional behavior using three different modes (reasons, causal histories, and enabling factors), they have only one mode for unintentional behavior, namely cause explanations, which operate much the same way as explanations of physical events. Cause explanations do not involve any complex conceptual assumptions about the agent's intentionality, subjectivity, or rationality. People conceptualize causes within a billiard ball model of causal forces: an event or process brings about another, with no necessary involvement of awareness, reasoning, or choice. Consider the following examples of cause explanations, extracted from original transcripts.

(4-17) I almost failed my exams. *Why?* **Oh, 'cause I didn't really prepare for them.**

(4-18) My dad got mad with me **because something was wrong with my computer and he did not know how to fix it.**

(4-19) A friend cried on the phone. *Why?* **She felt that no one loved her.**

Note that there are a variety of causes cited in these three examples. In the first we have a behavior ("didn't really prepare . . ."), in the second we have a situational fact ("something wrong with my computer") paired with a skill deficiency ("did not know how to fix it"), and in the third we have a belief ("felt that no one loved her"). The third example is particularly interesting because it shows how beliefs can serve as mere causes. To be a reason this belief would have to play a particular part in the generation of an intentional action—involving conscious consideration, rational support, and the mediating role of an intention. But that was not the case here. Clearly, believing that no one loves you can *cause* a number of things, among them sadness and crying, but that belief did not figure as a reason of an intentional behavior.

Types of Causes Cause explanations are the kinds of explanations attribution theorists have written about, and they can indeed be classified along such attribution dimensions as internal–external or stable–unstable (e.g., Peterson, Schulman, Castellon, and Seligman 1991; Weiner 1986). Of course, we have to examine whether these classifications have any empirical purchase, and I will take up this question in later chapters (e.g., 5.3.1, 7.6).

Besides the classic causal dimensions, other classifications may arise in future research (Ames, personal communication), such as causes that are mental versus nonmental or causes of which the agent is or is not aware. Work in our lab has focused on the theoretical development of explanations for intentional behavior; but there may well be unmined riches in the domain of unintentional behavior as well.

4.3 Comparison and Integration with Other Theories

After presenting the core claims of the folk-conceptual theory of behavior explanation, I now relate it to classic attribution theory and its various theoretical alternatives, focusing on divergent claims about the conceptual framework that underlies people's behavior explanations.

Because attribution theory after Heider failed to distinguish between intentional and unintentional behavior, four distinct modes of explanation (causes, reasons, causal histories, and enabling factors) were treated as if they were one. Moreover, this singular mode, labeled "causal attributions," was modeled after cause explanations of unintentional behavior. The mechanical cause–effect assumption fits this mode of explanation well, as do the many classifications of cause types proposed in the literature (person–situation, trait–nontrait, stable–unstable, etc.). As a result, attribution theory has always dealt comfortably with cause explanations of unintentional behavior.

The same cannot be said for the three explanation modes that people apply to intentional behavior—reasons, causal histories, and enabling factors. These explanation modes differ from cause explanations both in conceptual assumptions and psychological functions and therefore are not captured within the traditional causal attribution picture. The problem for traditional theory is twofold here. For one thing, it fails to discriminate three clearly distinct explanation modes and hence misses, among other things, the predictive power of the reason–causal history distinction (e.g., O'Laughlin and Malle 2002). Furthermore, traditional attribution theory applies the person–situation framework to all explanation modes, which leads to serious trouble in the case of reason explanations (as I analyzed in section 4.2.5). Thus, whereas lay people make numerous distinctions between modes and features of behavior explanations, attribution researchers have typically had only one dichotomy to offer—person (or dispositional) causes and situation causes. This confounding and collapsing of folk concepts is the central oversight of classic attribution theory.

This oversight was discovered long ago, but the research habits in the field were so firmly established that the discovery led to no more than a few debates (see chapter 1). Still today most published attribution studies use the simplified person–situation dichotomy, even for such complex and subtle issues as cultural differences in explanations (e.g., Choi et al. 2003; Morris and Peng 1994). It would be too easy, however, to fault researchers for holding conservative theoretical attitudes. Theory change is a slow process, especially in a field like psychology where there are few formalized theories that could be put to crucial experimental tests. In the case of attribution theory, moreover, alternatives were perhaps not fully worked out and did not get the exposure they needed to convince researchers to abandon a widely accepted framework. Nonetheless, it is valuable to track some of the early alternatives to attribution theory, if only to give credit to these brave critics and their innovative ideas. Moreover, I would like to point out parallels and differences between these theoretical models and the folk-conceptual theory of behavior explanation.

Among the alternatives to attribution theory, three proposals are of particular importance. The first came from Allan Buss (1978) who emphasized the distinction between causes and reasons, loosely relying on Heider's distinction between personal and impersonal causality. Buss used the cause–reason distinction to develop some specific ideas about actor–observer asymmetries that were later discredited (e.g., Locke and Pennington 1982). But his major insight stands strong today: that attribution theory confounded two types of explanation that function very differently in both conceptual and psychological respects. Unfortunately, none of the immediate replies to Buss's critique (Harvey and Tucker 1979; Kruglanski 1979), nor attribution research as a whole, dealt adequately with the collapsing of reasons and causes.

The cause–reason distinction picks out the two most diametrically opposed explanation modes, which hold prominent positions within the folk-conceptual theory as well. Beyond that, however, our theory clarifies why these modes are so different (because they reflect the distinct folk-conceptual assumptions about intentional and unintentional behavior) and introduces two other explanation modes that flow from the complexity of intentional behavior (CHR explanations and enabling factor explanations).

The second alternative to attribution theory was introduced and refined by a number of researchers, including Robert Abelson, Mansur Lalljee, John McClure, and Stephen Read (for a review, see McClure 2002). These scholars emphasized the importance of goal-based explanations and the corresponding assumptions people make about purposeful, planned behavior—assumptions that were simply not accounted for in causal attribution theory. By pointing to the unique role that goals play in behavior explanations, these researchers revealed clear limitations of the person–situation scheme. Despite success in various publication outlets, however, the goal-based movement, too, has had difficulties in changing the course of mainstream North American attribution research.

Goal-based explanations play a prominent role in our folk-conceptual theory, namely as reason explanations of intentional behavior. More specifically, goal explanations are one type of reason explanation: the kind that cites the object of the agent's desire or the desire itself (i.e., desire reasons). The folk-conceptual theory, however, clarifies that reason explanations don't always cite desires/goals but also cite beliefs and sometimes valuings, neither of which can be subsumed under the goal concept. Among explanations for intentional behavior, then, goals are one specific type of reason, and a detailed theory of reason explanation is needed to clarify the relationship between goals and other reasons, especially belief reasons.

A third model has gained some prominence recently, focusing on the distinction between goals and preconditions as complementary explanations for intentional behavior (McClure and Hilton 1997, 1998; McClure, Lalljee, and Jaspars 1991). Drawing on Heider's original analysis (under slightly different labels), John McClure and colleagues have carefully examined conditions under which one or the other explanation mode is preferred. No person–situation model could predict the patterns of results they have documented, because there is no room for goal explanations in such a model nor for a distinction between two different explanation modes with different psychological functions. Nonetheless, textbook and mainstream attribution research has yet to fully appreciate this work.

The distinction between goals and preconditions has a clear place in the folk-conceptual theory of explanation as well, but as part of the slightly more general distinction between reasons and enabling factors. Goals, as mentioned, are one type of reason explanation and answer a *why* (or *what for*) question. Importantly, goal and other reason explanations explain not only a completed action but also the motivation or intention to so act. Even if the agent never succeeded at performing the intended action, reason explanations clarify what motivated the agent to try to so act in the first place. "Preconditions" are perhaps more appropriately labeled *enabling factors* because they identify those factors that literally enabled the agent's intention to become action; hence, they answer the question of *how it was possible* that the action occurred—and, by implication, they don't explain anything about the agent's motivation to *try* to act in the first place. Further strengthening this connection, it has been shown that conditions that dictate folk explainers' preference for goals versus preconditions readily generalize to their preference for reasons versus enabling factor explanations (Malle et al. 2000, study 3).

In sum, the folk-conceptual theory of explanation integrates several insights from attribution theory and its alternatives to form a comprehensive picture of lay behavior explanations. Attribution theory has taught us about the logic of cause explanations, but several critics suggested that folk explainers use more than a single mode of explanation: they distinguish between reasons and causes, treat at least some reasons as goals, and also distinguish between reasons and enabling factors.

The folk-conceptual theory of explanation not only integrates these various theoretical advances but further expands the picture of behavior explanations by providing elements that have not been previously identified. An important novel element is the distinct mode of causal history explanations as a counterpoint to reason explanations. Even though both explanation modes clarify what motivated the action in question, reasons refer specifically to the agent's subjective and rational grounds of acting—what the agent had in mind when intending to act—whereas CHR explanations cite the broader causal background that led up to those reasons and, hence, the action. Another novel element is the detailed analysis of reason explanations, which reveals intriguing features at the conceptual, linguistic, and psychological level. Thus, the folk-conceptual theory of explanation provides a systematic model of the assumptions, concepts, and distinctions inherent in people's explanations of behavior. But this is only the first layer of the theory. The next chapters will examine the psychological processes that support the actual construction of explanations and thus introduce the theory's second layer. But before that, there is one item of unfinished business to attend to.

4.4   Meaning Reconsidered

Now that we have a full outline of the conceptual tools people use for explaining behavior, we can briefly look back at the elusive "meaning" that people search for when explaining human behavior. The present theory cannot account for every shade of this concept, but it does suggest what *meaning* means in the context of explanations.

The meaning of natural events is what the event indicates—often what caused it, sometimes what will follow it (as in the clouds that mean rain; Grice 1957). The meaning of an unintentional behavior typically lies in its causes as well, be they transient or stable, inside or outside the agent. The meaning of an intentional behavior, by contrast, lies typically in the reasons the agent had for acting, with desire reasons perhaps of primary importance because they express the point or purpose of the questioned action.

When the meaning of an intentional action in terms of its reasons is unknown or irrelevant, explainers have other tools available as well to create a coherent representation for themselves or their audience. Causal history of reason explanations offer the background to the agent's reasons and thus her action; enabling factor explanations clarify the forces that allowed the action to be successfully performed. Grasping the full meaning of an action might include all three of these aspects: the agent's own reasons for intending to act; the broader background and origin of those reasons; and the additional factors necessary for the agent's intention to become a successful action. Knowing all that provides people with a comprehensive, meaningful representation of an action. This will not be all we can ever say about the human search for meaning in action, but it is a decent first step.

5 Psychological Construction: A Theory of Behavior Explanations II

Chapter 4 presented the first major ingredient of a theory of behavior explanation—the folk-conceptual framework within which explanations are forged. This framework, centering on the concept of intentionality, sets the boundaries for what can be a behavior explanation; specifies the knowledge gaps that the explanation is expected to fill (e.g., what motivated the agent or what made the action possible); and provides the conceptual tools that in principle can be used in explanations (reasons, causal history factors, and the like). But a theory of behavior explanations has a second major ingredient, namely, the identification of psychological principles that guide the actual construction of explanations. This construction consists of the explainer's choices among the tools provided by the conceptual framework: selecting the appropriate mode of explanation and its specific features, identifying context-specific content, and formulating explanations in language (often with particular communicative purposes).

The claims and hypotheses put forth in this chapter come with somewhat more caution because work on the cognitive construction of behavior explanations is just beginning. But this research may be one of the most exciting directions the folk-conceptual theory of behavior explanations can go. Having made the necessary distinctions among modes of explanations (e.g., reasons, causal histories) and among specific features of these modes (e.g., reason type, mental state markers), we can set out to identify the various cognitive processes and psychological factors that underlie the construction of explanations.

I begin with a broadly painted analogy of this construction process and then peel apart its multiple layers.

5.1   Explanations as Shopping: An Analogy

Describing the actual process by which people cognitively construct explanations is a bit unwieldy. I will therefore make use of an analogy that illustrates important parameters of the construction process and makes the
entire process more intelligible. The analogy I offer may at first seem surprising but has a number of attractive features. In the end, the analogy
should be deemed only a stopover en route to a more formal cognitive theory that, I hope, will evolve from future research.

Our hero, a bachelor, lives in a small, old-fashioned town and has to make various
choices during his daily shopping. Depending on what he needs for the day, he may
go to the general store, the deli, the butcher, or the greengrocer.
    If he needs something for the house, he goes to the general store, where he may
choose between toiletry items, cleaning supplies, and so forth.
    If he needs something to eat, he has to make further decisions. In case he wants to
have a snack, he goes to the deli, where he may select cold cuts, cheeses, or the like.
In case he wants to cook dinner, he goes to the butcher or the greengrocer. Normally
he goes to the butcher first, and if he finds some tasty meat, the shopping's done. If
the butcher doesn't have much to offer, our shopper obtains some vegetables from
the greengrocer for a vegetarian meal. And sometimes he both buys meat and has vegetables as a side dish.
    When he does buy meat, he gets either chicken, beef, or game, and each of these
can be purchased either marinated or plain. Finally, when he does go to the greengrocer, he chooses greens, mushrooms, or various other vegetables.

At first glance, this shopping trip illustrates merely a large number of decisions. But the decisions are analogous to the kinds of choices a social perceiver makes when constructing behavior explanations. Figure 5.1 lays out
these choices in the explanatory domain and the following discussion re-
lates them to their analogues in the shopping context.

    When constructing a behavior explanation an explainer must make vari-
ous choices. Depending on what she[1] needs to explain, she may offer causes,
enabling factors, reasons, or causal histories. By analogy, our shopper needs
to decide, depending on what he needs, whether to go to the general store,
the deli, the butcher, or the grocer.

    The first decision is whether the behavior to be explained is intentional or
unintentional. If the explainer is puzzled over an unintentional behavior,
she will offer causes, and she may specifically cite person causes, situation
causes, or various interactions. Similarly, when our shopper needs some-

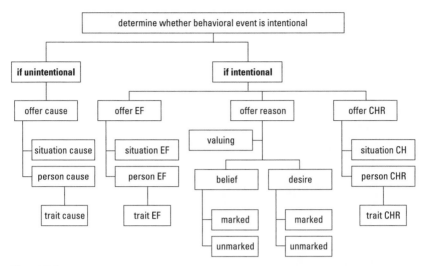

Figure 5.1
Choice points in constructing a behavior explanation.

thing for the house, he goes to the general store, where he may purchase toiletry items, cleaning supplies, and so on.[2]

If the explainer is puzzled over an intentional action, she must make further decisions, just as our shopper must make further decisions when he needs something to eat.

If the explainer tries to clarify how it was possible that an action succeeded, she offers enabling factors, which can again be located in the person, the situation, and so on. Likewise, if our shopper wants to have a snack, he goes to the deli for cold cuts, cheeses, and so on.

If, however, the explainer tries to explain what motivated the action in question, she offers reason explanations or causal history of reason explanations. Normally she tries to construct reasons first and, if she succeeds, ends there. If reasons cannot be constructed, she searches for a causal history explanation. At times she may even offer both reasons and causal history factors, with the latter complementing the former. In the analogous world, our bachelor goes to the butcher or the greengrocer if he wants to cook dinner. The butcher is the first option and if he finds good meat there, he stops. If the meat offerings are limited, he may go to the greengrocer for vegetables. Sometimes he even buys both meat and vegetables for a complete meal.

Finally, when an explainer does construct reasons, they can be either de-sires, beliefs, or valuings, and each one of them can be marked or unmarked (though valuings are virtually never unmarked; see below). Also, when she constructs causal history factors, she may as usual select person factors, sit-uation factors, and so on. Likewise, when our shopper buys meat, he selects either chicken, beef, or game, and each one can be ordered marinated or plain. And when he goes to the grocer, he chooses among greens, mush-rooms, and various other vegetables.

Now let me highlight a number of attractive features of this analogy. At the outset, it makes clear that constructing behavior explanations, like shopping, is a complex choice process.[3] In addition, the shopping analogy reflects various constraints that have meaningful correspondences in the domain of constructing explanations. For example, if the shopper needs cleaning supplies, it wouldn't be wise for him to go to the butcher—just as one wouldn't explain an unintentional behavior with reasons. Conversely, if the shopper needs dinner food, it would be bizarre to buy cleaning sup-plies—just as one wouldn't explain an intentional behavior with mere causes. Somewhat less eccentric, though still curious, would be a purchase of snacks for dinner—as it would be curious, though not incomprehensible, to respond to a why-question with enabling factors ("Why did she kill the intruder?"—"There was a gun in the house").

Certain combinations of shopping items are sensible, and so are certain combinations of explanation modes. One might at times buy both snacks and serious dinner food—just as one might explain both how it was possible that an action was performed (enabling factors) and what motivated the agent to perform the action in the first place (reasons and causal histories). And just as vegetables might nicely complement a meat dish, reasons and causal histories can peacefully coexist within one explanation.

Both explanations and shopping choices are sensitive to audience effects. For example, snacks will be more appropriate for an afternoon visit, whereas meat and vegetables will be appropriate for a dinner guest—unless of course the guest is vegetarian, in which case our shopper will omit the meat. Simi-larly, enabling factors will be the explanatory option of choice in, say, a sports interview whereas reasons and causal histories fit better in intimate conversations.

5.2 Psychological Determinants of Explanatory Choices

Now that we have a plausible map of the options and choice points in the construction of explanations (see fig. 5.1), we can turn to the identification of psychological factors that govern or determine these explanatory choices. In chapter 4, I introduced several of these factors when discussing current evidence on the conditions of occurrence for each explanation mode and for some of the specific features. Here I summarize these factors more systematically and develop a model that links psychological determinants to explanatory choices.

The psychological determinants of explanatory choices fall into three broad categories:

1. Judged behavior attributes
2. Pragmatic goals
3. Information resources

5.2.1 Judged Behavior Attributes

Before offering an explanation, social perceivers make several (often implicit) judgments about the behavior to be explained. One such judgment is about the *intentionality* of the behavior. If considered unintentional, explanations will refer to a cause; if considered intentional, explanations will cite a reason, causal history, or enabling factor (Malle 1999, 2001b). Among intentional behaviors, a second important attribute is the *difficulty* of the action. If the action is considered difficult to produce, the explainer will often choose enabling factors; otherwise, he is likely to choose reasons or causal histories (Malle et al. 2000; McClure and Hilton 1997, 1998). A third attribute is whether the to-be-explained behavior is singular or represents a *trend* (across time or agents). If the behavior is judged to be a trend, the rate of CHR explanations is greater than if it is singular (O'Laughlin and Malle 2002).

5.2.2 Pragmatic Goals

Pragmatic goals refer to the smaller or larger projects explainers try to accomplish with their communicative explanations, such as easing another person's confusion, managing their status in the interaction, or fending off

blame. Two groups of goals can be distinguished by their primary benefici-
ary: *audience design* (which chiefly benefits the conversation partner) and
impression management (which chiefly benefits the explainer). Audience design refers to the tailoring of an explanation so that the audience truly learns
what it wants to know (see section 1.4.4). The clearest case of such design is
when the explainer matches an explanation mode to the type of question
asked (Malle et al. 2000; McClure and Hilton 1998). This question can in-
quire either about the agent's immediate motivation ("What for?" → *reasons*), the background of that motivation ("How come?" → *causal histories of
reasons*), or about the factors that enabled successful action performance
("How was this possible?" → *enabling factors*). More subtle adjustments include offering a belief reason when it can be assumed that the audience
already knows the desire reason, or offering a CHR explanation when the
reasons for the action are likely to be obvious.

Whereas audience design falls under the conversational maxim of being
relevant (Grice 1975; Sperber and Wilson 1986), impression management
does not try to merely optimize communication but rather is an act of social influence (see section 6.3). The influence on explanatory choices can be
found at every level of analysis. People increase their use of causal history
explanations when accounting for negative actions (Nelson and Malle
2003); they increase their use of belief reasons when trying to appear rational (Malle et al. 2000); and they explicitly add a mental state marker to
their belief reasons when they want to distance themselves from the agent
(e.g., "Why is he looking at apartments?"—"He thinks I am moving in with
him"; Malle et al. 2000).

Even though the modifying influence of the explainer's goals is most
visible in the case of communicative explanations, it may also operate in
private explanations—when explainers attempt to influence themselves,
as it were. Explainers may lean toward certain explanation types, for example, when they try to justify to themselves an undesirable action or
when they engage in dissonance reduction, defensive pessimism, or self-
affirmation processes (Festinger 1957; Norem 2001; Steele 1988).

5.2.3 Information Resources

Deficits in relevant information about the agent, the behavior, or the context can limit the explainer's ability to accomplish his goals, and such defi-

cits often require adjustments to one's choice of explanation. This can be seen, for example, in the selection of belief reasons versus desire reasons. We find that observers, compared to actors, typically offer more desire reasons than belief reasons. The interpretation here is that desire reasons are easier to infer from contextual and cultural knowledge, whereas belief reasons are more idiosyncratic and sometimes only accessible to the actor. However, when observers know the agent and/or were present when the action took place, their rate of belief reasons increases to resemble that of actors (Malle, Knobe, and Nelson 2004).

A somewhat more complex case is the choice between reasons and causal history explanations. With reasons being the default mode for explaining intentional behavior, explainers will initially set out to provide the agent's reasons; but if they lack knowledge about the agent's relevant mental states they may be forced to search for a causal history explanation instead.

Knowledge, however, is not the only cognitive resource available. If an explainer does not actually know the agent's reasons, he may still infer or construct them. Indications in the agent's mannerism or past behavior, clues from the action context, and general cultural expectations about the kinds of motives that underlie certain behaviors usually provide a sufficient basis for inducing a reason (Bruner 1990).

This induction process becomes difficult when the action in question was not actually observed in context but rather described verbally, when the explainer does not know the agent, or when the action is so unusual as to make culturally typical motives inapplicable. In these circumstances, explainers are likely to search for causal history explanations.

But to provide such causal history explanations the explainer must know or infer some general facts about the agent or the action context. When even such general information is lacking, causal histories are not the solution to the explainer's problem (O'Laughlin and Malle 2002). The explainer will then provide, as a last resort, rather simpleminded *generic reasons* (e.g., "She wanted to," "He likes doing that," or "She thought it would be a good idea").

This multifaceted pattern can be formalized by four tacit rules for the use of reasons versus causal history explanations:

1. If every kind of information is available, provide reasons.[4]

2. If specific mental state information is unavailable, try to infer or construct it and provide reasons.

3. If mental state information cannot be constructed, search for general information about agent, context, or action and use it to provide causal history explanations.

4. If general information is not available (and cannot be constructed), provide generic reasons for the action in question—reasons for why *anybody* might act that way.

We have several pieces of evidence that are consistent with this pattern of rules (Malle, Knobe, and Nelson 2004; O'Laughlin and Malle 2002). When explaining their own intentional behaviors (as "actors"), people are in the best position to have every kind of information available and should, according to the model, predominantly offer reasons. Indeed, actors provide on average 80% reason explanations (and 20% CHRs), which is just about the highest rate of reasons observable (supporting rule 1). When explaining other people's behaviors (as "observers"), people lack various kinds of information and will try to infer or construct reasons, but this construction should reach a limit, resulting in an average reduction of reasons. Indeed, observers provide on average 65% reasons, a pattern that supports rule 2. A case that makes it difficult and cumbersome to infer reasons is when people explain the behavior of aggregate groups (see chapter 8). Aggregate group members all perform the same action but do so independently as an assemblage of individual agents (e.g., "The junior members of the psychology department worked hard throughout spring break"). Having difficulties in constructing the various mental states of these independent agents, people further reduce their reason explanations to 59%, a pattern that supports rule 3. Finally, when people don't know the agent at all and have not observed the behavior in question ("Why did 'Person A' work 70 hours last week?"), they cannot even construct causal histories and therefore return to a relatively high rate of reasons (77%). But the reasons they offer are generic (e.g., "They might like it") and many of them are pure guesses strung together, such as "Either they had to, given the demands of their jobs, they wanted to make a lot of overtime, or they had to work two jobs to support their families" (O'Laughlin and Malle 2002).

5.2.4 Modeling the Psychological Determinants of Explanatory Choices

We can now systematically relate the three groups of psychological factors (judged behavior attributes, pragmatic goals, and information resources) to the range of explanatory choices that occur at three levels: *mode* (cause, reason, CHR, enabling factor), *type* (either type of reason, e.g., belief versus desire, or type of cause, e.g., trait versus nontrait), and *form* (e.g., reasons with or without mental state marker). Figure 5.2 depicts their relationships and also highlights two important facts: that pragmatic goals are the most wide-ranging determinant of explanatory choices and that choice of explanatory mode is influenced by all three determinants.

One useful application of this model is to narrow down the psychological determinants that influence phenomena such as actor–observer asymmetries or self-servingness. By assumption, actors and observers explain the same behaviors, so we should expect any asymmetries in how they explain behaviors to be due to pragmatic goals and/or information resources. Self-servingness, by assumption, is not based on information resources, so we should expect any such effects to be due to judged behavior attributes or pragmatic goals.

Both sides of figure 5.2 can be expanded. On the right side, we can further distinguish between the diverse modes, types, and forms of explanation that were unveiled in chapter 4 and section 5.1. On the left side, we can break down some determinants into specific subtypes: behavior attributes such as intentionality, difficulty, or trend, and pragmatic goals such as answering specific explanatory questions or managing impressions. Using these expansions on both sides we can begin to write out regression equations[5] that connect a particular explanatory choice with a set of psychological determinants (see table 5.1). These equations represent some hypotheses that were already developed here and some that have yet to be developed in chapters 6 through 8. Among the equations we also find a mix of theoretical predictions (derived from the nature of a given explanatory tool; see chapter 4)

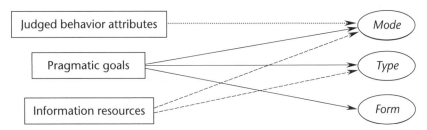

Figure 5.2
Psychological determinants of explanatory choices.

Table 5.1
Predicting selected explanatory choices from psychological determinants

(1)[a]	[REA, CHR, EF] vs. CAU = b_1 (behavior intentionality)
(2)[b]	EF vs. [REA, CHR] = b_1 (behavior difficulty) + b_2 (explanatory question) + b_3 (difficulty × question)
(3)	CHR vs. REA = b_0 + b_1 (behavior trend) + b_2 (impression management) + b_3 (information)
(4)	belief REA vs. desire REA = b_1 (impression management) + b_2 (audience design) + b_3 (information)
(5)	marked belief vs. unmarked belief = b_1 (impression management)
(6)	trait vs. nontrait = b_1 (information) + b_2 (behavior intentionality)

[a] See Malle (1999).   [b] See Malle et al. (2000).

and empirical discoveries. For example, equation (1) follows from the very meaning of cause explanations, whereas equation (5) was discovered when inspecting a sample of mental state marker usages. I fully expect these equations to be further modified with additional research, and new ones may be added in time. Importantly, however, the folk-conceptual theory of explanations puts constraints on such equations. For example, mental state markers will never reflect a difference in information because they operate at the linguistic level, not the level of explanation contents, whereas they may very well reflect an influence of audience design.

5.3   Cognitive Processes Involved in Selecting Specific Explanations

So far I have described choices among explanation modes and three psychological factors that govern these choices (judgments of behavior attributes, pragmatic goals, and information resources). But an explainer cannot just stop at a decision about a particular mode of explanation or a feature of that mode; he must select a *specific* cause or reason, one with a *specific* content (Hesslow 1988). This section explores the cognitive processes that are involved in this selection process.

Just as it may appear obvious that our bachelor who decides to shop for meat eventually has to pick a particular piece of meat, it should be equally obvious that people, when constructing a behavior explanation, must select a specific event, state, or object that they think brought about the behavior in question. But in a large number of attribution studies social perceivers were not allowed to take this obvious step. They were asked instead to pick one of two general classes of factors that presumably caused the behavior: person or situation causes. Imagine that you were asked by a colleague, "Why didn't you come to the talk yesterday?" and you answered, "It was due to something about me." Even if your colleague were familiar with attribution theory, she would not be satisfied with your response. Admittedly, there are circumstances in which a vague hint to a class of causes may be informative (e.g., when ruling out one set of possible explanations and turning attention to another possible set). But in most cases of naturally occurring explanations, choosing a mere class of causes will not do. This is obviously true for communicative explanations, which have to answer the specific wondering of one's conversation partner, but it is also true for private explanations. If my wife wonders why I am sad tonight, she won't be satisfied to determine that it was due to "something about the situation"; she would want to know which situation triggered my sadness and what about that situation did.

When explainers offer reason explanations, mere mention of a class of causal factors will be even less appropriate. A social perceiver who constructs a reason explanation will have to choose one or more particular reasons, and in so doing he has to identify them as beliefs, desires, or valuings; he has to settle on a particular content of that belief, desire, or valuing; and, in the case of communicative explanations, he has to decide whether these reasons are to be marked with mental state verbs or not. Obviously, broad person versus situation classifications illuminate nothing about these choices.

The psychological factors discussed in 5.2 determine only the kind of explanation one gives—at the level of *mode,* for example, a cause, a reason, or a causal history explanation. None of the determinants dictate which *specific* reason or cause the explainer will select. This selection must be a function of the particular behavior wondered about, the context, and the explainer's cognitive state—a triad of factors that will differ from one explanation to the next. But even though there is virtually an infinite number of specific explanations that social perceivers can and do form, there is only a limited number of cognitive processes involved in the search and selection of specific explanations. Identifying these processes and relating them to the different modes of explanation is the goal of this section. The discussion splits into two questions: (1) How are specific causes selected? and (2) How are specific reasons selected?

5.3.1 Selecting Specific Causes

The predominant belief among attribution researchers has been that causal attributions are driven by covariation calculation (e.g., Fiedler, Walther, and Nickel 1999; Försterling 1989, 2001; Hewstone and Jaspars 1987; Kelley 1967; cf. Cheng and Novick 1990; Glymour 2000).[6] If true, then at least for the three "mechanical" modes of explanation (causes, causal histories, and enabling factors), decisions about specific causes should be guided by covariation processes. However, there are several important limitations to this claim.

To begin with, in communicative explanations the choice of a particular causal factor is guided not only by perception and memory—processes that may be tied to covariation calculations—but also by impression management (i.e., selecting a cause that puts the agent or explainer in a certain evaluative light) and general audience design (i.e., selecting a cause that meets the listener's wondering or expectation). Choosing the best excusing explanation or selecting the causes that, say, one's psychotherapist wants to hear are decisions that are surely not driven by covariation information. (And it is not out of the question that impression management may even hold for some private explanations, as a form of mild self-deception.)

If covariation calculation does not solely drive decisions about selecting causes, we should at least be able to specify the conditions under which it is important. The empirical research on covariation, however, does not tell us much about these conditions, because most studies demonstrate merely that people use covariation information when it is provided by the experimenter (e.g., Försterling 1992; McArthur 1972; Shultz and Mendelson 1975; Van Kleeck et al. 1988). Hardly any study demonstrates whether and when people actively seek out covariation information in natural contexts. As a rare exception, Lalljee, Lamb, Furnham, and Jaspars (1984) asked their participants to write down the kind of information they would like to have in order to explain various events, and covariation information was not in great demand under these conditions. A few additional studies examined people's choices between receiving covariation information and some other information, and there, too, explainers were less interested in covariation information than in information about generative forces or mechanisms (Ahn et al. 1995) or information that would disambiguate a variety of spontaneously generated hypotheses (Lalljee et al. 1984).

Finally, even when one's search for causes could be supported by covariation information, collecting such information is difficult. It requires that the information is actually available (i.e., the explainer has encountered the behavior in question several times before) and that there is time to integrate the information. Outside the laboratory, neither condition is guaranteed to be fulfilled, so there would have to be some other, more efficient processes available for all the cases when either time or information is lacking.

All these considerations challenge the assumption that covariation calculation is the sole or even the main process by which people select specific causes. So what other selection processes might there be? At least four have been suggested:

1. Application of event-specific, agent-specific, or general *knowledge* (Abelson and Lalljee 1988; Fugelsang and Thompson 2000; Gopnik 1993; Gopnik and Wellman 1992; Lalljee and Abelson 1983; Lalljee et al. 1984; Leddo and Abelson 1986; Read 1987; Sagar and Schofield 1980; von Collani, Kauer, and Kauer 1991);

2. *Simulation* (i.e., imaginative representation) of the agent's mental states or *projection*[7] of one's own mental states onto the agent (Ames in press; Goldman 1989, 2001; Gordon 1986, 1992; Harris 1992; Krueger and Clement 1997);

3. Search for *generative forces* or mechanisms (Ahn et al. 1995; Ahn and Bailenson 1996; Ahn and Kalish 2000; Johnson, Boyd, and Magnani 1994; Cheng 2000; Wu and Cheng 1999); and

4. The *method of difference,* which contrasts the event in question with an alternative event and identifies the critical difference (e.g., Cheng and Novick 1990; Hilton and Slugoski 1986; Jones and Davis 1965; Kahneman and Miller 1986; McGill 1989; McGill and Klein 1993).

There are very few studies in the extant literature that have pitted these processes against each other. And perhaps for good reason, because several of the processes are intertwined. A search for generative mechanisms must rely on general knowledge or simulation to find the force that moved the agent; simulations may build on domain-specific knowledge; and the selection of an alternative event in the method of difference is likely influenced by projection ("What would I have done instead?") as well as cultural knowledge, while the search for critical differences between the events will likely aim at generative forces.

In light of the interconnections among these processes, and given that each of the processes has been found relevant for explanations in at least a handful of studies, it is compelling to conclude that folk explainers make use of all of these processes—as well as of occasional covariation calculation—when identifying specific causes, causal histories of reasons, and enabling factors (Malle 2001b). It is time, then, that research in this domain moved from the sole study of one broad causal selection process (such as covariation detection) to an investigation of the conditions under which each of these processes is used by explainers. In such an investigation, the folk-conceptual theory of explanation can play a pivotal role. By highlighting the distinct explanatory tasks explainers face and the conceptual tools (i.e., explanation modes) available to them for each task, the theory specifies some of the key parameters that guide the causal selection process. For example, the questions and demands that guide causal selection for an enabling factor explanation will be quite different from those that guide selection for a causal history explanation.

Because there is currently no systematic evidence available on the interactions among various causal selection processes and on the different selection processes dominant within each mode of explanation, I offer small samples of original explanations[8] and discuss the possible interplay among these processes separately for each mode of explanation.

Specific Causes in Cause Explanations   Cause explanations of unintentional behavior are perhaps the best candidate for finding covariation calculation at work. Many of Kelley's (1967) original examples were of this type, such as explanations for one's own enjoyment (p. 194) and other experiences, sensations, and reactions (p. 196). Covariation analysis is especially likely, as Kelley realized, in the case of self-perception—i.e., wondering why one feels a certain way or has a certain reaction. That is because the actor often has access to a wealth of covariation information that bears on the event in question. However, this covariation search may be used primarily in very difficult cases—when an explanation is otherwise hard to come by. If I wonder why I am having a headache and just cannot find an immediate trigger in things I ate or did, I may look back to previous headaches to try to find common denominators and then systematically rule some out that did not lead to a headache. But if I wonder why I feel tired in the early evening I may recall instantly that I got up early that morning.

Processes like these are of course difficult to study because they are entirely private wonderings and often do not lead to verbalized explanations. In one of our studies we asked participants specifically to recall behavioral events about which they wondered in private thought and then to recall the explanations, if any, that they had come up with at that time. Events that people recalled in this setting, however, were not the kinds of puzzling mental or bodily states that might demand covariation calculation. The states were more straightforward, and so their explanations were likely to be produced not by covariation analysis, but by conjecturing or recruiting knowledge about "generating" forces:

(5-1)   Why I think she likes me.—**Because I have too large an ego.**

(5-2)   How I managed to not notice something important.—**I was being silly and stupid, and I was in a hurry.**

(5-3)   Why I've felt so distracted lately.—**I felt that it was probably because I'm trying to settle in this quarter.**

When we turn to communicative explanations from the actor perspective, covariation is entirely absent. In such cases, the communicator typically knows why the event occurred but preemptively offers an explanation in case the listener wonders why:

(5-4)   I was really freaked out **'cause I had never seen anyone to have, like, a seizure.**

The speaker in this (recorded and transcribed) conversation may have felt that the intensity of his affect required clarification. But neither covariation nor simulation are of help in providing such a clarification. To render "being freaked out" understandable and acceptable, he refers to the specific stimuli in the situation and a lawlike principle that he presumably shares with his audience—that novelty can cause both surprise and fear and often triggers uninhibited, unprepared-for reactions.

Communicative explanations can also be about other people's behavior. In the following example, the explaining observer knows why the agent was angry and offers an explanation, perhaps again because the intensity of the emotion might seem surprising.

(5-5)   The bowling machine cleared his score. It's like, he was *really* pissed off, **because he was doing so good.**

For this explainer, the understanding of the event may have been formed already during the original situation, when she observed the machine clearing her friend's score after he had played very well. Because of the immediacy of the situation, it was easy for the explainer to simulate, or empathize with, the emotions that the agent must have had: joy about playing well, hope that it would continue or get even better, and then shock that his high score was deleted. The observer may have even had an "Oh no!" feeling not unlike the agent's own. The opportunity for direct observation and vicarious experience made other causal search strategies unnecessary in this case, because the explainer had a satisfying and immediate understanding of the friend's strong reaction, and this understanding was then communicated to her audience.

Consider now a situation in which the explainer doesn't literally know why the event in question occurred but does have a reasonable idea:

(5-6) Why didn't your sister want to work out?—**I think she is depressed because she just moved here and she doesn't have a job.**

By the method of difference, the contrast event of *wanting* to work out is easily inferred but fails to offer an explanation. Also, the explainer does not seem to simulate his sister's mind state because such simulation would be unlikely to generate the "distant" causal factors he cites but rather something more concrete like "She just didn't feel motivated to do anything." Nor does the explainer seem to rely on covariation patterns (and he may not even be able to if the behavior is novel). What the explainer relies on instead is agent-specific knowledge that is immediately activated when the question touches on his sister and her behavior: her depression and its presumed environmental causes as the generating forces of the behavior in question.

In the next example, the explainer also knows the agent well but doesn't actually know what happened.

(5-7)   Why didn't your friend give you the hot guy's answer [to a question the explainer had relayed]?—I just think **he might have forgotten.**

The explainer's conjecture is most likely based on cultural knowledge about what generating forces exist for this kind of behavior and which of these forces may apply to the agent (e.g., ruling out that the friend is spitefully withholding information). Alternatively, the speaker may have derived the explanation from a trait representation about the agent: that he is forgetful. Covariation analysis might have originally helped to form this trait representation, but the speaker most likely did not construct the explanation by calculating covariation information on the spot.

Let me turn now to explanations of a stranger's unintentional behavior. Without considerable historic information about the agent and her interactions with the relevant environment, the explainer cannot rely on covariation information. If the explainer was not even present at the time of the behavior, simulation is also quite unlikely. One might expect that explainers will offer traits, given well-known evidence that observers infer traits even from single behaviors (Jones and Harris 1967; Ross, Amabile, and Steinmetz 1977; Gilbert and Malone 1995). Interestingly, however, outside of forced inference situations we have found that observers use traits rather selectively—in cause explanations (offered spontaneously in conversation or as answers to why-questions), we see an average of 13% traits and actually *more traits* for agents whom the explainer knows well than for agents who are strangers (Malle, Knobe, and Nelson 2004). When explainers lack specific knowledge (including trait knowledge), they often resort to conventional explanations, based on cultural and contextual knowledge, as can be seen in the following example:

(5-8)   Do you have any idea why he was swearing and mad?—Uh, he sounds **overworked** and **he had little sleep.**

This explainer, who answers an experimenter's why-question, was not present in the situation and did not know the agent; she merely listened to a short story told by the agent in which the selected behavior was mentioned (Malle, Knobe, and Nelson 2004, study 4). The explainer thus uses the little information she has available (the agent mentioned at some point that he had been tired) and accounts for the emotional intensity by referring to general emotion knowledge (or conjecture): that stress and sleep deprivation make people emotionally labile.

A similar reliance on general knowledge can be seen in the following example (taken from the same study in which people listened to a brief story told by the agent before they explained a few of the agent's behaviors):

(5-9)   Do you have any idea why he liked the Harvard soccer program and coach better?—um [five seconds] uh [laughs] he might like them better because . . . um . . . **they're a better playing team** . . . an' . . . **the coach is more nationally known** . . . things like that . . .

The explainer neither knows the agent nor the answer (though he tried to search his memory for a while). The question format provides a clear contrast event and makes the search for comparison information most suitable, but the explainer conjures up only the most general comparative information.

To sum up, cause explanations of unintentional behavior can be constructed by a variety of causal search processes, and covariation analysis is by no means the dominant process. Lacking systematic empirical studies, we cannot say with confidence which search processes are used under what conditions; but several testable hypotheses suggest themselves:

1. Wondering why an unintentional behavior occurred that one directly observed, especially performed by familiar others, may most strongly pull for *simulation and projection*.

2. As familiarity with the agent decreases, and especially if the explainer did not directly observe the event, reliance on *general knowledge* is likely to increase.

3. Private wonderings for difficult-to-understand experiences in oneself may be most likely to pull for *covariation* analysis.

Specific Factors in Causal History of Reason Explanations   Causal history of reason explanations, to reiterate, are used in explaining intentional behavior to either complement or substitute for citing the agent's reasons for acting. The relationship between the CHR and the action explained can vary from tightly constraining the agent's possible reasons to vaguely ruling out some class of candidate reasons, as causal history factors encompass the broad spectrum from immediate context-specific triggers to background factors in the agent's personality, upbringing, culture, and the like. In examining the search processes that explainers rely on when picking out a particular causal history factor, I begin with an actor explanation.

(5-10)   The next morning I rode the school bus which I hadn't ridden in a long time, **'cause in town we lived right by the school.**

In this excerpt from a student conversation, the explainer felt compelled to explain to her partner why she hadn't ridden the bus in a long time. Because what requires explanation here is a behavior trend, a CHR explanation is more appropriate than a reason explanation (see section 4.2.6). No doubt the explainer knows this relevant causal history, but not from simulating her own past reasoning but from simply retrieving topic-relevant knowledge.

Even though the explanation in (5-10) is unlikely to have been generated by covariation reasoning, explanations for trends and patterns of actions may often pull for covariation analysis. Explanations of trends try to clarify what a whole series of actions have in common, and unless the explainer immediately retrieves that common causal history factor, a search for covariation patterns will be useful to suggest such a factor. In doing so, the explainer looks for factors that both covary with the class of actions considered and also have the generative power of triggering the variety of reasons for which those actions were performed.

An example I am particularly fond of is that of the mother who is asked to explain why she goes shopping many times a week. Her answer is: "Because I have three children." The series of actions in question is parsimoniously explained by offering this causal history of having three children because it underlies the variety of specific reasons she has for shopping each individual time (e.g., buying more milk, a new supply of diapers, or a special carpet cleaner for crayon stains). Covariation information is useful here because it helps pinpoint the one constant factor that causally contributes to virtually every individual action of the class in question.

In the next example, the explainer is an observer who is familiar with the agent but does not exactly know his reasons for acting.

(5-11)   Why did your brother try mushrooms?—I think he tried it **because his friend had it.**

The explainer could have relied on simulation to infer the agent's reasons, but that is not what she did. The explanation focuses instead on something the explainer believes she knows—specifics of the circumstances that help narrow down what *kinds* of reasons the agent might have had (possibly triggering in the audience a simulation of the agent's reasons). No covariation search could uncover this piece of situational information the explainer offers, because the brother never had performed the action in question before.

Sometimes the explainer has seen the agent perform the same action before but still does not need to engage in covariation calculations:

(5-12)   Why did she tell you who the guy was she was talking about?— She was just . . . **she's like that. She has nothing to hide.** She'll say any name, whoever, talk about anybody.

The explainer probably regarded the agent's reasons as obvious and offered a CHR explanation instead, portraying her action as part of a larger pattern. In explaining the pattern, the explainer relies on his representation of the agent's traits and habits, which no simulation could generate. Covariation likely entered at the earlier stage of forming the trait representation in the first place, but at the time of retrieving the representation, covariation analysis would hardly have to take place again.

Simulation is a useful tool to identify another person's reasons. But it also helps identify certain causal history factors at the level of the agent's experiences. In the following example, the explainer does not know the agent, nor the agent's reason, and has limited context information (once more, from an audiotaped description of the event).

(5-13)   Tell us why she wasn't saying anything.—Mmm . . . **probably 'cause she felt intimidated by the . . . um . . . comments of the director.**

The explainer has no historical information about similar behaviors available, so no covariation calculations are possible. The explainer thus seems to simulate the agent's experience in the situation and identifies an emotion that serves as a vivid and intelligible explanation.

To sum up, causal history of reason explanations, too, can be constructed by a variety of causal search processes. The sampled illustrations suggest the following hypotheses:

1. In generating CHR explanations, the predominant process is the recruitment of *knowledge* relevant to the context, the agent, or the action.

2. *Simulation* processes are dominant when the explainers searches for experiential causal history factors.

3. *Covariation* analysis is dominant when the explainer searches for a common causal history behind a trend of actions.

Specific Causes in Enabling Factor Explanations   As mentioned before, enabling factor explanations are relatively rare unless they are firmly elicited (e.g., by the questions "How was this possible?" or "Explain how . . ."; Malle et al. 2000; McClure and Hilton 1997, 1998; McClure et al. 2001). In our data sets of social behaviors (which include explanations spontaneously offered in conversation as well as responses to experimenter-posed why-questions), we find that less than 1% of explanations cite enabling factors. Nevertheless, it is instructive to examine the processes underlying the construction of such explanations when they do occur.

I begin once more with an actor explanation, one in which the explainer interprets a why-question as asking about what enabled a phone conversation with another person.

(5-14) Why did you talk to this guy initially (on the phone)?—He was like the shy, quiet one, and so . . . I, I went back and got like a card and a pen, and **I was like: "Are you gonna give me your phone number or not?"** basically.

The agent did not have to infer, simulate, or otherwise construct her explanation; she simply knew what enabled the successful phone contact because her audacious question itself was the enabling factor.

The second example is from the observer perspective and features an agent who managed to get all her work done while preparing for a test with her study partner.

(5-15) Do you have any idea why she got all her work done?—Um, because **she copied his half** [her study partner's half of the test material].

The explainer does not know the agent and only heard about the incident in a brief audiotaped story, but it is quite clear to him what it was that enabled the agent to get her work done. In arriving at the explanation, there was no simulation involved, and covariation analysis is equally unlikely, considering that this was the only such behavior encountered. The explainer seemed to directly remember the causal link between the agent's copying and getting her work done, picking it up while listening to the whole story initially and encoding the causal link right there and then (as people reliably do in text comprehension; Graesser, Millis, and Zwaan 1997; Trabasso and Magliano 1996).

Finally, consider two enabling factor explanations for fictitious behaviors elicited in a written questionnaire. In both cases, explainers have of course no agent-specific or action-specific knowledge, but they appear to recruit general knowledge that yields a plausible explanation:

(5-16) Mary, who is poor, bought a new car. *How come?* **She began to date a richer man.**

(5-17) Bob finished a difficult class assignment. *How come?* **He concentrated and took his time.**

Looking at the examples so far, the reader may be surprised at the apparent lack of covariation reasoning underlying enabling factor explanations. As I mentioned, these explanations are rare in data sets of social behaviors, and at least in these cases, covariation analysis is virtually absent. We have to turn to a different domain to find more enabling factor explanations

and more covariation analysis, and that is the domain of achievement outcomes. Numerous studies have shown that people are able to and do in fact
explain their own successes and failures (Weiner 1986). Because failures are
unintentional, they are explained by causes; but successes are usually regarded as intentionally achieved and are therefore explained by enabling
factors ("How was it possible?"). These explanations are not always informative, as interviews with victorious athletes attest ("We played hard"; "We
knew we had to dictate the tempo of the game"; etc.). When observers try to
determine what exactly brought about a pattern of achievements, the answer has to be more informative and will often pull for covariation reasoning. Teachers and admissions committees find themselves in such situations
when they examine the sources of academic success, as do sports analysts
when they try to determine what drives the winning record of a given team
or athlete. When we turn to artistic achievements, however, very little covariation information will be available, because the number of agents performing the same action is small and replicability is low. Perhaps this is one
reason why artistic feats are rarely explained—experts evaluate art, but they
do not dare explain what brought it about.

The hypotheses we can develop from these illustrative examples are
straightforward.

1. The construction of enabling factor explanations, too, relies primarily on
specific or generic stored *knowledge.*

2. In circumscribed domains of achievement, *covariation* analysis becomes
a dominant process.

3. Simulation is largely absent when constructing enabling factor explanations because people cannot easily simulate abilities, opportunities, and
context forces, which are the primary processes that enable actions to occur.

5.3.2 Constructing Specific Reasons

So far I have examined search processes for specific causal factors that
brought about events. Now I turn to reasons for intentional action, which
are constructed under assumptions of subjectivity and rationality and involve decisions about the type of reason offered (beliefs and desires), specific
reason contents, and (for communicative explanations) the use or omission
of mental state markers.

Some of the processes on which a search for causes relies are still going to be useful in the selection of specific reasons. In particular, simulation and activation of knowledge structures should do considerable work, and considerations of contrast events will be helpful to the extent that they unveil the competing options the agent considered in her decision to act. Covariation analysis, by contrast, is going to be of no use to actors (Knobe and Malle 2002) and of limited use to observers, except in constrained cases such as explaining repeated choices between well-defined options (cf. Jones and Davis 1965). Most important, there are two additional processes of significance here—*direct recall* and *rationalization*. As before, let me strengthen these claims with a number of examples, starting with a set of explanations that illustrate the actor's direct recall. In (5-18) below, the participant had talked about a recent life event, and the experimenter then selected a few behaviors to ask the participant to explain.

(5-18)   Why did you plan to buy your brother a video game? **'Cause it was his birthday** and **I wanted to have him get something that he would actually use.**

The actor might be echoing here what was actually going through his mind at the time—awareness of his brother's birthday and the desire to give him something useful.

A similar direct recall process seems to underlie the next two explanations, in which the actor mentions the actual sentiments that moved him to act (again, in response to the experimenter's why-questions about selected behaviors from a recent life event).

(5-19)   Why did you talk to your neighbors before the barbecue? **'Cause I knew that my friends were going to be over late** and **I didn't want to bother the neighbors late at night.**

(5-20)   Why did you decide to go hiking up the peak? **Just to kind of get a change of scenery. I was getting sick of what everyone else was doing, kind of.**[9]

Direct recall of reasons could be subsumed under knowledge processes, but it does have two unique features that deserve separate consideration. First, to the extent that the agent attended to her deliberation when deciding to act, the reasons that settled her decision will be highly available in explicit memory (Cowan 1995; Russell and d'Hollosy 1992) and, because directly experienced at the time of deliberation, they are likely to be quite accurately recalled (Brewer 1994).

Second, only actors can rely on direct recall of reasons, whereas observers recruit information about another person's reasons similarly to the way they recruit information about the causes of an event. Because direct recall is not possible for observers, this leaves two options: (a) recall of relevant generic or specific information, combined with inferences from that information, and (b) simulation of the agent's reasons. First the inferential process.

(5-21)   Why did your friends fish instead of hiking?—Probably **because they wanted to, you know, drink beer and be lazy.**

Here the explainer infers, from specific knowledge about his friends' fishing habits, what might be attractive to the agents. Note that covariation analysis isn't needed here: it is irrelevant what other people's reasons might be for going fishing.

In the next example, the agent is a complete stranger to the explainer, so the latter doesn't have any agent-specific information. But the context, the agent's observed interaction with objects, and generic assumptions allow for a plausible inference.

(5-22)   This teenager looked at the remote control car stuff in the hobby store and then stole something. *Why?* **He probably needed some things for a remote control car** and **did not have any money** or **he did not want to pay for it.**

In some cases, the explainer is able to acquire agent-specific and action-specific information—either from the agent directly or from other social sources.

(5-23)   Then he'd start getting marijuana **because he said it relaxes him.**

(5-24)   She [grandmother] went to the doctor's office **because she was having chest pains.**

In the second example, the explainer learned the relevant information either from the agent herself or from a family member, or it came out during the ordeal that followed in which the grandmother was rushed to the hospital with a heart attack.

The second major process on which observers rely when constructing reason explanations is simulation of the actor's reasoning process that led to the action.

(5-25)   Yesterday a friend and I were walking down the street and some random homeless guy bowed to us. *Why?* I have no idea why he did this. Maybe **because we were ladies** and **he felt obliged to do so.**

Without agent-specific knowledge, the explainer tries to take the homeless person's actual perspective. Through his eyes, they were ladies (the explainer wouldn't normally label herself as a lady), and in his perception, there was an obligation to bow to them.

The next two examples seem to involve not so much simulation but projection, the explainer's automatic assumption that others see or know the same things he does:

(5-26)   Brian had to, like, hold her back [his ex-girlfriend's mom] 'cause **she was, like, trying to come at me.**

(5-27)   One of my school friends came to comfort me. *Why?* **Because he knew that I was upset about that girl saying private stuff to the entire world.**

Projection is easier than simulation because it does not involve adjustment for the other person's unique perspective, knowledge, or feelings (Gordon 1992). It thus resembles the three-year-old's "heuristic" of mental state inferences: "What I know is true, so everybody else knows it too." Simulation is more elaborate in that the explainer tries to mimic the perceptions, thoughts, or desires that are unique to the other person and tries to go through the same reasoning steps that the agent herself took (Goldman 2001).

I close with the process of rationalization, which is primarily (though not exclusively) used by actors. We can define rationalization as the attempt to present a rational and justified reason for a given action, regardless of whether that reason was actually motivating the action. Rationalization cannot stand on its own but rather requires a basic construction process such as knowledge retrieval or simulation of a rational and desirable agent. Rationalization clearly serves pragmatic goals in that it treats the explanation as an opportunity to create a socially desirable image. As a result, rationalization will be most often used in conversational contexts, especially when the actor/explainer worries about his or her self-image.

In the first example below, the actor talks with a friend about her grandmother who, after a heart attack, was in the hospital (see 5-23).

(5-28)   I was asking my parents, What can I do? What can I do to help? **'Cause she wasn't dead, she was in a coma or something.**

The severity of the grandmother's illness made it perhaps questionable why the actor thought she could be of help at all, so she explains and justifies her reasoning by emphasizing that her grandmother was in a coma and so there were still meaningful things one could do.

The next example, a clear case of a contrast pair (why live in Atlanta rather than other places), may well contain truthful reasons cited by the actor, but the sheer number makes them appear to serve a strong rationalizing function.

(5-29)   I think probably when I'm done with school I'm gonna move to Atlanta. [Partner: *To Atlanta? Why?*] **Um, my brother lives there right now, and he's about to get married, and the rest of my family lives pretty close, and I really like it there.**

In response to the perhaps threatening question, the initially stated reasons about brother and family may not have seemed to the actor as sufficiently justifying her decision to move, so she adds information that makes Atlanta particularly attractive to *her* (cf. Brown and Van Kleeck 1989).

The hypotheses that flow from these examples bear out reasons once more to be the most distinct mode of explanation, in terms of both the unique selection processes and numerous actor–observer differences:

1. When selecting reason explanations, actors never rely on *covariation* calculation and observers only do so when explaining repeated choices between well-defined options.

2. Actors may often select the very reasons that moved them to act in a process of *direct recall*. This process should get decreasing use the less deliberation went into the action (because the memory trace for the action's reasons is weak) and the longer the time span between action deliberation and the explanation (because the memory traces may have washed out).

3. When actors explain undesirable actions or have to answer a challenge to their decision, they may (in addition to or instead of the other processes) rely on *rationalization*, which can itself be based on knowledge structures (what counts as a good reason) or simulation (why would a reasonable person act this way).

4. In contrast to actors, observers rely primarily on various *knowledge structures* and on *simulation/projection*.

5.3.3 Selection Processes in Overview

Table 5.2 summarizes the hypotheses (developed from original explanation examples) about the cognitive processes that help explainers select specific explanations, privately or in communication. The hypotheses are broken down only by explanation *modes* because selection processes are unlikely to be distinct for different *types* within each explanation mode, such as belief and desire reasons within reason explanations. The causal direction of these hypotheses is open: Explainers may sometimes decide first on a mode of explanation and then pick an appropriate cognitive selection process; or a predominant selection process may guide the explainer to a particular explanation mode.

Finally, what is the relation between the cognitive processes that constitute the selection of explanation modes and the psychological factors that determine those selections (behavior attributes, pragmatic goals, information resources)? Two main patterns can be expected, as displayed in figure 5.3. In pattern (A), a psychological determinant directly selects for a particular kind of explanation, which in turn activates particular selection processes. In pattern (B), a psychological determinant selects for a particular selection process, and both the determinant and the selection process jointly favor a particular kind of explanation.

As an example of pattern (A), judgments of behavior attributes can directly favor certain explanation modes (e.g., unintentional behavior → causes; difficult behavior → enabling factors), which in turn favor certain selection processes (knowledge structures and covariation assessment). Similarly,

Table 5.2

Cognitive processes of selecting specific explanations, broken down by mode

Explanation Mode	Knowledge Structures	Simulation/ Projection	Covariation	Direct Recall	Rationalization
Cause	✓	(✓)	(✓)		
Causal History	✓✓	✓	✓		
Enabling Factor	✓✓		✓		
Reason/actors	(✓)			✓✓	✓
Reason/observers	✓✓	✓✓	(✓)		

Note: No check mark in a particular cell indicates no use of the cognitive process in this column for the explanation mode in this row. A check mark in parentheses indicates use under only very limited conditions; one check mark indicates a fair amount of use; two check marks indicates frequent use.

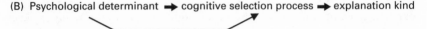

Figure 5.3
Relationships between psychological determinants, kinds of explanation, and cognitive selection processes.

audience design attempts can directly favor certain explanation modes or types, which then demand suitable cognitive search and selection processes. By contrast, limited information resources are an example of pattern (B), preventing the explainer from relying on direct recall and encouraging instead the use of projection or knowledge structures so that both limited information and the selection process lead up to causal histories or desire reasons as likely explanations. Impression management, too, follows pattern (B), encouraging the use of knowledge structures and rationalization in a search for suitable reason explanations.

5.3.4   Cognitive Architecture

A brief word on the cognitive implementation of these multiple causal search processes. Some sort of connectionist network is the most promising cognitive architecture for modeling knowledge recruitment in explanations (Read and Miller 1998; Van Overwalle 1998). Hearing words or observing behaviors automatically activates a large number of connected representations, some (perhaps many) of which are causal/generative, which are then immediately available for use in explanations. Modeling the process of simulation (or projection) in connectionist nets also appears possible (Cruz 1998), though it may be more difficult. Simulation involves the activation of one's own past experiences and plausible beliefs and desires, but it also involves "computations" on activated items, such as the practical reasoning that combines beliefs and desires into intentions and the demarcating of these operations with an "as if" or "off-line" or "other" tag.

Despite the promise of connectionist models, their networks capture only low to midlevel processes. To truly account for the phenomenon of explanations these processes have to be embedded in higher-order theories that incorporate content-full folk concepts (e.g., agent, belief), differential conditions of search processes (e.g., intentional versus unintentional behavior), and distinctions among explanation modes (e.g., reasons versus CHRs). Just as explanations are built, in part at least, from connectionist knowledge networks, they are arguably built from neural structures. But neither connectionism nor neuroscience is going to deliver the human folk concepts of mind and behavior or the cognitive principles of causal search and explanation construction (cf. Coltheart and Langdon 1998).

5.4 Summary

This chapter reviewed the second major ingredient of a theory of behavior explanation—principles that guide the psychological construction of explanations.

An analogy of a bachelor's shopping decisions highlighted the multiple choice points that explainers pass through en route to a full behavior explanation. These choice points include modes of explanation, specific types of reasons and causes, and linguistic forms. Three psychological factors were then discussed that govern the explainer's construction process: judged behavior attributes (e.g., intentionality or difficulty), pragmatic goals (e.g., communicating certain impressions), and information resources (e.g., knowledge, ability to infer or simulate).

But choosing *kinds* of explanation is not the last stage of construction; explainers must always settle on a *specific* cause or reason. In the absence of pertinent experiments, I used samples of original explanations to illustrate the diversity of processes on which people rely when constructing specific explanations. In light of this diversity, the traditional view of the everyday explainer as a covariation analyst (proclaimed in nearly all textbooks of social psychology) seems untenable. In fact, a person who relied only on covariation calculation when constructing explanations would display a serious deficit in social cognition.

The diversity of cognitive selection processes, moreover, appears to show systematic relationships with different modes of explanation. Reasons once more stand out as the distinct case, because they are usually constructed without any covariation analysis and, for actors explaining their own actions, from processes that are not used for other modes of explanation, such as direct recall and rationalization. Relationships between cognitive selection processes and psychological determinants of explanation choices exist as well, and these are yet to be explored in detail.

6 Behavior Explanations in Language and Communication

The previous three chapters introduced the conceptual and psychological principles that govern both private and communicative behavior explanations. Now I turn to some of the unique features of communicative explanations. When behavior explanations are used in communication, they are verbalized in specific linguistic forms, obey the rules of conversation, and have direct social consequences both for the speaker and the audience of the conversational exchange. Communicative explanations thus have several levels of analysis: linguistic, conversational, and social.

As linguistic events, behavior explanations reflect and express the basic ways in which language depicts behavioral and mental events. The first section of this chapter is therefore devoted to the language of behavior description and the causal and explanatory implications that these descriptions entail.

As conversational acts, explanations are subject to conversational rules, which govern both the mutual assumptions speakers and audiences make and speakers' choices of expression in light of these assumptions. Speakers are responsive, for example, to an audience's concerns and questions and adjust their formulations to their audience's presumed interest and knowledge. The second section of this chapter thus inquires into the way conversational rules shape the content and form of explanations.

As social acts, finally, explanations take on various interpersonal roles, such as informing, warning, soothing, persuading, and excusing. As has long been recognized in the sociological and communication literatures, people strategically use behavior explanations to accomplish social goals. Audiences are often aware of this process and therefore draw systematic inferences about the explainer's goals from the form and content of their explanations. Cognizant of that, explainers in turn alter their explanations to shape their audience's inferences and fulfill their goals in the social interaction; in short, they engage in impression management. The third section of this chapter therefore examines the impression-managing roles that behavior explanations play in social interaction.

Throughout this chapter I will use theoretical principles developed in chapters 4 and 5 to predict aspects of explanations as linguistic, conversational, and social acts. At times, additional theoretical principles will be introduced, which belong to the third, the language-specific layer of a folk explanation theory (see 4.1 for a discussion of these layers). The chapter (along with the two that follow) also offers applications of the folk-conceptual theory of explanation and suggests ways in which the theory goes beyond classic attribution models. From this perspective, the chapter first explores a phenomenon that has been described within classic attribution theory but, so I argue, can be better accounted for by a folk-conceptual approach.

6.1 Explanations and "Implicit Verb Causality"

All folk explanations of behavior attempt to provide, among other things, an answer to a causal question—"Why did this behavior occur, what brought it about?" To the extent that the behavior in question is described in language, the linguistic structures used in the description can bias the explainer's attempts at answering the causal question because causality is encoded in a variety of linguistic structures, including word semantics, morphemes, prepositions, and periphrastic constructions (e.g., Comrie and Polinsky 1993; Dirven 1995; Frawley 1992; Givón 1975; Shibatani 1976).

Psychological research has focused on causality encoded in verbs, especially *interpersonal verbs,* which are used to describe how one person affects another, such as when Anne helps Paul, or Holly dreads Aaron (Brown and Fish 1983; Garvey and Caramazza 1974). Descriptions of particular behaviors can be, and often are, contested by communication partners (Edwards and Potter 1993), in part because of their causal implications. However, often a particular behavior description is mutually accepted in a given discourse, and then the question arises how the verb choice influences people's perceptions of causality and their construction of explanations. This is the main issue of *implicit verb causality.*

6.1.1 Past Research on Implicit Verb Causality

The central question has been this: Which types of verbs have which kinds of causal implications? Nearly all researchers have framed causal implications in terms of the traditional dichotomy between internal (person) versus external (situation) causes. That is, an interpersonal episode could be caused by the person corresponding to the verb subject (internal attributions of causality), as in "Anne helps Ben because *she* . . . ," or an episode could be caused by the person corresponding to the verb object (external attributions of causality), as in "Anne dreads Ben because *he* . . ." Different classes of interpersonal verbs, according to this hypothesis, lead to distinct patterns of causal attributions, and this phenomenon is labeled the "verb causality effect" (for a review, see Rudolph and Försterling 1997). Specifically, action verbs imply person causes (e.g., A hit B because A was angry) whereas experience verbs imply situation causes (e.g., C heard D coming because D was very loud). In addition, some researchers suggested that each of the two verb classes further breaks into two subtypes that have opposite implicit causality patterns. Experience verbs are said to split into experiencer–stimulus verbs (for which the experiencer is in the subject position and the stimulus is in the object position) and stimulus–experiencer verbs (for which the positions are reversed). Action verbs, furthermore, are said to split into agent–patient verbs (for which the cause of the agent's behavior lies in the agent) and agent–evocator verbs (for which the cause of the agent's behavior lies in the patient). Finally, according to this hypothesis, all the implicit causality patterns can be accounted for by Kelley's (1967) covariation principles (Rudolph and Försterling 1997; Van Kleeck, Hillger, and Brown 1988).

Even though there is considerable evidence reported in support of this hypothesis (Rudolph and Försterling 1997), it suffers from serious shortcomings (Malle 2002c). First, the classifications into verb types have no clear theoretical foundation, and one verb class (agent–evocator) is entirely ad hoc. Second, empirical research has repeatedly confounded the *causal structure* of interpersonal episodes described by these verbs (e.g., who is affecting whom) with the *explanations* that are implied by these verbs ("*Why* did one person affect the other?"). Third, Kelley's covariation principles do not successfully account for the empirical data. I will elaborate here on the last two points, because they are most relevant to the topic of explanation. (For more detail on the first point, see Malle 2002c.)

6.1.2 An Alternative Perspective on Implicit Verb Causality

The pattern of "implicit verb causality" documented in the literature (see Rudolph and Försterling 1997) confounded two types of data: (a) the direction of causal transaction in interpersonal episodes (e.g., A behaves in a way that causes something in B; B experiences something due to A), and (b) explanations for these interpersonal episodes. The data patterns of causal transactions are conceptually inherent in interpersonal verbs. Action verbs describe one person acting on another and thus depict a *causing event* in which a *causer* affects a *causee;* experience verbs describe one person experiencing something due to another and thus depict a *resulting event* in which a causee is being affected by a causer.

Distinct from these patterns of causal transaction are the explanations of these transactions. When offering an explanation, the social perceiver indicates *why* the causer affected the causee, or why the causee was affected by the causer. Whereas the causal transaction structures are rather strict for most verbs, answers to why-questions can vary quite a bit with context. Table 6.1 displays a number of interpersonal verbs, their causal structure (causing event: *Beh 1;* resulting event: *Exp 1* and *Exp 2*), the rate of explanations referring to the verb subject, and some verbatim explanations from experimental participants. This pattern of data suggests that causal structure (e.g., does the statement describe the first person acting on the second person or the first person experiencing something as a result of the second person?) and the explanation content (e.g., mentioning the first person or the second person) are largely unrelated.

The causal structure of most interpersonal verbs can be predicted from the intentionality and observability ascribed to the depicted interpersonal episode (Malle 2002c). Behavioral events that are causing events (*Beh 1* in table 6.1) must be publicly observable; behavioral events that are resulting events (*Exp 1* and *Exp 2* in table 6.1) must be unintentional. The two by two scheme of intentionality and observability (see chapter 3) thereby provides a theoretical foundation for classifying verb types according to the behavioral event type they depict and for predicting which kind of causal structure is described by that verb.[1]

Past research, however, did not examine causal structure patterns. Rather, what was called "implicit causality" were in fact the explanations people offered for interpersonal episodes. This is most obvious for the case of "agent–evocator" verbs (see *praised* in table 6.1). The causal structure of these verbs

Table 6.1

Some interpersonal verbs, their causal structure, and their explanations

	Causal structure			"Subject"	
	Beh1	Exp1	Exp2	explan.	Examples
Maya understood Ian	0%	93%	3%	33%	Because she had gone through what he went through; Because he had a point.
James surprised Mary	40%	0%	40%	45%	Because it was her birthday; Because he wanted to make her happy.
Mick harassed Fran	97%	0%	3%	53%	Because she has his money; Because he had issues.
Nina praised Gerald	97%	0%	3%	31%	Because he was a good boy; Because he did well on the exam.

Note: Causal structure was assessed using a graphical response format. In a stick figure drawing of both interactants, participants marked off whether the verbal statement depicted the first person's behavior (Beh1), the first person's experience (Exp1), or the second person's experience (Exp2). "Subject" explanation refers to the percentage of explanations whose content featured the verb subject.

is rather unambiguously "causer's behavior affects causee" (averaged across ten such verbs, 88% of our respondents marked off the *Beh1* pattern). Explanations of these verbs, however, predominantly refer to the causee (true for 78% of our respondents). Because of this pattern of explanations, researchers felt compelled to split off agent–evocator verbs (which often elicit causee-focused explanations) from agent–patient verbs (which often elicit causer-focused explanations). But what is the psychological insight that comes with this split? All it tells us, I would argue, is that statements with certain interpersonal verbs (e.g., A praises B), when presented out of context, will elicit similar-looking explanations from most respondents, probably because, when lacking context, they have to rely on word meaning and cultural scripts to construct an explanation (e.g., B did something well). By contrast, the *causal structure* of the verb statement remains the same (A will always affect B with his intentional and observable act of praising).

In addition to this conflation of explanations and the causal structure of interpersonal verbs, that Kelley's (1967) covariation principles can account for implicit verb causality patterns (Rudolph and Försterling 1997; Van Kleeck, Hillger, and Brown 1988).

For one thing, we don't need any covariation information to account for the *causal structure* of an interpersonal episode, because this structure is derivable entirely from the behavioral event type that underlies the interpersonal verb. For example, action verbs, which refer to intentional and observable events, always depict the agent/causer bringing something about in the patient/causee.

An account based on covariation principles also runs into serious difficulties when we examine the *explanations* given for interpersonal verbs. To begin, experiencer–stimulus verbs such as *notice, envy,* or *dread* are claimed to imply high consensus and high distinctiveness (Rudolph and Försterling 1997). In other words, the statement "A noticed B" should imply that many other people noticed B and that A noticed few other people. This implication may be compatible with the sentence, but so is its opposite (that many others noticed B as well or that A also noticed C, D, and E). Either way, such implications are certainly not inherent in the meaning of the verb *notice*.

Furthermore, agent–patient verbs such as *hit, flatter, help,* or *obstruct* are expected to imply low consensus and low distinctiveness. That is, the statement "A helped P" allegedly implies that few other people helped P and that A helps many other people. But why? This implication does not follow semantically from the sentence or the verb. No different is the situation with agent–evocator verbs such as *hire, praise, recommend,* and their alleged implication of high consensus and high distinctiveness. Here, "A hired E" should imply that many other people hired E and that A hired few other people. In this case, the high consensus implication (that many others hired E) even borders on the absurd.

Why should covariation patterns be part of the verb meaning in the first place? Brown and Fish (1983) claimed that these patterns reflect real-world facts about the events depicted by those verbs. If this is so, we would have to be convinced that actions have *in general* low consensus and high distinctiveness (are performed by few people toward few objects) and that experiences have *in general* high consensus and low distinctiveness (are experienced by many people toward many objects). I don't know of any evidence that supports such a claim, and I very much doubt there ever could be such evidence.

In conclusion, the analysis of implicit verb causality I propose is this. First, there is an important difference between action verbs and experience verbs (interpersonal or not), because these verbs depict fundamental categories that people distinguish in their perception of behavioral events (chapter 3). Splitting these fundamental categories into subtypes makes little sense, however, except if one wants to catalog verbs that elicit explanations with a certain linguistic surface.

Second, knowing the fundamental event type depicted by an interpersonal verb—specifically, knowing the event's intentionality and observability—normally allows us to predict the *causal structure* of the depicted interpersonal episode, except for a small set of rarely used verbs that have ambiguous causal structure (Malle 2002c).

Third, the *explanations* people offer for psychological verbs in general and for interpersonal verbs in particular can vary considerably in content, though absence of context will limit that variation. Past research documented orderly patterns of generic explanation content but mistakenly interpreted them as "causal implications." I contend, instead, that these patterns reflect culturally shared, scriptlike knowledge structures that participants recruit to explain the context-free interpersonal statements prepared by the experimenter.

Fourth, the patterns of explanation content cannot be successfully accounted for by covariation principles, and I suspect that in a sample of verbs that are not preselected for their expected explanation patterns (or in a sample of respondents who do not share cultural scripts), the variation of explanation content will be far greater than previously documented and hence defy any systematic prediction. What is possible, of course, is to predict which *modes* of explanation a given verb type will elicit: Experience verbs (depicting unintentional events) will trigger cause explanations, and action verbs (depicting intentional events) will trigger primarily reason explanations. But these patterns are based not on the semantics of verbs, but on the folk concept of intentionality and its corresponding explanation framework.

6.2   Explanations as Communicative Acts

In the late 1980s, explanation research was invigorated by a new perspective that characterized explanations as communicative acts. Following philosophers of science (Bromberger 1965; Scriven 1962; Van Fraasen 1980) and a prescient essay by Kidd and Amabile (1981), a number of mainly

British psychologists began to examine the conversational features of explanations (Antaki 1988, 1994; Edwards and Potter 1993; Hilton 1990; Lalljee and Abelson 1983; Turnbull 1986; Turnbull and Slugoski 1988). Breaking a long period of dominance by cognitive models, this genuinely social approach to explanations provided several new insights, three of which are of particular importance.

First, researchers within this approach emphasized that communicative explanations are speech acts in dialogue and are therefore constrained by general principles of conversation. Paul Grice (1975) was the first to formulate such conversational rules, namely, the Cooperative Principle, and a set of maxims that help us satisfy that principle. The Cooperative Principle states that speakers should make their conversational contributions suit the accepted purpose or direction of the conversation as it stands at the given moment. The conversational maxims then help people satisfy the Cooperative Principle by demanding the speaker to be informative, truthful, relevant, and clear. Many scholars have argued that Grice's principles are too strong, and they subsequently suggested a variety of alternatives (e.g., Sperber and Wilson 1986). But Grice's fundamental insight remains valid today: that communication relies on implicit assumptions that both speaker and addressee capitalize on. These assumptions help speakers select the linguistic form that best communicates what they intend to convey to the other person; and the same assumptions help addressees infer what the speaker intended to convey with that communication.

A second insight of the communicative approach was that explanations are a particular type of speech act—they represent answers to other people's questions (Turnbull 1986). As such, explanations reflect the demands and presumptions underlying the other person's why-question because explainers engage in audience design. That is, they search for explanations that consider the questioner's background knowledge and try to identify the particular knowledge gap that is to be filled with the explanation (Slugoski et al. 1993; Todorov, Lalljee, and Hirst 2000). For example, when Quinn asks Erin "How come Mary bought a Mercedes?" Erin might answer "Because it's a good car." However, if Erin assumes that Quinn asks the question because he knows Mary is poor, a more appropriate answer would be "Because she inherited a load of money." (See McClure and Hilton 1997.)

Finally, the communicative approach highlighted a number of social-interactive functions of explanations, such as their contribution to negotiation, argument, and impression management (Antaki 1994; Antaki and Leudar 1992; Harvey, Orbuch, and Weber 1990; Tedeschi and Reiss 1981). Thus, variations in form and content of explanations reflect not just different causal perceptions but different social demands that the explainer tries to meet.

Despite providing sharp observations and novel insights, the communicative approach shared with the classic attribution approach its major weakness, which is the assumption that there is one uniform "causal explanation" process that applies equally to tumbling rocks, nervous feelings, and planned actions. Only the marriage of the communicative approach with the folk-conceptual approach promises to offer a successful account of the entire range of behavior explanations (Malle 2001a). In fact, the insights of the communicative approach are more clearly visible when we consider explanations within their folk-conceptual framework, because the modes and features of explanation distinguished therein map more systematically onto social and conversational functions than do the limited categories of person/trait and situation. There is no better phenomenon with which to illustrate this position than impression management.

6.3   Impression Management

Impression management—people's attempts to influence other people's perceptions and evaluations—is primarily used in communication (Barrett 1986; Goffman 1959). Because explanations are communicative acts they, too, can be used for impression management (Burke 1945; Mills 1940; Scott and Lyman 1968; Semin and Manstead 1983; Tedeschi and Reiss 1981). One thing that makes explanations especially useful in this regard is the fact that their primary function is *not* to manage impressions but to create meaning for one's audience. A skillful explainer may thus conceal his impression management goals, ostensibly providing the very information that the audience wants to know while at the same time slightly altering this information (or its form of presentation) to also meet impression management goals.

What makes folk explanations of behavior additionally useful for impression management is their complexity, as the multiple modes and features of explanation provide ample opportunity to subtly alter appearance and meaning without letting the distortion become too obvious. Within a standard attribution framework this complexity is grossly underestimated in that explanations are primarily classified as "person" versus "situation" and their only impression management function appears to be "self-servingness" (Bradley 1978; Miller and Ross 1975). As long as we remain in the domain of unintentional behavior, this model is satisfactory, though not without its complications (e.g., an internal cause can be excusing when it is uncontrollable but accusing when it is controllable; see Weiner 1986, 1995). However, once we consider intentional behaviors—the ones that are most often the focus of social scrutiny—the person–situation distinction fails to capture the underlying phenomena. The perpetrator of a socially undesirable act does more than just offer person versus situation causes. She manages impressions of intentionality, draws attention either to her own reasoning and thinking or to the complex causal web in which her reasoning and action were embedded, cites specific motives and portrays them as either idiosyncratic or common, and elaborates on the background and origin of those motives, anchoring them in anything from personality to immediate context to childhood, culture, or history.

The folk-conceptual theory of explanation avoids the ambiguities and limitations of a simple person–situation model and instead delineates the parameters that can be altered for impression management goals. These parameters, as laid out in chapter 4, include:

1. Implied intentionality (cause explanations versus other explanation modes);

2. Modes of intentional behavior explanation (reasons, causal histories, enabling factors);

3. Within reason explanations, type of reason (belief, desire), use of mental state markers, and content of reason;

4. Within causal history of reason explanations, type of causal factor (e.g., person–situation; trait–nontrait);

5. Within cause explanations, type of causal factor (e.g., person–situation; trait–nontrait).

The following discussion addresses the first three points; the remaining two will be taken up in chapter 7.

6.3.1 Implied Intentionality

Intentionality is not per se desirable or undesirable. When the intentionality of a positive action is in question, the conclusion that the action was indeed performed intentionally (rather than accidentally) will normally create a more desirable impression of the agent. However, when the intentionality of a negative action is in question, the conclusion that the action was performed intentionally (rather than accidentally) will create a more undesirable impression of the agent. In other words, perceptions of intentionality polarize impressions: Positive behaviors, if portrayed as intentional, lead to more praise; negative behaviors, if portrayed as intentional, lead to more blame (Shaver 1985; Weiner 1995).

But is this always the case? At times, one might argue, a positive behavior loses part of its praiseworthiness once it is recognized as intentional, deliberate, or "strategic." Don't we like spontaneous expressions of compassion or admiration better than those that were planned in advance? Though this is true, a distinction different from intentionality is at play here. The expression of compassion or admiration is intentional in either case—it wasn't that the agent meant to express fascination and accidentally expressed compassion, or that she meant to express compassion with Halle and accidentally expressed compassion with Holly. Rather, the deliberate nature of the act of expression makes us suspicious about ulterior motives behind the expression (Fein 1996). The same expression of such sentiments delivered spontaneously (though still intentionally) is considered genuine, "straight from the heart."

Portraying a behavior as unintentional is most effectively achieved by offering a cause explanation, and portraying it as intentional, by offering a reason explanation. However, changing an audience's perceptions of intentionality solely with an explanation is difficult unless the behavior's intentionality is ambiguous (e.g., "She knocked over your wine glass"). In such a case, offering a cause explanation (". . . because she didn't see it") leaves little doubt over the behavior's accidental nature, and offering a reason explanation (". . . to show her displeasure with your relentless flirting") leaves little doubt over its intentional nature (see Malle 1999, study 1). In many social situations, however, a behavior's intentionality is too obvious to deny. What options of influencing an audience's impressions do explainers have in that case?

6.3.2   Reasons versus Causal Histories

As outlined in chapters 4 and 5, intentional behaviors can be explained by three distinct modes: reasons, causal histories, and enabling factors. Of these modes, reasons and causal histories answer the motivational question of why the agent performed the action, whereas enabling factors answer the accomplishment question of how it was possible that the agent performed the action. This difference between motivation and accomplishment is at times exploited for impression management purposes, such as when the explainer directs attention away from the action's motives (which are subject to moral evaluation) and instead highlights how difficult it was to perform that action (which typically creates a favorable impression of the agent who overcame these difficulties).

But far more important for impression management of intentional behavior is the choice between offering reasons or causal histories. Because reasons are the default explanation mode for intentional behavior, the act of providing a causal history explanation is the rarer and therefore more salient event. Offering or withholding causal history or reason (CHR) explanations may thus be used as an impression management tool.

The conceptual meaning of causal history explanations dictates the kinds of impressions one can create with this explanation mode. CHRs shift attention from the agent's subjective deliberations to more "objective," distant causes, from her capacity to reason and choose to the impersonal network of causal forces that precede and influence that reasoning. We can predict, then, that explainers use causal histories when they attempt to reduce blame for a negative action. By doing so, they downplay the agent's reasons for acting and highlight what are presumed to be extenuating factors that led up to those reasons—intoxication, upbringing, imperfect reasoning, and uncontrollable circumstances, emotions, or traits.

It is relatively easy to find examples of this impression management strategy. Consider the following urban legend that has been circulated on the internet:

(6-1)   Kashima University has expelled four medical students for pelting other students with human brains. The expelled students said they didn't plan the brain fight. One of them said, "It just sort of happened." He blamed the odd behavior on **the pressure of constant study and lack of sleep.**

The explainer does not outright deny intentionality (which would be pointless) but tries in various ways to minimize impressions of deliberateness, premeditation, and full responsibility. He does so, in part, by offering a causal history of reason explanation—indicating that the pressure of constant study and lack of sleep caused whatever reasons they may have had for their unruly behavior.

In the following e-mail excerpt (from my personal archives), an undergraduate student volunteers an explanation for her sudden disappearance at the beginning of a class session:

(6-2) I just wanted to explain to you why I walked into class, turned in my paper, and left. This weekend my lacrosse team drove to Santa Barbara for a tournament. While driving back on Monday the van broke down in Ashland so we had to stay the night there—in the van. We drove the rest of the way Tuesday morning and got back at 10:30. **Because I was working off of zero sleep, a cramped body, and a frustrated mind, I thought it would be more productive if I went to bed for a while.**

The explainer fully admits to the intentionality of her action and even cites her key reason ("I thought it would be more productive . . ."). What carries the impression management load here is the extensive background information that culminates in three causal history factors: "zero sleep, a cramped body, and a frustrated mind."

Causal history explanations for more serious transgressions can be found in the legal world. In fact, over the past ten years, voices of concern have been raised over the alleged success of explaining intentional crimes by reference to (what I call) causal history factors, which seemingly get criminals off the hook (Dershowitz 1994; Wilson 1997). An infamous case is the so-called Twinkie defense, which convinced the jury that, when murdering San Francisco Mayor George Moscone and Supervisor Harvey Milk, defendant Dan White had diminished capacity due to job stress and ingestion of junk food. Equally infamous is the first trial against the Menendez brothers who had brutally shot their parents and whose defense council relied on discrediting background information about the parents, including drug use, depression, and one son's sexual abuse by the father. These causal history explanations all did their part in leading to a hung jury situation.

Occasionally, newspapers print people's expression of frustration with such cases, in which criminals apparently go blameless thanks to a fiendish causal history defense: "I am thoroughly sick of hearing the pathetic excuse that delinquent behaviour is the result of a disadvantaged childhood; of poverty, or inadequate education, or of dysfunctional family life," writes Christine Whitaker (2002) in a Canadian newspaper.

To be fair, the so-called abuse excuse (Dershowitz 1994) in legal proceedings is substantially rarer than people think and, when offered, frequently does not prevail (Wilson 1997). No murderer after Dan White succeeded in claiming diminished responsibility due to junk food; in a second trial, the Menendez brothers were sentenced to life in prison without parole; and very few abused, battered, or oppressed individuals receive mercy when killing their abusers.

Even when the crime is less serious than murder, causal history explanations are no guarantee for getting free. Consider this failed attempt (McClymont 2002, p. 24):

(6-3)   Former playboy and one-time Hard Rock Cafe owner Mark Coulton [. . .] had apparently pretended he was selling 100 per cent cotton tampons from California, when they were really inferior ones from Hungary. Giving reasons as to why the Palm Beach party boy should not have to do time in the slammer, his barrister, Charlie Waterstreet, explained that while his client had "acted in a way he was not proud of," **at the time of his fraudulent dealings Coulton was in "extraordinary medical and emotional turmoil."** [. . .] Coulton was given a 12-month suspended jail sentence yesterday, and ordered to serve 150 hours of community service and to repay $169,000.

The use of excusing CHR explanations in legal settings is in all likelihood just a pale reflection of the widespread practice of offering causal histories for impression management in everyday life. In a series of studies, Sarah Nelson and I tried to demonstrate this practice and examine its conditions of occurrence. To illustrate the explanations we worked with, consider the following examples:

(6-4)   I egged this girl's house and got caught. *Why?* **Because I was young, about 13 [CHR], and immature [CHR], she wasn't a friendly girl** [reason].

(6-5)   I slapped my mom. *Why?* **I was really angry and frustrated [CHR].**

(6-6)   This kid hit me. *Why?* **She was upset [CHR] and I had been annoying her [CHR]; we were both children [CHR].**

(6-7) She lied to many people about me. *Why?* **We had just broken off our long relationship** [CHR].

Across three studies, people used 22% causal histories when explaining socially desirable actions but 42% causal histories when explaining socially undesirable actions. Interestingly, this effect did not significantly interact with perspective (actor versus observer), individual differences in narcissism, or severity of the negative action (Nelson and Malle 2004). The consistency of the effect across these three variables is intriguing because it suggests that the increase in CHR explanations is not a self-serving bias (limited to actors) but a generalized social practice of accounting for negative actions.

One study in particular illustrates that CHR explanations are not used for merely self-serving purposes by actors (Nelson and Malle 2004). Respondents were asked to explain, in front of an audience, a number of socially undesirable actions they had recently performed. Moreover, just before providing their explanations actors were instructed either to "excuse" their actions, to "take responsibility" for their actions, or to "be honest." If CHR use were a self-serving tactic that actors routinely employ to excuse their undesirable actions, CHR rates should markedly increase in the excuse condition; but that was not the case. Causal history explanation rates were similar in all three conditions, ranging between 32% and 39%, which are fairly high CHR rates for actors. Other results of this study indicated that instructions were not merely inert—they did have effects on people's explanations, just not on causal histories. We therefore concluded that an increase in CHR explanations does not reflect a self-serving bias to excuse an action willy-nilly but rather the tendency to present the action in a context that makes the agent look intelligible and acceptable—an impression management tactic, moreover, that people extend to both self and others.

We were curious, however, whether actors would become more self-serving, and observers more derogating, when the action in question was more obviously negative. In an additional study we asked people to list actions that either they (or someone else) had committed and for which they (or the other person) had gotten into trouble. Naturally, we did not sample murder and mayhem with this instruction, but we did elicit behaviors such as lying, stealing, cheating, punching, mugging, damaging property, and house breaking. One may expect that, for sufficiently negative behaviors, people would increase their use of CHRs from the actor perspective (akin to the "abuse excuse") but decrease their use of CHRs from the observer perspective so as to not grant the perpetrator any deflection of responsibility. In previous studies, among explanations of positive and mildly negative actions, actors consistently used more reasons, and fewer causal history explanations, than observers did (Malle 2002b; Malle, Knobe, and Nelson 2004; see also chapter 7). If a true self-serving bias operated in explanations of *severely* negative actions, then this standard actor–observer asymmetry should disappear.

Our findings showed a 45% overall rate of CHR explanations (among the highest we have ever seen), but the standard actor–observer asymmetry emerged as strongly as it did in the past for positive actions ($\eta^2 = 10\%$). We concluded once more that people do not seem to use causal history explanations in a simply self-serving manner.

There was one trend that did distinguish explanations of highly negative actions from explanations of all other actions. We found a small number of cases in which a CHR explanation was used to actively *denigrate* the agent—in contrast to the typical deflection of responsibility. These denigrating uses are relatively rare but paint an unequivocally negative image of the agent, as the following examples illustrate.

(6-8)   He broke into our room and stole all our underwear. *Why?* **Because he is a pervert.**

(6-9)   This kid punched me in the face. *Why?* **Because he's an asshole.**

Ten out of eleven of the denigrating CHR explanations in this study were offered by observers and, of those, most referred to personality traits (7 out of 10). Even though such denigrating CHRs are quite infrequent (15% of observer CHRs), we do see here one indication of observers chucking their charitable attitude and turning a tool of favorable impression management into one of unfavorable impression management. Of course, more systematic studies would be needed to confirm this preliminary finding.

What both the mitigating and the denigrating use of causal history explanations have in common is the shift of attention away from the agent's subjective viewpoint and rational reasoning toward a more distanced causal assessment. Such a shift creates a more favorable impression of the agent when the reasoning was flawed or when there wasn't much reasoning to support the action. But that shift creates a less favorable impression when the agent's subjective reasoning would shed light on the action and perhaps make it intelligible whereas a causal history explanation subsumes the action in question under some undesirable trait.

Thus, even though we can predict that causal histories will increase in explanations of negative actions, we cannot as easily predict whether any given CHR explanation will be used to create a positive or negative impression of the agent. The base rates clearly favor the contention that CHR explanations are used (by actors and observers alike) as a mitigating device. To identify the conditions under which an explainer decides to use CHRs for a derogating purpose we would have to go beyond a model of folk explanation and design future studies by consulting a theory of social motivation and evaluation.

I have focused on impression management conditions that raise the frequency of CHR (rather than reason) explanations, in part because this is the rarer and hence more diagnostic explanation mode. However, there is at least one condition under which people appear to actively increase their use of reason explanations, namely when they try to appear rational (Malle et al. 2000). This use of reasons should be quite natural if people's conceptualization of reasons is tightly linked, as I have claimed, to a notion of rationality that pictures the agent's mind sorting through beliefs and desires and arriving, in light of them, at a decision to act.[2]

In our study (Malle et al. 2000, study 5), we asked participants to explain a small number of actions they had recently performed (some positive, some negative). All explanations were delivered in front of an audience that comprised an interviewer and other participants. In the experimental condition, participants were instructed to answer the interviewer's questions and try to appear as rational as possible; in the control condition, they received no special instructions. The results showed that, when reasons and causal histories were analyzed as multiple correlated variables ($r = .23$, $p < .05$), the impact of rational impression management was significant, but the effect was limited to the reasons variable. As expected, the rational group provided more reasons ($M = 1.7$) than the control group ($M = 1.4$), $F(1,85) = 4.8$, $p < .05$, $\eta^2 = 5\%$.

The same experiment also included a condition in which people were instructed to appear as self-centered as possible, and compared to the control group, they too increased their number of reason explanations, $F(1,85) = 8.0$, $p < .01$, $\eta^2 = 9\%$. Once more, we have to wonder how one explanation mode can deliver such different impressions—on the one hand to appear rational, on the other, to appear self-centered. The solution to this puzzle lies in the recognition that not all reasons are alike. When trying to create an impression of rationality or self-centeredness, people do not offer just any or all reasons they can think of—they specifically raise a certain type of reason. Which one they raise I explore next.

6.3.3 Features of Reason Explanations

When we look at the specific features of reason explanations, we find some very subtle but powerful impression management tools. Reasons, as chapter 4 laid out, can be either beliefs, desires, or valuings; they can be used with or without mental states markers; and they have a content that can be classified along a number of dimensions (e.g., person–situation, desirable–undesirable).

Reason Types   Because our research has not uncovered any psychological significance inherent in the choice of valuings, my discussion will focus on the far more frequent and socially significant reason types of beliefs and desires.

Desire reasons highlight what the agent lacks, wants, needs, or strives for. Mentioning a desire reason thus can portray the agent as deficient (i.e., "wanting") in some respect and as driven toward removing that deficiency. Such a portrayal does not put the agent in an especially favorable light, especially when she isn't striving for a socially valuable goal.

Belief reasons, by contrast, highlight what the agent believes, thinks, knows, deliberates about, or—when mental state markers are omitted—simply what appears to be the case. More often than not, belief reasons cast the agent in a favorable light by pointing to her reasoning and decision capacities, at times implying the triumph of thinking over wanting, reason over passion.

The choice of offering either a belief reason or a desire reason is driven in part by the explainer's information resources and assumptions about what one's conversation partner already knows. In addition, the belief–desire choice is driven by impression–management goals, one of which is the attempt to appear rational. This goal would be best achieved by specifically offering belief reasons, because they connote deliberation, thinking, and, well, rationality (see 4.2.4). We tested this hypothesis in the same experiment described earlier (Malle et al. 2000, study 5). When participants were asked to explain some of their actions in front of an audience, those instructed to appear rational offered significantly more belief reasons (M = 70%) than those in the control group (M = 50%) (Malle et al. 2000, study 5). This finding solves half of our puzzle from the previous section, where we found that people seem to increase reason explanations *both* when trying to appear rational and when trying to appear self-centered. The appearance of rationality is sought specifically by increasing belief reasons. (The other half of the puzzle will be solved in the next section.)

Another important impression management goal that reason types might help fulfill is to limit the blame one receives for performing undesirable actions. Here, however, the conceptual definitions of belief and desire do not generate a clear-cut prediction. Beliefs might be helpful when accounting for negative actions because they can indicate miscalculations, false assumptions, or purported facts that somehow make the action seem reasonable and justified (e.g., "Why did you throw away my notepad?"—"It had been lying around for months; I didn't think you'd still need it"). Desires, on the other hand, might be helpful because they can indicate the agent's actual goal in performing the action, a goal that may be more desirable than the action that resulted from it, as in the following example:

(6-10)   I made my best friend hide in my closet when I was a child (I was in so much trouble). *Why?* **I didn't want her to go home** [desire reason], **I wanted someone to play with after dinner** [desire reason].

In our empirical studies we also found mixed patterns of results. When explaining negative actions, people—both as actors and as observers—offered more desire reasons and fewer belief reasons than when explaining positive actions (Nelson and Malle 2004; Nelson 2003). However, there was also some indication that the severity of the action may moderate actors' use of reason types. In one study, we were able to analyze a full range of mild to severe negative actions (as rated by independent judges), and only the mildly negative actions were explained by a higher number of desires than usual, whereas the severely negative actions were explained by a *lower* number of desires than usual. A possible interpretation of this pattern is that proffering a desirable goal may succeed at making a mildly negative action appear acceptable, but it would rarely work with a severely negative action, for which a desirable goal just may not be credible. This pattern will have to be replicated, of course, before we can have faith in it.

Mental State Markers The social function of mental state markers is guided by both linguistic and conceptual features, and they combine to produce a number of impression management effects.

The first consists in the management of attention to the agent. At the linguistic level, verbs such as *think, want,* or *like* explicitly refer to the agent's mental state and thus highlight the subjective viewpoint of the provided explanation. But highlighting a subjective desire has, as argued earlier, different implications from highlighting a subjective belief. By explicitly using a desire verb, the explainer portrays the agent as needing, wanting, or striving for something that, in most cases, is to her advantage. The spotlight created by marked desire reasons can thus be used to forge an impression of the agent as egocentric or self-centered. Consider two examples:

(6-11)   Why did you give your grandmother a tour of your sorority?— **'Cause I wanted her to see my house and where I live** and **I wanted her to like it.**

(6-12)   I don't understand why [your parents] didn't talk to you about [going to boarding school] first.—I think **'cause they didn't want me to resist them,** you know.

Belief reasons, by contrast, highlight the agent's subjective representation of reality without hinting at the agent's selfishness. I suspect this is so in part because beliefs are viewed as caused by the world whereas desires are viewed as originating in the agent (cf. Wellman 1990), and in part because being selfish is largely defined on the basis of self-originating desires.

The goal of portraying somebody as self-centered may thus be achieved by specifically citing mental state verbs for desire reasons. (Conversely, the goal of avoiding the impression of self-centeredness may be achieved by omitting desire markers or citing belief reasons in the first place.) Empirical evidence for this impression management effect comes from the study mentioned earlier (Malle et al. 2000, study 5), in which we instructed some participants to portray themselves as self-centered when answering questions in front of an audience. Such "self-centered" explainers offered significantly more marked desire reasons ($M = 80\%$) than did the control group ($M =$

50%) (Malle et al. 2000, table 4). And though we tested this pattern only on actor explanations, the same results should hold for observer explanations as well.

The second social function of mental state markers lies in the explainer's choice to either embrace the agent's reasons or distance himself from them. Interestingly, this effect is limited to belief reasons; so I first describe the distancing–embracing function and then discuss why desire reasons do not have this function.

Belief reasons can be made to sound like they are statements of fact simply by omitting the mental state marker. A person might explain her watering the plants by saying "I thought they were dry," or she might say "They were dry." Similarly, we might say "She is taking an umbrella because she thinks it's going to rain," or we might say "because it's going to rain." In the second case of each of these examples, the explainer appears to state a fact, even though the action is of course still explained by virtue of the agent's (implied) belief about this fact (Malle et al. 2000).[3]

Thus, marked and unmarked belief reasons differ substantially from each other because the former ascribes a belief and the latter appears to state a fact. But the contrast between these two forms can be sharpened further. When an explainer offers a marked belief reason, he singles out *the agent's* belief and implies that he doesn't necessarily share or endorse that belief, thus distancing himself from the agent. When he omits a belief marker, he indicates that the belief is "fact," hence that he, the explainer, embraces the belief.

Compare the pairs of marked and unmarked belief reasons in table 6.2. In each case, the marked belief reason (in the middle column) indicates that *the agent*—and possibly no one else—had the cited thought or belief. By contrast, the unmarked belief reason (in the right column) mentions only the content of the agent's belief, and so the explanation sounds like a statement of fact. Because the explainer makes this statement of fact, he obviously believes it (Rosenthal, forthcoming) and thus embraces the agent's belief. (Note that in the third example, the agent is the explainer's "past self," whom he treats just like another person.)

This embracing–distancing function of belief reasons can have powerful communicative consequences. In one study we compared the effects of using a marked versus unmarked belief reason on the readers of the following brief vignette (Malle et al. 2000, study 6):

Table 6.2
Belief reason explanations with and without mental state markers

Behavior	Marked	Unmarked
She took the car to work	. . . because she believed she was late	. . . because she was late
He'll call her	. . . because he thinks she's interested	. . . because she is interested
I stayed away from him	. . . because I thought he was married	. . . because he was married

Cliff and Jerry are at a dinner party. Cliff asks Jerry: "Why did your girl-friend refuse dessert?" Jerry responds by saying:

"She thinks she's been gaining weight" *vs.* "She's been gaining weight"

The response on the left is a marked belief; the response on the right, an unmarked belief. After reading either one of the two scenario versions, participants rated (on a scale from 0 to 8) how happy Jerry was with his girl-friend's current weight. The difference between marked and unmarked belief reasons was substantial. Jerry was seen as almost three scale points happier with his girlfriend's weight when he used the marked belief than when he used the unmarked belief ($p < .01$, $\eta^2 = 20\%$). By using a mental state marker ("She thinks"), Jerry successfully distanced himself from his girlfriend's reason, implying that he did not believe (as she did) that she had been gaining weight.

The phrases "she thinks" or "he believed" are the most frequently used mental state verbs to mark a belief reason. However, there are others as well, and table 6.3 displays a range of such belief markers, ordered from most distancing (top) to most embracing (bottom).

At least in English (but I suspect in most languages), desire reasons are recognizable as mental states, whether or not the explainer uses a mental state verb to mark them. Even without a mental state marker, the syntactic form in which desire reasons are expressed—"(in order) to," "so (that)," "for . . . (sake)"—reveals them as desires:

(6-12)   She moved to Kentucky *to* **have this baby.**

(6-13)   We used to hitchhike, like, into town . . . *so* **we could get to the general market.**

(6-14)   Why did you initially enroll in dance class?— **I kind of use it** *for* **exercise.**

Because desire reasons always signal the agent's subjective motivational state, there is no linguistic room for the explainer to indicate whether he embraces the agent's reason or not. Just consider any of the above explanations and add a mental state marker—the explainer's attitude toward the agent's reason does not change.

But do desire markers have no social function besides the highlighting of self-centeredness? They do, but these functions are subtle. Marked and unmarked desire reasons sometimes differ in the degree of formality of the reason ascription. In response to the CEO's question "Why did she leave early?," a friend might say "To pick up her daughter," whereas an assistant might say (using a mental state marker) "She needed to pick up her daughter from school."

In addition, by choosing carefully among different desire verbs, explainers are able to convey the intensity of the agent's desire. For example, when explaining why Lana worked overtime all year, we might choose a variety of desire markers: because she *needs; would like; wants; longs for; craves; passionately wants; lusts after* a new car.

These impression management effects of mental state markers are not solely predictable from the conceptual meaning of reasons. The third level of a theory of explanation must come into play as well, which concerns the

Table 6.3
Reason explanations with varying mental state markers

Behavior	Marker	Reason Content
She changed the party from Saturday to Friday because she . . .	mistakenly believes jumped to the conclusion thinks/believes assumes/presumes expects heard/inferred concluded/deduced saw/discovered realizes/knows	. . . that he's leaving on Saturday

Note: The belief markers are ordered from most distancing (top) to most embracing (bottom).

specific linguistic options that explainers have available in a particular language. We have every reason to believe that most languages besides English will have options to ascribe beliefs and desires, but which specific linguistic options allow explainers to embrace or distance themselves from the agent's reasons is an open empirical question.

6.3.4 Outlook: How Effective Are Impression-Managing Explanations?

While examining the specific choices explainers make when they are engaged in impression management, my collaborators and I have also begun to explore the effectiveness of these choices for *actually* impressing an audience. From this ongoing research, I select one example that demonstrates an audience effect, though I do not want to suggest that these effects will be numerous or easy to find. It should not surprise us, for example, that people who try to manage others' impressions often fail to fully take their audience's perspective into account and may therefore miscalculate what kinds of explanations would best achieve their impression management goals.

In the aforementioned experiment investigating the effects of rational self-presentation on modes of explanation (Malle et al. 2000, study 4), we also examined the effects that actors' choices of explanations had on their audience.[4] After each participant provided explanations of up to four actions, audience members ($N = 79$) wrote down their impressions of the actor using a variety of seven-point (0 to 6) rating scales that formed, among others, the dimensions of *rational* (logical, thoughtful, rational; $\alpha = .75$) and *self-centered* (self-absorbed, selfish; $\alpha = .88$). As predicted, participants who had been instructed to present themselves as rational were perceived as more *rational* ($M = 3.8$) than the control group ($M = 3.5$), $F(1,74) = 2.9$, $p = .05$, $\eta^2 = 14\%$, whereas participants who had been instructed to present themselves as self-centered were perceived as more *self-centered* ($M = 2.5$) than the control group ($M = 1.6$), $F(1,74) = 14.4$, $p < .01$, $\eta^2 = 16\%$. Because we know that instructions to appear rational led to an increase in reasons, especially belief reasons, and instructions to appear self-centered led to an increase in mental state markers, especially for desires, we also examined the question of whether these explanation features mediated the audience impressions. Indeed, explainers were seen as more rational the more reasons they provided ($r = .40$, $p < .01$). Specifically, audience impressions of rationality were a function of the explainer using belief reasons ($r = .46$, $p < .01$) but not a function of the explainer using desire reasons ($r = -.01$). Perceptions of selfishness were also, as expected, associated with the use of mental state markers, but this effect was relatively weak ($r = .17$, $p = .14$).

6.4 Summary

A study of the linguistic, communicative, and social functions of behavior explanations requires a model of the conceptual framework that underlies these explanations. Using this model, I analyzed the hypothesis of "implicit verb causality," according to which interpersonal verbs semantically imply patterns of causality. However, the patterns of findings actually break into two distinct phenomena: the causal structure of interpersonal episodes; and the explanations that are given for such episodes. The patterns of causal structure found in the literature can be accounted for by the folk classification of behavioral events that is based on the concepts of intentionality and observability (see chapter 3). The patterns of explanations found in the literature, I suggested, primarily reflect cultural consensus over how to explain canonical interpersonal episodes; rules of covariation are not needed to account for these findings.

I also showed in a number of ways how the folk-conceptual theory of explanation can help us pinpoint specific impression management tactics that people employ in social interaction. Some of these tactics can be directly predicted from the conceptual meaning of such explanatory parameters as causal history factors or belief reasons. Others require the addition of the third layer of folk explanation theory—that of linguistic options available in a particular language for attempting certain impression management goals. Obviously, none of these predictions or explorations can be accommodated by classic attribution theory and its theoretical vocabulary of person and situation causes.

Future research will have to continue to explore explainers' choices of particular explanation parameters when pursuing specific impression management goals but should also examine which of these choices, and under what conditions, have their desired effects—when impression management actually manages other people's impressions.

7   Explaining Behavior of Self and Other

Humans have evolved the capacity to interpret social behavior of enormous complexity by grasping its roots in mental states, personality, and the social context. This folk interpretation of behavior centers on the appreciation that people are agents who can act intentionally on the basis of their reasons but who also exhibit a large number of unintentional experiences, emotions, and behaviors. These fundamental assumptions apply equally to others and the self—that is, there is only one conceptual framework within which humans perceive and reason about both their own and other people's behavior and mind (Barresi 2000; Barresi and Moore 1996).

Few would deny, however, that the way people perceive and reason about themselves is different from the way they perceive and reason about others. Behavior explanations, in particular, should show such *self–other asymmetries*. If, for example, people know more about their own actions and experiences than about others' actions and experiences they should be in a better position to explain them than other people are.

How can we reconcile these two postulates? That is, how can there be a single folk theory of mind and behavior that nonetheless allows for significant self–other asymmetries? To answer this question we must heed the distinction between the conceptual framework of behavior explanation and the cognitive processes that it interacts with. A conceptual framework (such as the folk theory of mind) selects input, classifies it into certain categories, and engages subsequent processing that operates on those categories. There is every reason to believe that humans have only one such conceptual framework that handles information about mind and behavior in both self and other. However, several psychological processes modulate which input reaches the framework in the first place, which information is translated into specific explanations, and which of them are publicly expressed. These psychological processes—such as attention, information access, or interaction goals—are responsible for self–other asymmetries in explanation. To clarify the impact of these processes, we have distinguished between three levels at which self–other asymmetries in explanation can occur (Knobe and Malle 2002):

Level 1—which behavioral events people try to explain;

Level 2—what explanatory hypotheses people construct about these events;

Level 3—how people publicly formulate these explanatory hypotheses.

At each of these levels, the folk theory of mind and behavior sets the boundaries within which the relevant information is categorized, but it does not control the information itself or the processes that operate on the categories. At Level 1, the folk theory classifies behavioral events into particular categories (actions, experiences, etc.; see chapter 3), but psychological processes such as attention, information access, and motivational relevance dictate *which* events are selected for explanation. And because actors and observers differ in these psychological processes, their selections of which events they explain differ as well (Malle and Knobe 1997b).

Similarly, at Level 2, the folk theory constitutes the kinds of explanatory hypotheses people can form (e.g., reasons, causal histories of reasons), but any particular hypothesis an explainer constructs will depend on such processes as knowledge recruitment and mental simulation (see 5.3). Again, because actors and observers can differ in these processes, their explanatory hypotheses will differ as a result (Knobe and Malle 2002; Malle 1999, 2002b; Malle, Knobe, and Nelson 2004).

Finally, at Level 3, the verbal expression of explanations is bounded by available folk concepts (e.g., belief and desires), but specific formulations also reflect the explainer's attitudes and pragmatic goals. Once more, actors and observers frequently differ in those attitudes and goals, yielding asymmetries at the level of linguistic formulation (Malle, Knobe, and Nelson 2004).

Chapter 3 dealt with the processes that modulate the initial selection of events for explanation (level 1), resulting in asymmetries regarding *which* behavioral events actors and observers explain. This chapter explores the processes that govern the construction and formulation of explanations (levels 2 and 3), resulting in asymmetries regarding *how* actors and observers explain behavior.

7.1   Actor–Observer Asymmetries in How Behaviors Are Explained

Both actors and observers construct their explanations within a folk-conceptual framework. Inherent in this framework are distinctions among types of behavior, modes of explanation, and specific features within each explanation mode (chapter 4). As a result of these distinctions, actors and observer must make numerous choices, from judging the intentionality of the behavioral event to adding versus omitting mental state markers. These choices were initially discussed in chapter 5 and are illustrated once more in figure 7.1.

When referring to *choices,* I am not implying that explainers necessarily make conscious choices. Sometimes they may well, but most of the time consciousness is directed at the *content* of cognition relevant to the explanations, leaving the construction of the actual form of explanations to well-practiced unconscious operations. In this construction process, we find subtle differences between explanations of one's own behavior and those of other people's behavior, generated to a large extent by differences in information resources and pragmatic goals (Malle 2002b). I now discuss these asymmetries at each of the choice points identified by the folk-conceptual theory of behavior explanation.

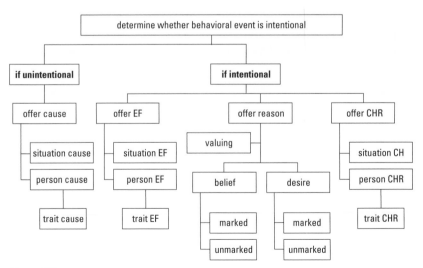

Figure 7.1
Choice points when constructing a behavior explanation.

7.2   Intentional or Unintentional?

Before people can offer an explanation for a behavioral event, they must first determine the intentionality of the event[1] because people's models of causality and ensuing modes of explanation differ qualitatively between intentional and unintentional behavior (see chapter 4).

What shapes these judgments of intentionality? Obviously, they are influenced by the actual nature of the behavior and by the depth of the explainer's information about it. In general, actors will have an information advantage over observers in determining intentionality, because they have critical information available about their own planning, choice, and execution of intentional behaviors (Gollwitzer 1996; Knobe and Malle 2002; Kuhl 1987; McClelland 1987; White 1980). But there is little evidence that this information advantage yields a *systematic* actor–observer difference in the readiness to judge behaviors as intentional. At times actors will know better than an observer that they acted intentionally; at other times actors will know better that they *didn't* act intentionally. In addition, actors may be more motivated to see their behavior one way or the other depending on pragmatic concerns in the particular context. Here too, the pattern is anything but straightforward (see 6.3.1). Sometimes it may be opportune to portray a socially undesirable behavior as unintentional in order to reduce blame, but at other times it may be more effective to portray the undesirable behavior as performed intentionally for a good, justified reason (Scott and Lyman 1968; Tedeschi and Reiss 1981).

But perhaps there is a bias among observers toward assuming intentionality when they are in doubt about a behavior? It has been suggested that young children overattribute intentionality (Premack 1990; Lyon 1993), and we know that humans are quite ready to attribute intentionality to numerous phenomena that are in all likelihood unintentional, such as natural catastrophes (e.g., interpreted as "acts of God") as well as a wide range of animal and machine behaviors (Dennett 1987). On the other hand, it has been argued that people, as actors, sometimes overattribute intentionality to their own behaviors even when the circumstances do not seem to justify it (Langer 1975; Wegner 2002).

Thus, the data we have available do not unequivocally support the hypothesis of a general observer bias toward intentionality. There is, however, some recent evidence suggesting that observers show such a bias of ascribing intentionality when the behavior is harmful. Knobe (2003a) reports the results of a series of studies in which people were far more likely to consider a behavior intentional when it had negative moral consequences than when the same behavior was described as having positive or neutral moral consequences. Whatever the exact interpretation of this finding (see section 4.2.2), it does suggest that observers are biased toward assuming intentionality for harmful behaviors. Such a bias might even be justified from a signal detection viewpoint, because the costs of falsely designating a negative behavior as intentional (when it is not) will be much smaller than the costs of failing to recognize a harmful behavior as intentional (cf. Lopes 1982; Plous 1993). Consider the enormous costs of falsely assuming that an explosion was an industrial accident when in fact it was a deliberate terrorist attack. Whether these patterns suffice to produce a general actor–observer asymmetry in intentionality judgments, however, cannot be determined without further research.

Even if there were a general actor–observer asymmetry in intentionality judgments, its implications for actor–observer asymmetries in *behavior explanations* would be negligible. If, say, the actor considers a behavior unintentional, she will offer a cause explanation; if the observer considers that same event intentional, he will likely offer a reason explanation. The two explanation modes differ, but they differ in such an obvious a way that the resulting debate, conflict, or negotiation between actor and observer will not play out at the level of explanation but at the level of intentionality judgments.

In discussing the choice points at which actor and observer explanations diverge I will therefore presume an already agreed-upon intentionality judgment for the behavior in question. Any discrepancy, debate, or negotiation would then have to be settled at the level of explanations so that we are dealing with genuine actor–observer asymmetries in explanation.

7.3 Reasons or Causal Histories of Reasons?

The first genuine actor–observer asymmetry in explanation lies in the choice between reasons and causal history of reason (CHR) explanations, the two major modes for explaining intentional behavior.[2] Of the psychological determinants identified in section 5.2, both information resources and pragmatic goals should differentially influence actors' and observers' choices among these explanation modes (Malle 2002b).[3]

Indeed, actors typically have excellent—some would say, privileged—information access to their own reasons. When deciding to perform a particular behavior, an actor normally thinks about reasons that count in favor of it, and when she is later asked to explain that behavior, her first impulse will be to mention the very reasons she considered during her deliberation. No such privileged access holds for the causal history of reasons, because this history is not part of the agent's deliberations. Observers, of course, have no privileged access to any explanatory information. They will occasionally know the agent's reasons (e.g., when the agent told them) or be able to infer them. But at times they will have no idea for what reasons the agent acted and therefore resort to a causal history explanation. Thus, differences in information resources predict that actors use more reasons (and fewer causal histories) than observers do.

Pragmatic goals, too, push the asymmetry in the same direction, because reason explanations better serve actors' impression management goals. Research shows that reason explanations make the agent appear more rational (Malle et al. 2000) and can be used to justify the behaviors they explain (Schueler 2001). To the extent that actors are trying to make their behaviors appear rational and justified, then, they may prefer reason explanations over causal history explanations. Except in unusual circumstances, observers will not have that same motivation to portray the agent in a rational, justified, or generally desirable light.

Thus, consideration of two psychological determinants of explanation choice (information resources and pragmatic goals) predicts that actors use more reasons (and fewer causal histories) than observers do.

Evidence   The hypothesis of a reason–CHR asymmetry received consistent support in a series of studies that examined over 4000 explanations (Malle, Knobe, and Nelson 2004). Across these studies, actors offered 1.5 reasons and 0.4 CHRs per intentional behavior explained, whereas observers offered 1.0 reasons and 0.7 CHRs. Below are sample reason explanations by actors and causal history explanations by observers that put this asymmetry in relief:

Reason explanations by actors:

(7-1) Why did you plan to buy your brother a video game?—'**Cause it was his birthday** [reason] and **I wanted to have him get something that he would actually use** [reason].

(7-2) Why did you decide to go hiking up the peak?—**Just to kind of get a change of scenery** [reason]. **I was getting sick of what everyone else was doing, kind of** [reason].

Causal history of reason explanations by observers:

(7-3) Her family like had these family get-togethers all the time '**cause they had quite a few aunts and uncles in the family** [CHR].

(7-4) Sometimes he [divorced father] would break in and put gifts all around the house, **because for a long time he was torn between still loving her and hating what she'd done** [CHR].

The above examples are of course more illustrative than representative, because even observers use reasons as their default. However, they do so less than actors, often replacing reasons with CHR explanations.

What supports the claim that observers *replace* rather than complement reasons with CHRs? Could observers not add more causal histories to their reason explanations and thereby only appear to use more CHRs? The evidence suggests otherwise. Across our series of studies, we examined the frequency of explaining a given intentional action (a) with reasons only, (b) with causal histories only, and (c) with a mix of reasons and causal histories. The results, broken down by perspective, are displayed in table 7.1.

Observers do not substantially differ from actors in their rate of mixed reason–CHR explanations. Rather, they differ in their decreased rate of

Table 7.1
Rates of explanation mode for intentional behaviors

	Actors	Observers
Reasons alone	68%	52%
CHRs alone	10%	24%
Reason/CHR mix	22%	25%

Note: CHR = causal history of reason explanation

reasons-only explanations and their corresponding increased rate of CHR-only explanations. This is the pattern we would expect if observers sometimes had difficulties coming up with a reason explanation and therefore offered a causal history explanation instead.

To get more clarity about the underlying determinants of this actor–observer asymmetry, we examined in one study whether the reason–CHR asymmetry is moderated by the degree of knowledge an observer has about the agent (Malle, Knobe, and Nelson 2004, study 4). We compared "close observers," who knew the agent well and were actually present when the behavior occurred, with "distant observers" (cf. Schober and Clark 1989), who didn't know the agent at all and learned about the explained behavior and its context from a narrative. We found no difference in the use of reasons and CHRs for these two types of observer—both offered significantly more CHRs and fewer reasons than actors did. How is this possible?

As argued earlier (section 5.2.3), knowledge does not have a straightforward effect on explanations. Observers may lack knowledge about the agent's mental states, in which case it will be difficult to provide reason explanations, or they may lack knowledge about the agent's personality, background, or culture, in which case it will be difficult to provide CHR explanations. Even though distant observers have less knowledge overall, they may not have specifically less mental state knowledge or specifically less background knowledge, and so their relative use of reasons and causal histories remains unaffected. Thus, what may be driving the actor–observer asymmetry in reasons is not so much learnable knowledge about the agent but rather a more fundamental difference between actors and observers in their cognitive access to reasons. In section 5.3.2 we saw a number of examples that suggest actors often use a method of direct recall when constructing reason explanations—a process that is simply not available to observers, even those who know the agent well.

The second determinant of the predicted reason–CHR asymmetry—impression management—is currently under investigation in our lab. If the hypothesis is correct, observers who try to put the agent in a rational, socially desirable light should decrease their causal history explanations, increase their reason explanations, and thus close the actor–observer gap. The extent to which this gap cannot be closed by an impression management manipulation would, in turn, be indicative of the power of information resources to generate this asymmetry.

7.4   What Type of Reason?

The second hypothesis about actor–observer asymmetries in explanations concerns the choice between belief reasons and desire reasons.[4] We know from chapter 4 that desire reasons provide the most direct answer to the questions "For what purpose?" or "To what end?" This makes them the paradigmatic motive of intentional action, because the end or purpose is what the action is driving at, the change in the world that the agent tries to bring about. Belief reasons, by contrast, are considered the "map by which we steer" (to use a metaphor by Armstrong 1973, following Ramsey 1931). In belief reasons the agent represents primarily the action's context and circumstances, its causal relation with the aimed-at outcome, details of planning and execution, and navigations around obstacles.

Once more, differences in information resources and pragmatic goals predict an actor–observer asymmetry in the use these two types of reason. Whereas for actors either type should be easily accessible, observers are likely to have more trouble with belief reasons than with desire reasons. That is because the kind of information that desires represent is more easily gleaned from the action itself, from social rules and cultural practices (Bruner 1990), and from one's own experience (Harris 1996). Belief reasons, by contrast, represent information that is more idiosyncratic to the agent and the specific context, such as considered alternatives, anticipated outcomes, and perceived obstacles. Thus, observers quite easily infer what somebody's desire or purpose would be in acting a certain way, but they will have difficulty inferring what the agent's specific thoughts were in choosing this action, at this location and time, and in this manner.

Another way of putting the difference between desires and beliefs is that to infer an agent's belief reason one must truly take *this particular* agent's perspective and represent her mental states. By contrast, inferences of desire reasons can rely on the explainer's recognition of strong external attractors, goal objects, and outcomes that people in general are after ("for money"; "to get attention"), and such recognition requires far less genuine perspective taking. Parallel to this difference in inferential requirements, developmental research has shown that children learn to attribute desires before they learn to attribute beliefs (e.g., Nelson-LeGall 1985; Wellman and Woolley 1990) and that they explain actions using desires before using beliefs (Bartsch and Wellman 1989).[5]

Besides the difference in information resources, there is also a difference in pragmatic goals that predicts an actor–observer asymmetry in the use of reason types. Specifically, actors are normally interested, more so than observers, in presenting the image of a smart, rational agent; and it is beliefs, not desires, that help create this rational impression (Malle et al. 2000; see also section 6.3.3).

Thus, on the basis of the same two psychological determinants relied on earlier—information resources and pragmatic goals—we can predict that actors use more belief reasons (and fewer desire reasons) than observers do.

Evidence   The hypothesis of a belief–desire asymmetry received consistent support in the series of studies referenced above (Malle, Knobe, and Nelson 2004). Actors offered on average 1.0 belief reasons and 0.6 desires reasons whereas observers offered 0.5 belief reasons and 0.6 desire reasons. Once more, I provide sample belief reasons by actors and sample desire reasons by observers that put this asymmetry into relief:

Belief reasons by actors:

 (7-5)   I wanted to pick up a friend **'cause he was just at home doing nothing** [belief].

(7-6)   And I looked in this pack and got out this little Band-Aid case in this pack or something like that, **'cause I thought it would have something that I needed in it** [belief].

Desire reasons by observers:

(7-7) Dad refused to move out for two months after [wife/mother] filed for divorce **just because he wanted to be with his kids** and **he didn't want to leave the house we had in West Linn** [desires].

(7-8)   So she put the knives under her bed **to protect herself** [desire].

This time, the study that compared close and distant observers favored a knowledge account of the data pattern (Malle, Knobe, and Nelson 2004, study 4). Whereas distant observers displayed the familiar prevalence of desire reasons, close observers were very similar to actors in their predominance of belief reasons. One might ask whether close observers benefit more from their knowledge about the agent as a person or from the context-specific information they gathered when observing the agent perform the action in question. We have currently no decisive data to answer this question.

7.5 Add a Mental State Marker?

We saw in the previous chapter (6.3.3) that mental state markers in belief reasons play different roles from those in desire reasons. Whereas marked and unmarked belief reasons convey quite different meaning and hence attain different social functions, marked and unmarked desire reasons are semantically highly similar. Thus, only within belief reasons might the adding or omitting of mental state markers show an interesting actor–observer asymmetry.

The factors of information resources and pragmatic goals are, once more, key in deriving the hypothesis about actors' and observers' differential use of mental state markers. First, actors' cognitive access to their belief reasons is such that in their minds they directly represent the *content* of their beliefs—e.g., belief [the plants are dry]. They do not normally represent their own belief qua *mental state;* that is, they usually do not have the conscious meta-state of belief [I *believe* the plants are dry] (Rosenthal forthcoming). When formulating their belief reasons in language, actors will often express simply what they represented, and so they usually leave their belief reasons unmarked: "Why did you turn on the sprinkler?"—"The plants were dry!" Observers, by contrast, typically represent the agent's thinking qua mental state—that is, belief [*she thought* the plants were dry]—and are therefore more likely to express a belief reason with a mental state verb: "Perhaps *she thought* the plants were dry."

But this first process may only set the cognitive defaults (actors start with the unmarked case, observers start with the marked case), which may be overridden by factors influencing actual linguistic formulations. A second process supporting the belief marker hypothesis directly influences the formulation of reasons. By adding or omitting belief markers, explainers can convey an evaluative attitude toward the cited belief reason (Malle et al. 2000; see also chapter 6). That is, by omitting a belief marker the explainer embraces the agent's belief whereas by adding such a marker the explainer distances himself from the agent's belief. Now, this linguistic device for embracing or distancing oneself from a belief reason will more often be used by observers than actors, because when explainer and agent are different persons some of their beliefs will diverge. Thus, suppose a man is trying to explain why his lady friend has been looking for a new home. If he says that she is looking for a new home "because we are going to get married," he thereby affirms the truth of her belief that they are going to get married. But if he says "because she thinks we are going to get married," he seems clearly to be casting doubt on the truth of that belief.

When explainer and agent are the same person (i.e., in actor explanations), a divergence of their beliefs is less likely. Actors can use mental state markers to distance themselves from their own past reasons ("I locked the door only because I thought you had already left"), but such cases will be the exception. In fact, actors will often be motivated to omit belief markers for impression management purposes because they thereby make their reason sound as if it were an objective fact ("because we can afford it") rather than a subjective belief ("because I think we can afford it"). (See Malle et al. 2000.)

Thus, both the representational form in which beliefs are accessed and the impression-managing functions that unmarked belief reasons can serve jointly support the prediction that actors more often omit belief reason markers than observers do.

Evidence   The belief marker asymmetry emerged in all five studies in which it was tested (Malle, Knobe, and Nelson 2004). Observers gave twice as many unmarked as marked beliefs (0.4 versus 0.2) whereas actors gave four times as many unmarked as marked beliefs (0.8 versus 0.2). The following explanations highlight this reliable pattern.

Unmarked belief reasons by actors:

(7-9)   I'm probably taking next fall off **because my boyfriend lives in Florida** and **that in itself is a very difficult situation** [unmarked beliefs].

(7-10)   I went to the east coast with a friend. *Why?* Umm, **I'd never been to the east coast,** and then **my friends are going there to visit their friends at MIT** [unmarked beliefs].

Marked belief reasons by observers:

(7-11)   I'm guessing that he waited [to die] till I left **'cause he knew that I was leaving** [marked belief].

(7-12)   He told me that my other brother was getting married. *Why?* **I think, I guess he thought I should know** [marked belief].

We also examined whether the belief marker asymmetry was moderated by knowledge (acquaintanceship), but no such moderation was found (Malle, Knobe, and Nelson 2004, study 4). Studies are currently under way that manipulate the impression management goals of both actors and observers and examine whether, when holding constant these goals, actors still use more unmarked belief reasons than observers do.

7.6   Trait or Not?

Jones and Nisbett's (1972) classic postulate of an actor–observer asymmetry was formulated in terms of attributions to dispositions versus situations. The term *disposition,* however, has two different readings (e.g., Ross and Fletcher 1985). In one reading, dispositions are stable traits (Jones and Davis 1965; Shaver 1975); in another, dispositions are any kind of "person cause" or "internal cause" of behavior (Kelley 1967; Nisbett et al. 1973). Thus, we must distinguish between two distinct traditional actor–observer hypotheses: (1) observers may provide more *trait* explanations than actors do; (2) observers may provide more *person* explanations than actors do. I begin by discussing the trait hypothesis and devote the next subsection to the person–situation hypothesis.

In our studies (Malle, Knobe, and Nelson 2004), we defined traits as those person factors that referred to temporally stable attributes of the agent's personality. Nontraits encompassed all remaining person factors, ranging from fleeting feelings to moderately stable preferences or desires (unless they clearly characterize someone's personality, such as "He has always hated confrontation").[6] All counts of traits and nontraits occurred in cause explanations (for unintentional behaviors) and causal history explanations (for intentional behaviors). Enabling factor explanations were virtually nonexistent in our samples of social behavior explanations, and reasons, if counted, would all be nontraits, thereby artificially inflating that category's frequency.

Across five studies we found support for the hypothesis that observers generate more trait explanations than actors do. Whereas actors offered 12%

traits, observers offered 22% traits.[7] However, we also identified two important qualifications to this overall pattern. First, in one study that tested for effects of knowledge, observers highly familiar with the agent offered significantly *more* traits ($M = 21\%$) than observers unfamiliar with the agent ($M = 8\%$), with the latter offering even slightly fewer than actors did ($M = 10\%$). Thus, it is not as though observers resort to traits when they are generally ignorant of the causes of a given behavior (and would use fewer trait explanations if only their knowledge improved). In order to give an elevated number of trait explanations observers actually have to know the agent reasonably well.

A second qualification is that the trait asymmetry was more reliable for explanations of *unintentional* behavior than for explanations of intentional behavior. An inspection of the relevant means suggests that the asymmetry is weakened for intentional behaviors because actors offered a fair number of traits within their person CHR explanations ($M = 30\%$), barely fewer than observers did ($M = 34\%$). By contrast, actors used only 8% traits in their person cause explanations, reliably fewer than observers did ($M = 18\%$).

Looking beyond these qualifications, how do we explain the overall trait asymmetry? Jones and Nisbett (1972) suggested three psychological mechanisms that might account for observers' greater use of trait explanations. According to the first account, observers use dispositions (traits) because the agent's behavior is especially salient to observers. This claim of salience is well supported, and it produces an actor–observer asymmetry in the kinds of events actors and observers explain (chapter 3). But as an account of the greater use of traits in observer explanations, the salience claim fails. From the fact that observers attend to the agent's observable behavior it just does not follow that they should be especially likely to explain this behavior in terms of traits—factors that lie *inside* that agent. It would seem plausible to hypothesize that explainers who attend to behaviors offer explanations that refer to behaviors; or that explainers who refer to internal factors do so because they attend to those internal factors. But the claim that explainers refer to traits because they find behavior especially salient remains puzzling and unfounded. In fact, it also remains empirically unsupported. When Taylor and Fiske (1975), McArthur and Post (1977), and Uleman, Miller, Henken, Riley, and Tsemberis (1981) directly manipulated salience, none of them found an effect on trait explanations.

Jones and Nisbett (1972) offered a second account of the actor-observer asymmetry in dispositional explanations. Because observers have less information available than actors do, observers resort to trait explanations, especially when they do not know the agent. This account is not supported by the data (Hampson 1983; Kerber and Singleton 1984; Malle, Knobe, and Nelson 2004). Our studies showed that observers increase, rather than decrease, their use of traits when they know the agent well. Conversely, observers barely use traits at all when they don't know the person.

Thus, observers do not use traits as their default explanation, and they certainly do not favor them when unfamiliar with the agent. Observers select traits, I surmise, when they don't quite know the specific cause that brought about the behavior in question but recognize that the behavior fits under a general trend that they are familiar with—a habit or trait they have learned about from interacting with the agent. Consider the following examples in which the explainers, who know the respective agents well, do not offer a context-specific cause for the behavior in question but subsume it under a supposed general pattern.

(7-13)   And we went and told my coach, and he just like laughed, [Partner: *Why?*], **'cause he's so mean** [laughs], no—**that's just the way he is** [laughs].

(7-14)   Why is she in such a good mood today?—**She is always enthusiastic.**

Still, why don't actors, too, make use of their own trait knowledge (which they undoubtedly have)? Here, Jones and Nisbett's (1972) third account comes into play—the claim that actors are reluctant to ascribe traits to themselves for fear of losing their sense (or public image) of being a freely choosing agent.[8] This is a plausible hypothesis, but it is not clear how it would answer two important questions: Why would actors ever offer a trait explanation if the costs of losing their sense of freedom are so high? And why, specifically, do actors offer a good number of traits in their causal history explanations (30% of person CHRs) compared to their cause explanations (8% of person causes)?

If we return to the psychological factors of information resources and impression management, we may have a better chance of answering these questions and thus account for the actor–observer asymmetry in traits. In short, differential information access accounts for the asymmetry in cause explanations, and impression management accounts for the absent asymmetry (and actors' reference to traits) in causal history explanations.

When actors explain their own unintentional behaviors, they usually experience them as a singular event and have some hypothesis about its immediate triggers. As long as they have such a hypothesis, there is no need for them to refer to a trait as an explanation of that singular event. Observers, by contrast, sometimes have no idea what the trigger of another person's unintentional behavior might be (especially if they were not immediately present when the behavior occurred). They might therefore search for other information useful for explaining it and, if they know the agent, may come up with pertinent trait knowledge.

The situation is somewhat different in the case of causal history explanations. Actors may already choose CHR explanations because of impression management goals (especially for undesirable behaviors). So it is no far stretch to argue that they may occasionally choose a trait CHR when it helps in their impression management. Observers, on their part, may sometimes use CHR traits because they lack more specific causal information or because they themselves are engaged in impression management (perhaps to denigrate the agent; see 6.3.2).

To sum up, observers do exceed actors in their use of traits, but only in cause explanations of unintentional behavior and only if observers actually have decent knowledge of the agent's habits and character. Two of the three classic accounts of the actor–observer trait asymmetry do not hold up to scrutiny (cf. Knobe and Malle 2002). The third one—actors' reluctance to ascribe traits to themselves because they constrain their freedom—is plausible but awaits further study. Joint reference to differential information resources and impression management goals currently appears to be the most promising account of the actor–observer asymmetry in traits.

7.7   Person Cause or Situation Cause?

I now turn to the second reading of the classic actor–observer asymmetry, according to which "dispositions" are any kind of person cause and observers are said to provide more person causes (and fewer situation causes) than actors do. However, we were not able to find any evidence for this hypothesis. In five studies, the person–situation asymmetry was statistically significant only once, and in one study an opposite trend emerged (Malle, Knobe, and Nelson 2004). Across all studies, actors offered 1.5 person explanations and 0.6 situation explanations whereas observers offered 1.5 person explanations and 0.5 situation explanations.[9]

Why, then, did past studies seem to find evidence for the person–situation asymmetry (e.g., McGill 1989; Nisbett et al. 1973; Robins, Spranca, and Mendelsohn 1996; Storms 1973)? At least three factors may have contributed to what seem to have been spurious person–situation findings.

First, in many actor–observer studies the term *disposition* was left ambiguous. As a result, researchers may have measured traits in their studies (e.g., Storms 1973) and found evidence for the trait asymmetry (which does seem to hold) but falsely interpreted the results as a person–situation asymmetry.

Second, most studies did not assess people's explanations in their own words but rather analyzed their checkmarks on causal rating scales. Such responses are unlikely to reflect genuine behavior explanations because the experimenter-provided scales do not match up well with the conceptual framework that underlies people's spontaneous explanations. People's behavior explanations vary in substantially more parameters than do attribution rating scales, so the limited scale responses are highly ambiguous. For example, respondents may use the "person" pole on a causal rating scale to express a judgment of perceived intentionality, a reason with person content, a person CHR, or even a person cause of unintentional behavior—four substantially different explanatory parameters that the person–situation scales cannot disentangle.

Third, in the few studies that did examine people's free-response behavior explanations (McGill 1989; Nisbett et al. 1973), the coding of explanations was probably more sensitive to patterns of linguistic surface than to the conceptual meaning of the explanations themselves (Antaki 1994; Malle et al. 2000; Monson and Snyder 1976; Ross 1977). For example, the explanation "She chose psychology because it helps people" would traditionally be coded as a situation attribution, whereas the explanation "She chose psychology because she feels it helps people" would be coded as a person attribution. But the two statements refer to the same belief reason; they differ solely in their use of mental state markers. Because belief reasons most often have as their content an aspect of the means to act or the action's consequences (which all could be read as "about the situation"), and because omitting a belief marker reveals this content directly on the linguistic surface (e.g., "it helps people"), actors who use unmarked belief reasons *appear* to provide "situation attributions" when in fact they differ from observers in the way they linguistically express their belief reasons (Malle 1999).

In sum, past studies that reported findings of an actor–observer asymmetry along the person–situation dimension suffered from a variety of methodological and conceptual problems. When we examined folk explanations in their naturally occurring verbal context, we failed to unearth any evidence for such a person–situation asymmetry (Malle, Knobe, and Nelson 2004). Of the traditional attribution claims of actor–observer asymmetries, only the trait asymmetry was supported, and it came with important qualifications.

7.8 Conclusions

The classic actor–observer asymmetry in behavior explanations, cast in terms of the disposition–situation dichotomy (Jones and Nisbett 1972) is a simple and elegant effect. Unfortunately, we will have to forgo simplicity if we want to provide an accurate account of how and why actors and observers differ in their explanations of behavior. The complexity of these asymmetries is of course a direct result of the complexity of folk explanations in general. There isn't just one distinction or dimension along which explanations differ but a variety of modes (e.g., reasons and causal histories) and, within each mode, a variety of specific features (e.g., reason type, mental state markers). People's behavior explanations cannot be forced into a disposition–situation scheme, and therefore we meet with multiple actor–observer asymmetries, not just one.

The first and perhaps most important asymmetry is the tendency for actors to offer more reason explanations (and fewer causal history explanations) than observers do. What makes this asymmetry so important is that it puts at center stage the attempt to capture an agent's own subjective reasoning—an attempt that is unique to the explanation of intentional action and represents a fundamental achievement of the folk theory of mind (see chapter 2). It is not difficult to see that actors have more reliable access to their reasons than observers do, and so information access is one likely mechanism that underlies the reason asymmetry. But the subjectivity of reasons also allows actors to adjust their reports of reasons in the service of managing other people's impressions, and impression management is a likely second mechanism that underlies the reason asymmetry. Both of these hypotheses about mechanisms still await direct empirical tests.

Among the other actor–observer asymmetries there is, first, the tendency for actors to offer more belief reasons (and fewer desire reasons) than observers do. Our findings suggest that this belief asymmetry can be overcome by observers who know the agent well and were copresent at the time of action. Whether general knowledge and copresence are both important in overcoming the asymmetry, or whether one of them suffices, has yet to be determined.

Next, the belief marker asymmetry is the tendency for actors to offer more unmarked (and fewer marked) belief reasons than observers do. Though slightly smaller in effect size, this asymmetry is reliable as well. Actors' use of unmarked belief reasons increases when they attempt to present themselves in a rational light (Malle et al. 2000), so it seems likely that actors' inclination for impression management is one force behind the belief marker asymmetry. In addition, there appears to be a fundamentally different way in which belief reasons are cognitively represented. Actors typically represent the *content* of their beliefs (e.g., belief [the plants are dry]) whereas observers typically represent the agent's belief qua mental state (e.g., belief [*she thought* the plants were dry]), a pattern that biases observers toward using more mental state markers than actors do. This hypothesis still awaits empirical tests.

Finally, we found support for one version of the classic actor–observer asymmetry, namely that actors use fewer trait explanations than observers do. However, this asymmetry holds reliably only for explanations of unintentional behaviors and requires a good deal of knowledge on the part of observers—strangers use very few trait explanations (Malle, Knobe, and Nelson 2004). Our results suggest that traits are neither the default option for observers (because the overall incidence of trait explanations is low) nor are they the fall-back option whenever an observer doesn't know why the agent behaved a certain way. Instead, observers ascribe traits when they don't know the local causes of a given behavior but are familiar with a broader pattern under which the behavior falls. Actors, for their part, rarely use traits in explanations of their behavior, and if they do, the trait is likely to serve an impression management goal that no other explanation can fulfill.

This detailed picture of actor–observer asymmetries in behavior explanations offers rather interesting applications in the domains of relationships and interpersonal conflict. It would be worthwhile to explore which specific asymmetries are most strongly related to the frequency of misunderstanding and conflict. Of importance is also the question of what could be done to reduce the various actor–observer asymmetries. Is it enough to provide the observer with more knowledge about the agent, or does he have to be copresent when the specific action is performed? Can active attempts to empathize with the agent bring observers closer to the subjective perspective that the agent occupies? And, finally, how can actors be prevented from using their behavior explanations too heavily in the service of impression management goals?

8 Explaining Behavior of Individuals and Groups

Everything said so far about behavior explanations presumed that the agent of the behavior is an individual. Virtually all examples of explanation have featured individuals, and all theoretical propositions were formulated in terms of individual agents, with no regard for the question of whether explanations of group agents are any different from explanations of individual agents. This is, in fact, quite in keeping with the entire literature on explanations, attributions, and accounts, where no theory of explanation has commented on the potentially unique features of genuine group behavior. Intergroup attribution work examined differences in explanations for members of various groups (Hewstone 1990; Islam and Hewstone 1993; Pettigrew 1979; Susskind et al. 1999), but the explained behaviors were always behaviors of *individual* group members as opposed to behaviors performed by entire groups. One recent article explored attributions to groups and individuals (Menon et al. 1999), but it focused on ascriptions of dispositions when assigning responsibility, still several steps removed from a general study of group behavior explanations. The literature on theory of mind, too, has limited itself to the social cognition of individuals. Inferences about beliefs, desires, and intentions are always considered to be inferences about a single person's mind, and hardly any research has examined whether and when children ascribe mental states to groups (Ames et al. 2001).

One might wonder whether this omission appropriately reflects a reality in which people don't ascribe mental states to groups and, likewise, don't explain group behaviors. However, just a brief glance at the news media casts doubt on this claim: Countries, governments, sports teams, interest groups, genders, and ethnicities are all described as performing actions and as having mental states. Consider just a small set of examples, taken from a newspaper, a newscast, and a web site, respectively.

(8-1)   The executives were not forced to resign but left because of the company's financial problems and because they had limited decision-making power. (Stoughton 1999)

(8-2)   Democrats, I think, would ultimately like to keep Trent Lott in there, no matter what they're saying now, because he's a good target. (Lehrer 2002c)

(8-3)   While China wants an official apology, and desires the world to know about the largest single city massacre in the history of the world, Japan is simply annoyed that people are still dwelling on what is to her a "hazy past." (Cook 2002)

In a sense it is surprising that the literatures on behavior explanation and theory of mind have attended so little to group agents, given that both these literatures have taken significant inspiration from philosophy of mind, where the topic of collective action and collective intentionality has received ample attention (e.g., Bratman 1993; Clark 1994; M. Gilbert 1989; Searle 1990, 1995; Tuomela 1995; Tuomela and Miller 1998; Wilson 2001; Zaibert 2003). However, a number of philosophers deny the existence of "group minds" (e.g., Searle 1990). Perhaps as a result of such philosophical skepticism, or perhaps due to their own skepticism (since Allport 1924), psychologists have found little value in pursuing the topics of group agency and group minds. But it is of course unimportant whether there really are group minds in the world. What counts is whether people ascribe mental states to groups and explain groups' behaviors by reference to mental states. There should be little doubt that they do.

I will assume, as a working hypothesis, that people use their folk theory of mind to make sense of groups just as they use this folk theory to make sense of individuals. If so, then group behavior explanations should display the same distinctions and parameters that we have documented for explanations of individual behavior. That is, people will see groups as agents (Morris, Menon, and Ames 2001); distinguish intentional from unintentional group behavior; explain unintentional group behavior with causes; explain intentional group behavior either with reasons, causal history factors, or enabling factors; and select reasons as the beliefs or desires that the group agent was aware of and in light of which the group decided to act.

But not all groups are alike (Lickel, Hamilton, and Sherman 2001). College graduates, ethnic groups, or nations comprise individuals that are at best loosely connected to each other. Members of a work group, a decision board, or a family are more tightly connected. Ascribing reasons to the latter groups is more compelling because the social perceiver can more clearly picture the reasoning process that the group as a whole underwent—such as the family members weighing their beliefs and desires and making a joint decision to act. In the case of a precinct's voting behavior, a welfare institution providing a service, or an ethnic group striving for equal rights, the image of a coherent agent or joint decision process is more difficult to maintain.

In the following sections I begin with a brief overview of psychological research on the social perception of groups and collect useful insights from this literature on two main questions: Do people in fact explain group behaviors the same way they explain individual behaviors? And if so, what are the limits of this likeness? With these insights in hand I then discuss potential social consequences of group behavior explanations in propaganda and political discourse.

8.1   Social Perception of Groups

The last ten years have seen a rapid increase in research on the social perception of groups (e.g., Abelson et al. 1998; Brewer and Harasty 1996; Brewer, Weber, and Carini 1995; Hamilton and Sherman 1996; McConnell, Sherman, and Hamilton 1997). Whereas previous research on stereotyping, prejudice, and ingroup–outgroup attitudes focused on the social perception of individual group members, the novel perspective has turned to whole groups as the targets of social perception. One question guiding this work has been whether people perceive groups as coherent and unified entities similar to the way they see individuals as such entities (Campbell 1958). The general consensus is that people often do, and the perception of groups as entities is typically referred to as perceived "entitivity."[1]

Donald Campbell (1958) characterized entitivity as a function of a group's proximity and similarity among members, joint movement, and common fate. The first wave of research in the 1990s, however, focused more on the coherence and unity of group impressions, and such coherence is typically characterized in terms of trait inferences (e.g., Hamilton and Sherman 1996). The conceptualization of entities as a coherent structure of traits has a long tradition in social psychology. At least since Jones and Davis (1965) researchers have assumed that people divide the causes of all behavior into dispositions (enduring traits) and situations (see D. T. Gilbert 1995; Shaver 1975). Traits are taken to be people's "way of packaging the behavior of others" (Hastorf, Schneider, and Polefka 1970, p. 59) and as the "lay view of behavior" (Nisbett 1980, p. 109). People appear to readily ascribe traits to individuals (Ross, Amabile, and Steinmetz 1977) and do so because they regard individuals as coherent entities (Hamilton and Sherman 1996). The question then becomes to what extent people see groups, too, as having traits and, hence, being coherent entities.

Research suggests that groups are overall perceived as less "entitive" (i.e., less coherent) than individual persons. When perceivers face a group, they infer less extreme traits from behavior than when they face an individual (Susskind et al. 1999). Perceivers also recall less information about group behaviors than about individual behaviors and base their impression more on memory than on "on-line" processing (McConnell, Sherman, and Hamilton 1994). And when perceivers receive initial information about a target and then find this information disconfirmed, they are more ready to adjust their initial impressions if the target was a group rather than if it was an individual (Weisz and Jones 1993).

It makes intuitive sense that groups, compared to individuals, are seen as less coherent overall, because there is more variation possible when several individuals are bound together (even if they are similar in some respects) than there is variation within a single individual. But is this difference in coherence best described as a difference in how easily traits can be ascribed to the two types of targets? Do social perceivers really conceptualize the unity of groups in terms of traits, just looser bundles of traits than they assume in individuals?

In the chapters of this book so far, which focused on the social perception of individuals, I have presented evidence that (a) traits play only a minor role in people's conceptual framework of mind and behavior (chapter 2), (b) traits are used rather infrequently in folk explanations of behavior (section 7.6), and (c) when traits are used in explanations, it is often because the explainer has intimate information about the target agent. Considering this limited role of traits in the context of individual behavior explanations, it is rather unlikely that traits should play a far more substantial role in the explanation of group behavior.

We can more directly examine the limitations of the trait approach to group perception by considering how the trait notion handles variations in perceived entitivity. Recent research has shown that people see some groups as more coherent, or more entitylike, than other groups (e.g. Hamilton, Sherman, and Lickel 1998; Lickel et al. 2000). These variations appear to be shaped by such factors as physical proximity, group size, communication among members, and common fate (Brewer and Harasty 1996; Campbell 1958; Knowles and Bassett 1976; Lickel et al. 2000; Wilder and Simon 1998; Yzerbyt, Rogier, and Fiske 1998). Surely, willingness to ascribe traits to a group is not the fundamental force that directs variations in such coherence-shaping features as physical proximity, communication, and common fate. Rather, willingness to ascribe traits is likely a consequence of perceived entitivity (Yzerbyt, Rogier, and Fiske 1998), which is itself a consequence of those coherence-shaping factors.

A second wave of research on group perception has indeed turned away from a trait-based conceptualization of group entitivity and focused more on joint goals and interaction within groups (e.g., Abelson et al. 1998; Lickel et al. 2000; Welbourne 1999; Wilder and Simon 1998). In line with this trend, I suggest that the key concept that helps account for perceptions of coherence in groups and for group behavior explanations is the concept of agency (Abelson et al. 1998; Morris, Menon, and Ames 2001; O'Laughlin and Malle 2002).

As detailed in chapter 2, the conceptualization of human beings as agents is a fundamental and early-developing aspect of social cognition. According to this conception, individual agents are self-propelled, capable of intentional action, and have mental states as reasons to guide those actions. Applied to the domain of group perception, we should expect that a group is considered an agent if it is seen, qua group, as self-propelled, capable of intentional action, and guided by its mental states.

This consideration of perceived group agency has two important implications. First, a group-as-agent will be perceived as highly coherent if it is seen as "unitized" by group-level beliefs, desires, and intentions—mental states that *the group* had when preparing to act. As a corollary, variations in perceived coherence should be associated with variations in features of agency. The more a group can be considered a self-propelled intentional agent who acts on the basis of its own reasons, the more the group will be seen as coherent and entitive.

Second, when a group performs an intentional action, people will be able to use the same tools of explanation that they use for individual actions—

reasons, causal histories, and so on. Reason explanations are of particular importance, because they ascribe mental states of deliberating and deciding to the whole group—precisely the image of a "group mind" that some philosophers have shunned. The following sections examine these two implications in turn.

8.2 Aggregate and Jointly Acting Groups

I have argued that when a group seemingly acts as an agent, people will have the most powerful perceptions of unity and coherence for that group— perceptions that closely resemble those observed for individuals. For example, singular names for nations are often used to convey a unity that makes a group action sound like an individual's action. Consider the following claims about Japan's handling of the massacre in the Chinese town of Nanking in 1937 (Cook 2002):

(8-4)   But in the case of the Rape of Nanking, instead of learning from past mistakes and crimes, Japan hides it, or worse, denies it. By doing so, it creates tensions within Sino–Japanese relations, it affects the world's perception of Japan, and it prevents Japan's younger generations from understanding the full implication of their country's role in World War II.

Even an entire political movement can be depicted as a unified agent, as in the following passage by Secretary of State Dean Acheson (1951, p. 272):

(8-5)   The real significance of the North Korean aggression lies in this evidence that, even at the resultant risk of starting a third world war, communism is willing to resort to armed aggression, whenever it believes it can win.

When the label used for a group agent is a plural noun, the implication of a tightly organized unit can be conveyed just as easily, illustrated by this news analysis dialogue (Lehrer 2003):

(8-6)   (LEHRER) . . . Why are the Democrats filibustering a Latino [appointee to the U.S. appellate court]? (SHIELDS) Democrats feel, I think, they have to make their own case, that they can make the case themselves that they stand for the Latinos as opposed to George W. Bush. . . . And the Democrats don't think they'll suffer as much among the broader population because it's an appellate court nomination.

Senate Democrats are treated here as a unified agent who feels and thinks, a coherent group that acts on the basis of its jointly deliberated reasons and plans.

Some descriptions of group actions make explicit how the members of a coherent group are seen as acting *together*. In this excerpt from the libertarian *New American Magazine*, William Norman Grigg (1996) quotes Admiral Chester Ward as characterizing the Council on Foreign Relations (CFR) as follows:

(8-7) [The] CFR, *as such*, does not write the platforms of both political parties or select their respective presidential candidates, or control U.S. defense and foreign policies. But CFR members, as individuals, acting in concert with other individual CFR members, do.

The Admiral appears to reject the idea of a mythical conspiracy and instead links political control to individual members, but he powerfully invokes the notion of an organized, jointly acting group of individual CFR members.

Not all groups, however, are seen as unified agents. Many groups are described as performing "plural actions" with no implication that the group acted as one. For example, a financial analyst describes a time when "people would buy stock because their hairdresser's second husband suggested it" (Lehrer 2002c); there is no doubt in the audience that all these people acted independently of each other. Another analyst speaks of unemployed people "who say that they are available to work, they would like to work, but they haven't looked because they just feel that there are no jobs there for them" (Lehrer 2002b). Again, the implication is clear that the people in this collection acted similarly but independently of each other (if with similar reasons, or so the analyst suggests). In such cases, the group referred to is really an aggregate of many individuals who each operate as separate agents and thus do not deliberate, plan, decide, or act together-as-one.

We must therefore distinguish between two types of group representations (O'Laughlin and Malle 2002). Closest to the concept of an individual agent is the notion of a *jointly acting group*, in which the members deliberate, decide, and act together as a unified group agent (e.g., a board decides on a policy or a family prepares for a picnic).[2] By contrast, in *aggregate groups* the members all perform the same action but do so independently as a mere collection of individual agents (e.g., CEOs nationwide cut down company benefit packages; American families prepare for the fourth of July picnic).[3]

Members of jointly acting groups have to be in proximity to one another in order to communicate and interact with each other in reasoning about a joint action. Moreover, they will have to share at least some goals and some beliefs to arrive at a joint intention to act. Finally, they cannot be too large, or else their joint planning and acting will fail. Thus, jointly acting groups naturally incorporate such critical features of "entitivity" as proximity, communication, common purpose, and moderate size (Campbell 1958; Knowles and Bassett 1976; Lickel et al. 2000; Wilder and Simon 1998; Welbourne 1999). The prototype of a highly entitive group then is a jointly acting group. One might even wonder whether the notion of entitivity merely re-describes with a more technical term people's folk concept of agency as applied to groups. Be that as it may, we do now have an *explanation* for why proximity, communication, size, and common goals are factors that make people's perception of coherence and entitivity more likely—because these are the very factors that allow a group to jointly plan and act.

Members of aggregate groups, by contrast, do not have to be in proximity to one another; they do not have to communicate with each other; and they neither deliberate nor make plans together as an organized unit. Rather, members of aggregate groups independently deliberate and decide to act, each member based on his or her own reasons. The perceiver literally aggregates these independent members into a (linguistic) group category, such as "high school seniors," "college athletes," or "yuppies." What elicits this aggregation is a complicated problem akin to the question of how people form social categories (Krueger and Rothbart 1990; Rothbart and Park in press). Reacting to superficial similarities, cognitive economy, and overgeneralization may each play a role. Regardless, what is most important for our purposes is that people see aggregate groups as qualitatively different from jointly acting groups.

This model of group perception has much in common with the research on group entitivity reviewed in the previous section, but it also differs in two important respects. First, the distinction between aggregate and jointly acting groups is taxonomic, whereas many entitivity researchers accept an "entitivity continuum" (Hamilton, Sherman, and Lickel 1998). I do believe that people, if asked to, can judge groups along such a continuum, but I also believe that in their everyday cognition and explanation of group behavior people rely primarily on the distinction between aggregates and joint agents. In much the same way, people can judge the intentionality of behaviors along a continuum (and actually show very high agreement in these judgments), but there is every reason to believe that they use the dichotomous distinction between intentional and unintentional behavior when solving everyday problems of social cognition and behavior explanation (Malle 1999; Malle and Knobe 1997a; Malle, Moses, and Baldwin 2001b). In fact, Lickel et al. (2000) analyzed people's continuous judgments of entitivity for a large number of groups and empirically derived a taxonomy of four group types—intimacy groups, task groups, social categories, and loose associations—that can be readily classified into the joint agent category (intimacy and task groups) and the aggregate category (social categories and loose associations).

A second difference between the entitivity approach and the agency approach is that entitivity is treated a bit more like a stable group trait, whereas joint agency is context specific (O'Laughlin and Malle 2002). For example, one and the same high-entitive task group (such as a design team) may be seen as a joint agent in one context (when it decides on a project schedule) and as an aggregate in another (when all team members work hard at their desks). Thus, when groups are viewed as performing actions in particular circumstances, their abstract entitivity may be psychologically less relevant than their contextualized status as aggregates or joint agents.

If we adopt this working model of two kinds of groups—those that are perceived as unified agents and those that are mere aggregations of individual agents—we can begin to ask what consequences this distinction has for people's explanations of group behavior.

8.3   Differences between Individual and Group Behavior Explanations

In light of the above considerations, a fruitful approach to the issue of group behavior explanations is to distinguish among three types of targets—individuals, aggregate groups, and jointly acting groups—and examine whether people's behavior explanations differ for these targets. But the folk-conceptual theory of explanations requires us not just to examine "differences in explanations" but to select specific parameters of explanation. Are we investigating intentional or unintentional behaviors? If intentional, are we investigating the reason–CHR choice or the relative use of enabling factors? And so on.

With regard to the first selection choice, we have favored intentional over unintentional behaviors. For one thing, from an observer perspective intentional behaviors are more frequently attended to, explained, and evaluated (Malle and Knobe 1997b; Malle and Pearce 2001; Shaver 1985); and this pattern should hold for any agent, whether singular or plural. In addition, pilot testing in our laboratory showed that it is difficult to identify a sufficient number of unintentional stimulus behaviors that can be reasonably performed by both groups and individuals (except for unintended consequences of intentional behaviors). Of course, interesting questions could be posed about the explanation of unintentional group behaviors, such as the degree of falsely ascribed intentionality as a function of ingroup–outgroup status (see Abelson et al. 1998). However, a first investigation of differences in individual and group behavior explanations does well to focus on intentional behaviors.

With regard to the second selection choice, we should favor examining the distinction between reason explanations and causal history explanations and, at least provisionally, set enabling factors aside. Enabling factors are a bit too rare in social discourse and too question specific to promise interesting individual–group differences. In addition, the distinction between reasons and causal histories allows us to derive fairly precise predictions because the processes that drive the reason–CHR choice in general (see chapter 5) are very much applicable to the question of individual versus group agent explanations. (Once this investigation bears fruit, we can ask next whether there are any differences at the level of belief and desire reasons or at the level of mental state markers.)

Guided by these considerations, Matt O'Laughlin and I conducted a series of studies to examine differences between individual and group behavior explanations with respect to the reason–causal history choice (O'Laughlin and Malle 2002). Our experiments were designed to test two hypotheses: that behavior explanations of individuals differ from those of aggregate groups (hypothesis one) and that behavior explanations of aggregate groups differ from those of jointly acting groups (hypothesis two).

8.3.1 Hypothesis 1: Individuals versus Aggregate Groups

As specified in chapter 5, reason explanations are the default response to why-questions about intentional actions, with 84% of such explanations containing at least one reason (Malle 1999; Malle et al. 2000). The other mode of explaining intentional action consists of offering causal histories of reasons. This mode is less frequent, but under certain conditions CHR explanations can substantially increase in frequency. Two of these conditions are of particular importance here, because they suggest that aggregate group actions will elicit a higher number of CHR explanations than will individual actions.

The first condition falls under the category of judged behavior attributes (see section 5.2.4). Specifically, CHR explanations should increase when a why-question is directed at a trend of action rather than a singular action. A trend consists of either a single agent performing multiple actions or multiple agents performing a single action. Because reasons are designed to capture a particular agent's deliberations that favor performing a particular action, behavior trends are not especially well explained by reasons. It would be cumbersome to identify each specific reason that favored each action in a trend—either the single agent's multiple actions or the multiple agents' single action. Due both to cognitive economy and conversational principles (Grice 1975), explainers will therefore seek out a parsimonious account of the entire trend of actions without having to enumerate each and every action's reasons. Citing a causal history factor is such an account.

The second condition falls under the category of information resources. When explainers do not have specific information about the particular agent performing the particular action, they will try to recruit general information that is available about the type of agent or the type of action performed.[4] General information, such as about the agent's traits, the situational context, or the historical background of the action, is best expressed in CHR explanations. For example:

(8-8)   Why didn't she speak to him?—**The dynamics of their relationship has always been peculiar** [CHR].

The explainer apparently did not know the agent's specific reasons for not speaking to the other person, but he had general information available about the broader context of the action, which he used to construct a CHR explanation.

Applying these two conditions to the comparison between individual and aggregate group actions, we can predict an increase of CHR explanations for aggregate group actions. Such group actions (e.g., "More than half of Americans did not vote in the presidential election") involve multiple agents who act with multiple different reasons, in which case causal history factors would present a parsimonious explanation ("The political process is in shambles"). Moreover, aggregate group actions readily activate general (often stereotypic) information about groups' social conditions, action tendencies, and dispositional attributes (e.g., Devine 1989; Reicher, Hopkins, and Condor 1997; Wittenbrink, Gist, and Hilton 1997), which are likely to be expressed in CHR explanations ("Americans don't care about politics").

To test this hypothesis we presented participants with a series of actions that were described as having been performed either by an individual or by an aggregate group (see table 8.1). For each action, participants wrote down their explanations, which were framed as answers to somebody's conversational question as to why the group/individual performed the given action. All explanations were classified by two coders into the reason/CHR categories (κ's = .84 to .88), using the F.Ex coding scheme of folk explanations (F.Ex 1998; see appendix).

The results supported the first hypothesis: Whereas per-behavior explanations for individuals contained 0.5 CHRs and 1.1 reasons, explanations for groups contained 0.8 CHRs and 1.0 reasons.

If both postulated conditions (action trend and information limitations) produce the increase in causal history explanations for aggregate group actions, we should be able to eliminate that CHR increase by eliminating either one of its favoring conditions. For one thing, when explainers have action- or context-specific information available about an aggregate group, they should be less likely to use a large number of CHR explanations (at least in cases when that information suggests common reasons across the whole

Table 8.1
Sample targets and actions used in O'Laughlin and Malle (2002, study 1)

Nina/ High School seniors	used drugs
Tonya/ Native Americans	opened a casino
Joe/ Males	voted Republican
James Thuton/ Inner City Youth	Committed murder
Sara/ High School Students	Attempted suicide

group aggregate). One instance in which explainers have a greater level of specific information holds when they are themselves members of the aggregate group:

(8-9)   Everyone just let everything out. *Why?* **We all knew there was a problem** [reason] and **we all care about each other** [CHR] so **we knew we just needed to talk it out** [reason].

(8-10)   There was an awkward pause and we both hung up. *Why?* **We could see the conversation was going nowhere** [reason].

From a data set of more than one thousand explanations (Malle, Knobe, and Nelson 2004), we culled explanations people had given for aggregate group actions from this "we" perspective and contrasted them with explanations for aggregate group actions from the "they" perspective (O'Laughlin and Malle 2002, table 5). Supporting the predicted role of information resources, social perceivers used only 0.1 CHRs and 1.5 reasons when explaining group actions from the "we" perspective, compared to 1.1 CHRs and 0.9 reasons when explaining group actions from the "they" perspective.

The second attempt to eliminate the CHR increase for group actions started with the observation that CHR explanations are recruited for explaining group actions that are behavior trends. If a group action were not a trend but one unified action, then CHR rates should not increase because the group's action can be parsimoniously explained by shared reasons that led the group to act as one. This consideration led to our second hypothesis.

8.3.2   Hypothesis 2: Aggregate versus Jointly Acting Groups

CHR explanations for aggregate groups are more frequent, we argued, in part because the target of explanation is a set of agents performing the same behavior but presumably for different reasons. The situation is different when the behavior of jointly acting groups is explained. Such groups deliberate and act together as one unified agent and may therefore be seen as having their own group-level reasons for acting (M. Gilbert 1989). As a result, an explainer could parsimoniously explain the group's action by their joint reasons.

Two data sets support this prediction (O'Laughlin and Malle 2002, study 3). In an experimental study, we constructed sets of four behaviors that were described as being performed either by an aggregate group (e.g., "High school seniors nationwide vandalized the high school gym") or by a jointly acting group ("The seniors at Davis H.S. vandalized the high school gym"). Participants explained one set or the other. The results showed that jointly acting groups elicited significantly fewer CHRs ($M = 0.2$) and somewhat more reasons ($M = 1.0$) than aggregate groups did ($Ms = 0.5$ CHRs, 0.9 reasons).

The second data set was again culled from a series of separate studies (Malle, Knobe, and Nelson 2004), this time selecting explanations of aggregate groups and jointly acting groups ($\kappa = 0.85$) and coding them for the reason–causal history distinction. Supporting our hypothesis, aggregate groups elicited a significantly higher number of CHR explanations ($M = 1.1$) and fewer reasons ($M = 0.9$) than did jointly acting groups ($Ms = 0.2$ CHRs, 1.2 reasons).

8.3.3 Interim Conclusion

The reported studies document that people have no difficulties ascribing reasons—that is, mental states that are rational grounds for acting—to whole groups, whether aggregate or jointly acting. On average, explanations for group actions contain about one reason per behavior explained, slightly more than they contain causal histories. Thus, the working hypothesis that social perceivers use the same conceptual framework (their folk theory of mind and behavior) for explaining groups as they do for explaining individuals has received substantial support, and the claim that people credit "plural subjects" with minds (M. Gilbert 1989) can hardly be doubted.

Beyond the important similarity of individual and group explanations, however, systematic differences exist as well. First, explanations of aggregate group actions elicit more CHR explanations than do explanations of individual actions. This discrepancy appears to be due to differential information resources (social perceivers tend to have more general than specific information available about aggregate groups compared to individuals, inviting more CHR explanations) and due to their handling of action trends (social perceivers frequently use CHR explanations to parsimoniously explain such trends). Second, whereas actions performed by aggregate groups elicit an increase in CHR explanations, actions performed by jointly acting groups do not. Such groups are seen as deliberating, planning, and acting together as one agent, which requires no managing of action trends and makes reasons more easily available to explainers.

One remaining question is how explanations of jointly acting groups compare to explanations of individual agents. Surprisingly, we found in two data sets that explanations for jointly acting groups showed even *fewer* CHRs (and somewhat more reasons) than did explanations for individuals, though both showed significantly fewer CHRs than did aggregate groups (see figure 8.1). This finding cannot be an artifact of unusually low levels of knowledge about the individuals in question, because the pattern held across known and unknown individuals; and it cannot be a simple artifact of methodology, because the pattern was consistent across experimentally elicited and spontaneously uttered explanations.

Interpreting the particularly high rate of reasons for jointly acting groups is challenging without further study, but a few intriguing possibilities suggest themselves. To begin, a jointly acting group's reasoning process may be particularly salient or easily imaginable because joint deliberation and joint decision are the key features social perceivers use to identify this type of group. If this is correct, then reasons should decrease to the extent that the group's joint deliberation and decision making are downplayed.

Moreover, a jointly formed group intention has presumably overcome the different interests of various group members and might therefore be seen as stronger than an individual's intention. Highlighting the diverging

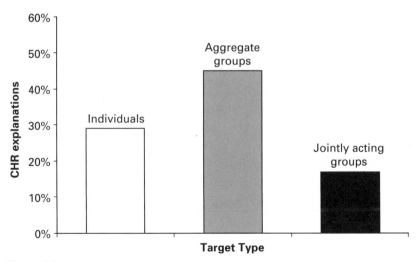

Figure 8.1
Rates of CHR explanations across three different target groups.

interests that have been integrated in a joint decision should therefore further increase the use of reasons.

Finally, the high level of organization attributed to jointly acting groups may be interpreted as a powerful determination to act, which then directs attention toward the elements that best reflect this determination: intentions and reasons. Portrayals of tight levels of organization and action readiness should therefore increase the number of reasons ascribed to jointly acting groups.

8.4 The Social Function of Group Behavior Explanations

I now turn from the cognitive question of how people represent groups and, through explanations, find meaning in their actions to the genuinely social question of how people use behavior explanations to manage an audience's impression of a particular group. This social aspect of explanations, important in the case of individual targets, may be even more important in the case of group targets because people interact less with groups than they talk about them, which renders verbal commentaries a prominent source of information. One need only observe the numerous descriptions of group behaviors in the news media and consider how few of these descriptions are matched by anybody's actual interaction with the described group *as a whole* (e.g., the Iraqis, the House Democrats, troops deployed in the Pacific, survivors of an earthquake in India, and so on). Most of the time, people talk about groups, especially aggregate groups, without ever interacting with them. As a result, people form impressions of these groups, not on the basis of interacting with them and building up meaningful representations of their actions and motives, but on the basis of other people's descriptions, conjectures, and explanations (cf. Hirschfeld 1994).

If these considerations are correct, explanations of group behavior will have a significant impact on the social cognition of groups. In the following sections I focus on two major aspects of such group cognition: the perception of unity or joint agency and the development and maintenance of stereotypes.

8.4.1 Perceptions of Group Unity and Agency
If behavior explanations differ systematically by type of group, as section 8.3.2 suggested, then the mode of explanation that the explainer selects

(CHR or reason) may be able to shape the perception of a group's unity and joint agency. That is, in the case of an action description that does not by itself imply joint agency, the offering of a reason explanation should lead to greater perception of unity than the offering of a causal history explanation. Systematic empirical investigations of this hypothesis are not yet available, but it is easy to imagine the kinds of stimuli that would be needed to test this hypothesis:

(8-11)   Number Five Group Air Force Bombers raided Dresden **because the allied strategic air offense was progressing toward the Eastern front** [CHR].

(8-12)   Number Five Group Air Force Bombers raided Dresden **because they wanted to break the German soldiers' will to resist** [reason].

The prediction is that people faced with the first, causal history explanation should form an impression of the bombers as a sizable aggregate, bound together merely by their role in the larger military operation, whereas people faced with the second, reason explanation should form an impression of the bombers as more of a jointly acting group.

Assuming that the mode of explanation can alter people's impressions of groups as more or less united (i.e., jointly planning and acting), what consequences does this heightened perception of unity have?

Abelson and colleagues (1998) argued that jointly acting groups are seen as particularly menacing, and Insko, Schopler, and Sedikides (1998) suggested that there may be a biological predisposition in humans to distrust other groups, especially those that are coordinated and tightly organized as a unit. Communicators should therefore portray groups as jointly acting units when they want to instill in an audience feelings of fear and rejection of that group or when they express their own such feelings. Indeed, Robert Jervis (1976) documented that conflicting nations display a bias to see each other's behavior as more coordinated and centrally planned than it really is. He writes: "If two actors simultaneously increase their hostility toward a third, the latter will believe they are acting in concert even if there is evidence that such cooperation is unlikely" (pp. 321–322). And a "state's behavior is usually seen as centrally controlled rather than as the independent actions of actors trying to further their own interests" (p. 324).

Often, however, it is not cognitive bias that leads to perceptions of unity but rather cunning propaganda. For example, in justifying the impending attack on Poland in 1939, Hitler reportedly characterized the Eastern neighbor in this way (United States 1946, p. 390):

(8-13)   In spite of treaties of friendship, Poland has always had the secret intention of exploiting every opportunity to do us harm.

The tactic of portraying the hated group as highly organized, scheming, and jointly acting is used by propagandists of many colors. Here are two examples from an antihomosexual document (Baron 2003), both of which emphasize the alleged tight organization of the "homosexual movement."

(8-14)   There is no single reason the media increasingly refers to homosexuals as gay rather than queer. But one reason is undoubtedly that the homosexual movement is extremely well organised, and has made powerful allies and friends who lobby on its behalf and as a quid pro quo.

(8-15)   In recent months, the organized homosexual movement has been lobbying vociferously, and sometimes violently, for a reduction in the age of consent.

The device of ascribing group intentions and group agency is of course not limited to right-wing propagandists. Australian undergraduate students discussing "race relations in Australia" strategically used the portrayal of agency when describing Aboriginal people (Augoustinos, Tuffin, and Rapley 1999). For most of the discussion, students characterized Aboriginal people as primitive, passive, and dead weights (which is akin to the denial of agency), but when it came to discussing colonial history, the portrayal suddenly turned to Aborigines as active agents (e.g., "they *keep bringing up the point* that umm they were here sort of in Australia before the British"; ibid., p. 360, emphasis added). Both passive and active portrayals can reveal negative attitudes, but a characterization of passivity reveals feelings of pity or disdain whereas a characterization of intentional agency reveals feelings of apprehension and, in some cases, dread.

In legal contexts, too, an attorney may want to portray a group of people as jointly acting—for example, to highlight that a defendant acted out of self-defense against a threatening, coordinated group of attackers. Conversely, a prosecutor may want to emphasize coordination ("conspiracy") among individual defendants committing a series of crimes. In a powerful example from history, the Allied prosecutors in the Nürnberg indictments treated the twenty-four principal Nazi war criminals as a group of *conspira-*

tors—a jointly acting group. Even though some of the criminals had actually worked together in creating and maintaining the reign of Nazi terror, the group as a whole, strictly speaking, probably never deliberated, planned, and acted jointly. Understandably, however, the prosecutors' aim was to paint the picture of a coherent, organized group agent, as the following examples illustrate.[5] Note the emphasis on phrases of planning ("aims and purposes," "prepared to seize," "program") and on desires reasons ("in order to," "designed to"), underscoring the motivation, resolution, and intentionality of the collective atrocities.

(8-16)   In order to accomplish their aims and purposes, the Nazi conspirators prepared to seize totalitarian control over Germany to assure that no effective resistance against them could arise within Germany itself. (International Military Tribunal 1947, p. 31 [count IV. (D) 1.])

(8-17)   Implementing their "master race" policy, the conspirators joined in a program of relentless persecution of the Jews, designed to exterminate them. (Ibid., p. 33 [count IV. (D) 3. (d)])

At some point in the Nürnberg indictment we can also observe an expansion of the group agent's boundaries, from the conspirators to Germans in general, accompanied by the same powerful phrases of purpose and intentional agency:

(8-18)   At the beginning of 1944, in the Ozarichi region of the Bielorussian SSR, before liberation by the Red Army, the Germans established three concentration camps without shelters, to which they committed tens of thousands of persons from the neighbouring territories. They intentionally brought many people to these camps from typhus hospitals, for the purpose of infecting the other persons interned (ibid., p. 48 [count III. (A) 2. (a)])

A particularly powerful technique for increasing perceptions of unity is to use singular nouns when referring to whole groups. I mentioned earlier the common practice of labeling nations and organizations with a singular term. Yet more striking is the use of the singular for social or ethnic groups— a case when, in the perceiver's representation, the typical group member merges completely with the group as a whole (cf. Rothbart and John 1985). For example, at the end of World War II many people in Central Europe were deeply afraid of "the Russian" (in Germany and Austria, they called "him" *der Russ)*. Just a few decades earlier, anti-Semitic propaganda disparaged "the Jew" (e.g., Schulz and Frercks 1934). And around the same time in the United States, racist propaganda spoke of "the Negro" (e.g., Dixon 1905). I don't know of any systematic exploration of singular terms for disparaged groups, but I would venture the hypothesis that the use of such terms is rare and emerges only under conditions of strong and relatively widespread social rejection of a minority. Today, for example, one finds only very few White supremacists who refer to "the Black" (e.g., Hale 2003).

So far I have argued that the portrait of a group's unity—achieved by high-lighting a group's organization and coordination and by referring directly to its reasons, intentions, and deliberate actions—is used to invoke or express perceptions of the group's menace and threat. I believe that this is by far the most frequent use. Occasionally, however, a portrayal of group agency may aim at eliciting greater admiration for the group in question. For example, in a speech delivered at the thirty-fifth anniversary of East Germany's national youth organization, communist head of state Erich Honecker (1984) emphasized the unity and togetherness of this organization:

(8-19)   On that fall evening 35 years ago, the young generation of our republic pledged its loyalty to our republic, because it "wanted to, and will, bring peace and a better life."

What both the admiring and the disparaging portrayals of group agency have in common is that the perceived unity prohibits considerations of diversity—hindering the perception of group members as individuals who differ from each other (cf. Judd, Ryan, and Park 1991). This representation of groups as being of one determined mind naturally connects to the second potential function of group behavior explanations: the evocation and maintenance of stereotypes.

8.4.2   Stereotypes and Group Explanations

In the social-psychological literature, a stereotype is usually seen as a bundle of trait representations that perceivers have about a group (Ashmore and Del Boca 1981; Devine 1989; Stangor and Lange 1994). To the extent that stereotypes influence a person's explanation of group actions, we should therefore expect that behavior explanations for stereotyped groups will often refer to such traits (Tajfel 1969; Yzerbyt, Rocher, and Schadron 1997). But herein lies a puzzle. If, as concluded in the previous section, portrayals of joint group agency make a group appear of one mind and of limited diversity, should not reason explanations (which increase for jointly acting groups) be most strongly associated with stereotyping? And does this implication not contradict the literature on stereotyping?

The first thing to note is that in our studies of group explanations, just as in the studies of individual explanations, we found that only around 10% of explanations referred to traits. So whatever role traits may play in stereotypes, their role in behavior explanations is not paramount. There may be indirect ways by which stereotypic traits can influence behavior explanations. For example, to the extent that traits can be broken down into networks of beliefs, desires, and values (Kammrath, Mendoza-Denton, and Mischel 2003), we might imagine that stereotypic traits could be translated into more context-specific reason explanations of group behavior (cf. Ames et al. 2001). But the actual work in conveying an image of a group would then be done by those reason explanations.

The second point to make is that traits are not the only contents of stereotypes. For example, stereotypes can comprise social conditions, group organization, and action tendencies (Deaux and Lewis 1984; Reicher, Hopkins, and Condor 1997; Wittenbrink, Gist, and Hilton 1997), with the latter most likely captured by reference to desires, intentions, and goals. As a result of the diversity of stereotype contents, we cannot make the straightforward prediction that the presence of a strong stereotype will automatically lead to more causal history explanations (or more reason explanations, for that matter). Rather, it depends on the content of the stereotype. Stereotypes referring to broad social conditions will elicit more causal history explanations; stereotypes referring to specific action tendencies will elicit more reason explanations; and stereotypes referring to trait attributes may elicit either trait causal histories or reasons that "break down" the trait into context-specific forces. We should therefore expect to see stereotypes reflected in the full variety of behavior explanations, be they different types of reasons or different kinds of causal histories. (Conversely, any kind of behavior explanation can in principle evoke or buttress a stereotype.) This diversity, however, will only be visible once we move away from a strict trait view of stereotypes.

One variable that may systematically moderate the influence of stereotypes on group behavior explanations is the explainer's political orientation. Research suggests that people with left-wing political affinities analyze the behavior of groups at a more remote level, using sociological descriptors, whereas people with right-wing affinities analyze group behavior at a more psychological level, emphasizing individual accountability, motives, and intentions (Gaffie, Marchand, and Cassagne 1997; Pandey et al. 1982). We should therefore expect that when people with left-wing attitudes explain group behavior they will offer a substantial number of causal histories, which may refer, for instance, to social conditions. When people with right-wing attitudes explain group behavior, however, they will offer a substantial number of reason explanations, referring to specific goals the group was allegedly pursuing.

Let me illustrate this hypothesis with an example. In an anti-Semitic text, Bernard Lazare (1995/1894) wrote that "the Jew spoke the language of the country he inhabited, but he spoke it only because it was indispensable in his business transactions" (chap. 11). This is a reason explanation (an unmarked belief reason), and it alleges that Jewish people performed a deliberate cultural assimilation for the sheer purpose of economic gain. A more charitable, sociological explanation would be that Jews spoke the language of the country they inhabited "because of the monolingualism in all economic exchanges," which would be a causal history explanation.

But here, again, is a complication. For many target groups, the right-wing/left-wing difference is confounded with the difference between hostile and favorable attitudes. That is, certain target groups will elicit more hostile feelings from one political orientation but more favorable feelings from the other (contrast, for example, welfare recipients and the World Trade Organization). It would therefore be important to investigate which explanation mode predominates when, say, people with left-wing attitudes explain the behavior of a disliked group such as neo-Nazis. Does the more "remote" approach prevail such that they offer, as usual, causal history explanations? If so, are the cited causal histories still social structures or now undesirable traits? Or will, alternatively, the dislike for this target group elicit a greater number of reason explanations, portraying the group as a deliberate, malevolent agent?

Earlier I rejected the hypothesis that stereotyping is reliably associated with a particular mode of explanation, such as trait causal histories. But a broader hypothesis was recently formulated according to which group behavior explanations generally maintain stereotypes about that group (Yzerbyt, Rocher, and Schadron 1997). That may be because explanations have the power to strengthen people's confidence in the explained event (Anderson, Krull, and Weiner 1996; Koehler 1991) and because explanations remove inconsistent, stereotype-threatening information (e.g., Kunda and Oleson 1997). As one case of stereotype maintenance, consider the following excerpt from a nationalist propaganda essay, attributed to a writer from the John Birch Society (Propaganda 2003).

(8-20)   Perhaps some of these individuals accepted CFR [Council on Foreign Relations] membership without full knowledge of the organization's history and subversive goals. Perhaps others joined **because they are determined to create an all-powerful world government—run by them—that would supplant an independent America.**

The passage offers a reason explanation that makes a strong (and stereotypic) claim about the Council on Foreign Relations ("because they are determined to create an all-powerful world government"), a claim that is repeatedly found in documents promoted by the John Birch Society.[6]

Even though behavior explanations can perform stereotype-invoking and maintaining functions, this function is not limited to stereotypes but rather holds for all knowledge structures from which explainers recruit explanation-relevant information. Moreover, behavior explanations are unlikely to be the primary force in maintaining stereotypes because they are just too rare to carry this weight. To create or maintain a group stereotype through language, the methods of choice will be behavior descriptions and group predications (e.g., using trait adjectives; Maass 1999), which have both the necessary frequency and flexibility to be used in virtually any context of speech.

Another function ascribed to explanations of group behavior is that they express or evoke essentialist beliefs about the group (Yzerbyt, Rogier, and Fiske 1998). Psychological essentialism is the postulate that ordinary people assume there are "essences" that define natural kind categories, such as animals, materials, mental illnesses, or ethnic groups (Haslam and Giosan 2002; Haslam, Rothschild, and Ernst 2000; Gelman and Wellman 1991; Gil-White 2001; Medin and Ortony 1989). Some authors have argued that essentialist beliefs about social categories (e.g., men, Jews, Germans) foster stereotypes for that category (Yzerbyt, Rocher, and Schadron 1997) and that stereotypes based on essentialist beliefs are particularly difficult to change (Rothbart and Taylor 1992). Yzerbyt, Corneille, and Estrada (2001) also suggested that seeing a group as an entity (i.e., with high levels of similarity and organization among group members) will foster essentialist beliefs (and vice versa). By transitivity, we might have to conclude that seeing groups as entities will increase stereotyping.

However, the relationships among these constructs—entitivity, essentialism, and stereotyping—are complex (Hamilton, Sherman, and Rodgers in press), and the precise role of explanations within this triad is unclear. One aspect of entitivity, namely perceived similarity among group members, is likely to increase stereotyping, and it may plausibly encourage inferences about a group's "essential" characteristics. But evidence is mounting that trait similarity is not a felicitous way to conceptualize entitivity; that in fact agency and shared motives better capture people's discrimination between genuine groups and mere collections of individuals (Hamilton, Sherman, and Rodgers in press; O'Laughlin and Malle 2002; Welbourne 1999; Wilder and Simon 1998). It is doubtful that such perceptions of agency are frequently accompanied by essentialist beliefs, given that the very point of agency is a focus on context-specific beliefs, desires, and actions. Moreover, perceptions of agency do not seem to have a privileged connection to stereotypes, considering that some of the most elaborate stereotypes are for social categories that are not very agentive groups (Hamilton, Sherman, and Rodgers in press).

So where does this leave us with the alleged relation between behavior explanations and essentialism? I argued earlier that both reason explanations and causal history explanations are capable of conveying stereotypes. Of these two, causal history explanations would be ideally suited to convey an "essential" group attribute (whereas reasons will be too context bound to have the causal force and inferential richness expected of an essence). At the same time, Yzerbyt and colleagues (2001) have claimed that highly entitive (i.e., jointly acting) groups are most apt to elicit essentialist beliefs. So we should expect that people offer causal history explanations to express their essentialist beliefs about these entitive/jointly acting groups. But, in fact, the opposite is the case (O'Laughlin and Malle 2002): jointly acting groups' actions are explained primarily by reasons, not by causal histories. So either behavior explanations have little to do with essentialism, or essentialism has little to do with entitivity—or both, as the following arguments seem to suggest.

Hamilton, Sherman, and Sack (2001) argued specifically against the potential connection between essentialism and entitivity. They point out that some types of groups, such as social categories like gender and ethnicity, show a relatively low degree of entitivity but a high incidence of being essentialized, whereas other types of groups, such as families and work groups, show a relatively high degree of entitivity but a low incidence of being essentialized. Of course, these counterexamples notwithstanding, there may still be a general correlation between the two variables, but the difficulty is to actually come up with groups that *do* show high entitivity and a high likelihood of being essentialized. One might have to turn to small-group societies in which one band of fifty may see a neighboring and competing band as both tightly organized and driven by essential attributes (cf. Gil-White 2001).

Another argument casts doubt on the potential connection between essentialism and behavior explanations. If we expect that certain explanations have the power to persuade the audience of a group's essence, which explanations might these be? Haslam, Rothschild, and Ernst (2000) proposed that essentialist thinking involves beliefs that a category (e.g., a social group) has a crisp boundary, necessary or defining properties, a natural basis, has endured throughout history, and comes with immutable membership. It seems difficult for a behavior explanation to convey all or even many of these rather strict requirements—a simple trait causal history, for example, would not do. Not surprisingly, therefore, a search through our database of group explanations did not uncover any obvious essentialist explanations. Furthermore, a search for examples of essentialist claims in propaganda documents brought to light very few instances of essentialist perceptions to begin with, and only a single one that even resembles a behavior explanation:

(8-21)   The causes that gave birth to this agitation, which kept it up and perpetuated it in the souls of some modern Jews, are not external causes such as the tyranny of a ruler, of a people or ferocious code: they are internal causes, i.e., such as pertain to the very essence of the Hebrew spirit. (Lazare 1995/1894, chap. 12)

In sum, we can draw four conclusions about the social functions of group behavior explanations. First, when people explain group behavior, the chosen mode of explanation (reason versus causal history) covaries systematically with the type of group considered (jointly acting versus aggregate groups). To the extent that this portrayal of group type is used to stereotype or disparage a group, explanations help in this function. Second, group stereotypes influence behavior explanations via the supply of relevant knowledge structures. However, this influence is not limited to any particular explanation mode—stereotypes can be reflected in reason explanations just as in causal history explanations (and even cause explanations). Third, the reverse influence, that of explanations on stereotypes, is much less clear. Though a behavior explanation that relies on stereotypical information will reactivate and thus perhaps maintain the underlying stereotype, behavior explanations—owing to their relative infrequency—can play only a small role in the larger process of stereotype maintenance. Fourth, there is little doubt that strongly negative attitudes toward a group can be conveyed by referring to "essences," and essentialist causal history explanations may be part of this parcel. But such essentialist behavior explanations appear to be quite rare, and inferring a deeper relationship between essentialism and behavior explanation seems, at this time, unwarranted.

9 Looking Back and Ahead

This book presents four major claims about ordinary people's explanations of behavior. First, behavior explanations are both a cognitive tool and a social tool. As a cognitive tool, behavior explanations provide meaning; as a social tool, they manage interactions.

Second, behavior explanations are embedded in a conceptual framework of mind and behavior. Within this conceptual framework, people distinguish between different types of behavior and employ different modes of explanation for each.

Third, the distinctions among these modes of explanation and their specific conceptual assumptions make up the primary (conceptual) layer of a theory of behavior explanation. The second layer encompasses both the psychological forces (such as pragmatic goals, information resources) that govern the use of each explanation mode and the cognitive mechanisms (such as inference, simulation, and information retrieval) that do the processing work when explanations are constructed. The third layer consists of the specific linguistic features of each explanation mode in a particular language and the features' concomitant psychological functions.

Fourth, this three-layered theory succeeds better than attribution theory at describing and accounting for the complex phenomena of behavior explanations.

In this last chapter I look back at each of these claims, identify open theoretical questions, and look ahead to a number of possible applications of the folk-conceptual theory of explanation.

9.1 Functions of Explanations: Meaning and Interaction Management

What does it mean that people find *meaning* in explanations? I suggested in chapter 3 that people search for meaning when a link is missing in their representation of reality—when something is "strange" in light of previous knowledge, assumptions, and expectations (Moravcsik 1998). An explanation restores coherence in the representational system by harmonizing the strange element with the previous elements (Read, Druian, and Miller 1989; Read and Miller 1998; Thagard 1989). What are, then, in Heider's (1958) words, "the psychological entities that bring consistency and meaning to . . . behavior" (p. 34)? The theory of folk behavior explanations presented here is quite specific in answering this question.

The meaning of an *unintentional* behavior lies in its causes. What does it mean that the child is coughing, the old man trembling, or the young lover stuttering? Cause explanations make unintentional events meaningful by clarifying what brought the event about—which could be a state or trait of the agent, a situational trigger or obstacle, or interactions among these factors.

The meaning of an *intentional* behavior will often lie in the action's "point" or purpose, expressed as a desire reason. If we ask, after seeing *Donnie Darko*, "What was the meaning of her waving at the dead boy's mother at the end?" we want to find out what the agent hoped to achieve by that action (show her sympathy? express her deep understanding?). More generally, people look for the meaning of an intentional action in the reasons the agent had for acting—which are the beliefs and desires in light of which the agent decided to act, the considerations that *favored* this particular action. The meaning of an action is, in other words, the role that the action plays in the agent's deliberations, how it is connected to the agent's network of beliefs and desires.

Sometimes, however, the meaning of an intentional action in terms of its reasons may be unknown or irrelevant. An explainer can then offer a causal history explanation that at least offers distal causes contributing to the action, in which case meaning lies either directly in the causal background or in the class of possible reasons that are compatible with, or are suggested by, this background. Alternatively, the meaning of an intentional action can lie in the conditions that enabled the action to be successfully performed. If I hear that my seven-year-old nephew hit several three-point baskets and if I wonder what this means, I am not wondering about his reasons but rather whether he succeeded because he practiced hard, has an unusual ability, or because the shooting distance to the basket in minileague is less than I expected.

Explanations thus provide meaning by connecting the behavior in question to other knowledge—knowledge about the agent, the situation, past events or anticipated future outcomes. This achievement of meaning occurs in the mind of the person who wondered about the behavior and is the classic cognitive function of explanations—increasing the perceiver's understanding and, as a likely benefit, prediction and control.

If finding meaning were the only function of explanations, this book would have been half its size. What demanded the other half is the social function of behavior explanations that allows people to create impressions, manage interactions, and influence social outcomes. Explanations, in this sense, are speech acts delivered in communicative exchanges. They therefore play a variety of communicative roles, such as providing meaning for another person, influencing others' beliefs about the agent or the explainer, and expressing evaluations of the action, the agent, or associated events.

Whereas the cognitive aspect of behavior explanations has been studied in the attribution and social cognition literature, the social aspect has been studied primarily in the sociological literature on accounts (e.g., Blumstein 1974; Orbuch 1998), the communication literature on rhetorical devices (e.g., Barrett 1986; Burke 1943), and the social-psychological literature on impression management (e.g., Schlenker 1980; Tedeschi and Reiss 1981) and social argument (Antaki 1994; Edwards and Potter 1993). Different names have been given to related phenomena—such as *accounts, justifications, excuses*—but these phenomena are still first and foremost explanations. They all offer a link that restores meaning, but in this case the explainer tries to create a meaningful representation in another person, often not merely to fill a cognitive gap but to smoothen the ongoing interaction, avert negative evaluations, or gain a social benefit.

One may argue that the cognitive function of explanations is primary, for an explanation may exist without serving a social function but no explanation can exist without serving a cognitive function, as there has to be *someone* who gains, or is expected to gain, meaning from the explanation. But from this primacy of the meaning function we should not conclude that the social functions are any less important. In the evolution of the human behavior explanation capacity, it may well have been the social functions that drove explanations to greater differentiation and sophistication; and in contemporary children's development of behavior explanations it may well be the communicative practice that feeds their mastery (Bartsch and Wellman

1995). Moreover, what we know of behavior explanations today we know primarily from verbally expressed explanations, and it remains to be seen whether purely private explanations (to the extent that they can be measured) show the same degree of sophistication as public explanations do.

Cognitive and social functions merge quite elegantly when explanations are used by one person to provide meaning for another. Such an act of clarification can create *shared meaning,* or shared representations of the social world (Hastorf, Schneider, and Polefka 1970; Higgins 1992; Moscovici 2001). Because explanations create meaning that is always to some extent causal, the shared meaning thereby created has multiple uses: fostering coherence in understanding a past event, providing confidence in predicting that kind of event in the future, and pointing to mechanisms that permit changing such an event.

Creating shared meaning between two people, however, requires the prior existence of a number of shared assumptions—for example, regarding the language they speak and the conceptual frameworks they bring to the situation. In the case of explaining human behavior, I argued, this shared framework is the folk theory of mind and behavior. And if that framework is shared among conversation partners and underlies communicative explanations of behavior, then, by implication, it will lay the foundation for private explanations as well. Thus, both functions of behavior explanations—finding meaning and managing interactions—are fundamentally tied to the human folk theory of mind.

9.2   The Magic of a Theory of Mind

Humans, and perhaps no other species, have the capacity to interpret behavior in terms of its underlying mental states. Such an interpretation, in its general form, is already an explanation, because behavior is seen as not only accompanied by but resulting from mental states. Thus, the theory of mind is at heart a causal-explanatory framework. However, it is also an ontological framework in that it classifies phenomena into broad categories, such as intentional action, beliefs, desires, and emotions. These categories structure perception by filtering and ordering the complex stream of human behavior, and they make this ordered information available for explanation and prediction. Because of the fundamental ties between mind and behavior within this framework, social perceivers who try to understand a particular behavior will often infer mental states to form an explanation. But the explanatory system flexibly permits other causes as well, including nonmental forces inside and outside the person.

The key contribution of the folk theory of mind lies in its conception of intentional agency. According to this concept, most living beings are seen as self-propelled and capable of purposeful actions—which are, put simply, actions that result from the organism's desires and beliefs about the world. The very concept of intentional action requires the monitoring of other people's mental states, because what drives, explains, and predicts their actions will be a particular set of desires and beliefs. As one default feature in this monitoring process, humans assume that another person has similar desires and beliefs as they have. Infants may even need such an implicit assumption of *other* = *self* to get their developing theory of mind off the ground (Goldman 2001; Harris 1992; Meltzoff and Brooks 2001). But many times the assumed similarity is proven wrong, so humans learn to amend their *self* = *other* assumption and become able to suspend it. In this way, the folk theory of mind confronts humans with the subjectivity of motivation and cognition and the ensuing individual variations in human behavior. Moreover, it also provides the tools that account for this variation—in the form of a conceptual network that guides the search for and interconnection among mental states that explain action.

Attribution and social cognition research has not paid sufficient attention to this rich conceptual framework of mind and behavior, despite Heider's groundbreaking work on some of its core elements. As a result, the unique explanation mode of *reasons* has been largely ignored in the social-psychological literature.[1] Among all explanations, reason explanations most clearly embody the influence of the folk theory of mind because they are defined as ascriptions of mental states in light of which the agent formed her intention to act. The relevant mental states are conceptually differentiated (beliefs, desires, and valuings) and are seen as resulting, by means of at least rudimentary reasoning, in the formation of an intention—another key mental state characterizing intentional action. Without a folk theory of mind, humans might still be able to provide causal explanations, even for intentional behavior, but they would be incapable of providing reason explanations.

The folk theory of mind not only organizes the social perceiver's interpretation and explanation of behavioral events but also coordinates interpersonal communication about human behavior. Using this folk theory when explaining behavior, the speaker can detect specific missing links in the other person's representation of the situation and select which kinds of elements (e.g., reasons, enabling factors, causes) will restore coherence and meaning for the other person. Selecting merely a *kind* of explanation will of course not suffice to make such a communication successful; shared knowledge about the domain at issue and about the specific context in which the behavior occurred will be needed to settle on the specific contents of, say, beliefs, desires, and causal histories.

When explanations are used as social tools to manage status, impressions, and evaluations, the conceptual framework of mind and behavior continues to be essential. The speaker will have to manipulate the other person's judgment of intentionality as well as the specifically ascribed reasons (or causes) for the behavior in question. To present an *excuse* for a negative outcome (e.g., being late) is thus often tantamount to providing a cause explanation—implying lack of intentionality—for what might otherwise be construed as an intentional behavior. When judgments of intentionality cannot be fended off, explainers must resort to *justifying* their actions—that is, offering a plausible, rational, and defensible reason explanation.

Precisely because reason explanations not only fulfill a cognitive function but also have considerable force as a social tool do people use and abuse reasons to meet social demands. What sounds like a "good reason" can compel a conversation partner to do unusual things (Langer, Blank, and Chanowitz 1978) or convince a decision maker to take a surprising course of action (Shafir, Simonson, and Tversky 1993; Simonson and Nowlis 2000). The desire to appear rational can be so strong that reason explanations are effectively invented, or constructed from plausible assumptions (Wilson et al. 1989), even if the behavior in question is not obviously an intentional action. One's professed "reasons" for holding a certain view, attitude, or value, are rarely the actual beliefs and desires that led one to intentionally adopt that view (because one probably did not adopt that view deliberately and intentionally) but rather the best-sounding answers to a face-threatening question such as "Why do you love her?," "Why do you support the war?," or "Why do you like strawberry jam?" But this abuse of reasons should not mislead us into believing that all reason explanations are mere rationalizations and inventions for the purpose of impression management. Only because they normally carry meaning and hold up to scrutiny can reason explanations occasionally be used for distorting social functions; and only if they conform to the rules of the folk theory of mind can reason explanations achieve their meaning and social management functions.

9.3   The Folk-Conceptual Theory of Explanation and Attribution Theory

For a long time, the decisive word on lay behavior explanations came from attribution theory. One goal of this book has been to persuade the reader that this decisive word was wrong. Not always, but often; not when dealing with explanations of unintentional behaviors and outcomes, but when dealing with explanations of intentional behaviors. So am I arguing for theory change? For a theoretical revolution? Revolutions rarely happen in social psychology, and the literature on attribution is so large (and the researchers familiar with the traditional theory so numerous) that only over considerable time can any new model replace attribution theory. Moreover, previous attempts at replacing it were not very successful, as the textbooks still describe mostly Kelley's covariation model, Jones's trait inference model, and person–situation attributions by perspective, self-servingness, and the like. Finally, the person–situation distinction is so seductively simple and the issue of dispositional inference so easily described and researched in the lab (using one of a handful of paradigms) that the field will be reluctant to abandon these tried approaches in favor of any alternative, especially a more complex model of explanation. Whence, then, the optimism for the theory of explanation proposed here to make a difference and perhaps eventually supersede attribution theory?

Good science has to study the phenomena as they exist, and that is where attribution theory's greatest weakness lies. In imposing a conceptual framework on folk explanations that just isn't the *people's own* framework, much of attribution research has provided data that are simplified, difficult to interpret, and have led to false conclusions. The overarching view that behavior explanations are just like causal judgments of any other event can be proven wrong rather quickly—simply by analyzing naturally occurring explanations in all their conceptual and linguistic complexity. To even describe these explanations one needs additional distinctions among modes and features of explanations, as proposed in the folk-conceptual theory (F.Ex 1998, see appendix to this vol.; Malle 1999). However, this theory not only describes but also *accounts for* many of the regularities of these modes and features of explanation, from their conditions of occurrence to some of their specific functions. Furthermore, we have been able to show that the concepts and distinctions in this new theory have predictive power when it comes to investigating impression management (Malle et al. 2000), asymmetries between individual and group targets (O'Laughlin and Malle 2002), asymmetries between actor and observer perspectives (Malle, Knobe, and Nelson 2004), and self-servingness (Nelson and Malle 2004). And whenever we analyzed the explanation data in terms of a person–situation attribution model, virtually no such predictive power was found. These findings suggest that the folk-conceptual theory better captures the breakpoints, or joints, in the framework that underlies people's behavior explanations and in the patterns they display when actually explaining behavior in private or social contexts.

But how can it be that previous research on attribution phenomena failed to uncover its own limited predictive power? I believe that this failure arose from two methodological biases. First, participants were typically asked to express their explanations on predefined person–situation rating scales rather than in the form of natural verbal utterances. As a result, people had to transform their complex explanatory hypotheses into simple ratings, which probably invited guessing strategies as to how the ratings were to be interpreted and surely led to severe ambiguities in the ensuing data. Second, in the few cases in which unfettered verbal expressions were analyzed, the coding was quite limited, often picking up no more than trends in the linguistic surface of explanations (e.g., in the use of mental state markers; McGill 1989; Nisbett et al. 1973; for evidence and discussion see Malle 1999, study 4, and Malle et al. 2000, study 4).

The shortcomings of traditional attribution theory are not confined to the conceptual level; they extend to the process level as well. The central proposition that explanations are constructed from covariation assessments (Kelley 1967) has garnered no supportive evidence except for demonstrations that people can *respond to* covariation information if provided by the experimenter. In the absence of systematic evidence for spontaneous covariation analysis, I examined samples of explanations (in section 5.3) and suggested that people rely on multiple psychological processes to construct explanations, including retrieval of general and specific knowledge, mental simulation, and occasional covariation analysis. This is an issue that has yet to be settled by empirical research, but the textbook tenet that explanations are constructed from covariation assessments is almost certainly false in its general form.

Despite my critical analysis, I don't claim that classic attribution research has contributed nothing. Quite the contrary. It posed questions and pointed to phenomena that had simply not been considered before—the power of behavior explanations in the first place (Heider 1958; Jones et al. 1972; Quattrone 1985); the many interesting factors that create systematic variations in explanation, such as actor–observer differences (Jones and Nisbett 1972), self-servingness (Bradley 1978; Heider 1958; Miller and Ross 1975), and impression management tactics (Tedeschi and Reiss 1981); and the larger network of cognitive and social antecedents and consequences of behavior explanations (Anderson, Krull, and Weiner 1996).

But these impressive results and insights of attribution research emerged *in the context* of attribution theory, not as *predicted results* of that theory. For example, nothing in Kelley's (1967) or Jones and Davis's (1965) theory predicts that there must be actor–observer asymmetries, much less that these asymmetries are of a particular kind (Knobe and Malle 2002). Likewise, none of these theories predicts impression management tactics, a self-serving bias, or other interesting phenomena. What attribution theory does explicitly claim is that people form explanations as ascriptions of person (disposition) causes versus situation causes and do so on the basis of covariation assessment. But these are precisely the tenets that were not put to the test, because no alternative predictions were even considered. In light of the data presented in this book, moreover, these predictions are quite likely false. Consequently, the most celebrated insights and findings of attribution research cannot actually be derived from attribution theory, and those patterns that can be derived either remain untested or appear to be incorrect.

How does the folk-conceptual theory of explanation fare in comparison? The central contribution of this theory is to identify the conceptual framework that underlies lay explanations of behavior, including the key role of intentionality and the resulting distinctions between modes of explanation (e.g., reasons, causal histories, enabling factors) and their specific features (e.g., beliefs, desires, mental state markers). This first, conceptual layer of the theory—directly tested and supported in recent work (Malle 1999; Malle et al. 2000)—precisely describes the tools people use to explain behavior, ties together the primary functions of behavior explanations of finding meaning and managing interactions, and clarifies a number of puzzling findings in past attribution research (see sections 4.2.5, 7.7).

In addition, the conceptual framework of behavior explanations substantially influences the psychological processes that help implement explanations as cognitive and social acts. However, the conceptual layer does
not, by itself, entail which psychological determinants govern explanatory
choices or which cognitive selection processes underlie the construction of
specific explanations. Postulates about these phenomena constitute a separate, second layer of the theory, introduced in chapter 5. For one thing, three
primary psychological determinants (judged behavior features, pragmatic
goals, information resources) guide people's choices of modes and features
of explanation, and these determinants also provide the theoretical tools to
account for actor–observer asymmetries and individual–group asymmetries
(see chapters 7 and 8). Moreover, explainers must select specific contents of
explanations in specific situations, and they do so by relying on a variety
of cognitive processes, including knowledge structures, direct recall, simulation, and covariation analysis.

The conceptual and the psychological layers of the present theory are, of
course, closely related. The primary psychological determinants are tailored
to the particular attributes of explanatory modes; for example, behavior features and information resources that elicit reason explanations are quite distinct from those that elicit enabling factors (Malle et al. 2000). Likewise, the
conceptual attributes of explanation modes put constraints on the cognitive
processes that are recruited to construct specific explanations (Knobe and
Malle 2002). Reason explanations, for example, rely on cognitive selection
processes that are quite different from those used for other modes of explanation. Which particular cognitive processes are activated in an explanation
episode also depends on the primary psychological determinants and the
explainer's perspective (actors or observer). A number of hypotheses about
these complex relations were developed in section 5.3 and remain to be
tested.

The final, linguistic layer of the folk-conceptual theory includes an analysis of the grammar of beliefs and desires and of the logic of mental state
markers (see sections 4.2.4, 6.3.3) as well as an orderly treatment of the in-
tricate connections between surface appearance and conceptual structure of
reason explanations—connections that cast serious doubts on previous attempts to study free-response explanations of behavior (see section 7.7).

Over time, more relations among the three layers of the folk-conceptual
theory will be discovered. It would of course be naive to hope for a grand

unified theory in any domain of psychology, let alone social psychology; but by distinguishing different layers of theorizing and slowly connecting these layers, we can pinpoint which layers need improvement and thus work toward a mature scientific theory.

9.4   Open Theoretical Questions

With further theoretical progress we should also be able to answer some of the questions that are left unanswered by the current formulation of the folk-conceptual theory of explanations. First, we are still lacking an exact cognitive model of the processes involved in explanation construction. At this time, we have identified the choices explainers make, from modes to types and features of explanation; three primary antecedent variables (behavior features, pragmatic goals, information resources); and a series of cognitive processes that are recruited to construct specific explanations (information retrieval, simulation, covariation analysis, etc.). Initial predictive equations describe the relationship between explanatory choices and various antecedents (table 5.1), and a series of hypotheses describe the relations between cognitive processes and specific explanation parameters (sections 5.3.1–5.3.3). But exactly how all three sets of variables—antecedents, cognitive processes, and explanation parameters—relate to each other is not yet clear. Chapter 5 offers starting points for a unified model (figures 5.2 and 5.3), but more theoretical and empirical work is needed before we can develop such a model.

Second, little is known about the behavior characteristics that pull for certain explanation modes and features. We have identified behavior intentionality and behavior difficulty as broad predictors of certain modes of explanation (e.g., reasons and enabling factors), but several other predictive characteristics remain to be uncovered. For example, what facet of behavior elicits the explainer's choice of belief reasons versus desire reasons? In chapter 5 (note 9), I speculated that initiation of movement or changes of location might often demand desire reasons, and one might expect choices between options to elicit (unmarked) belief reasons. To take another example, I recently drove in the Oregon countryside and noticed vaselike containers hanging precisely from the midpoint of wire lines (see fig. 9.1). Why were these containers hung there? The answer, I expect, that most people would search for is a desire reason[2]—the purpose of the action. Why is that?

Figure 9.1
Why were vaselike containers hung in the midpoint of these wire lines?

Another unresolved question is the relation between behavior explanations and explanations of other events (ranging from mythical to scientific, from religious to mathematical). Is there one thing called explanation? Or are there in fact many forms of causal inference, many forms of explanation (Keil and Wilson 2000)? Explanations answer questions of *why, how possible,* and *how.* There is certainly one thing that all these answers have in common: they fill a gap, solve a cognitive puzzle. But to complete any explanation, a number of other cognitive processes are necessarily engaged as well. Explanations involve memory, some modicum of audience design (even if the audience is oneself), implicit or explicit consideration of patterns, rules, or laws, and assumptions about causality (e.g., intentional versus physical causality). In addition, some explanations are based on perception, information retrieval, or inference, whereas others are based on mental simulation. Will we thus have to give up the notion of one "pure" explanatory process that holds across social and nonsocial domains? Moreover, if explanation is not one thing, there is little sense in looking for neural substrates of explanatory processes. Depending on whether explanations are based on simulation, direct recall, data-based inference, or statistical covariation detection, they will engage very different neural mechanisms. Moreover, explanations rely heavily on the conceptual framework for the domain in question (e.g., the folk theory of mind and behavior for the domain of psychological explanations) and it seems rather unlikely that there is a unique neural substrate to a conceptual framework—and even if there were one, it would be very different from the neural mechanisms of inference, simulation, or recall.

In chapter 2 we saw that research on autistic children and adults can be highly instructive when exploring the folk theory of mind. Similarly useful would be a specific investigation of autistic children's behavior explanations. For example, we would expect that autistic children do not show an early emergence of mentalistic explanations of human behavior. If, beyond that, autistic children have generalized difficulties with explaining *any* kind of event, then we would have some evidence that a theory of mind, and the mentalistic explanation of behavior it supports, is a foundational capacity for explanations in general. If, on the other hand, autistic children have no problem offering explanations of physical events and perhaps even non-mentalistic explanations of behavior, then explanation skills are not fundamentally rooted in a theory of mind but rather in a more general cognitive capacity.

Taking one step back, what is the evolutionary history of the capacity to explain? Does explanation require language? Or at least a representational system like a protolanguage? Has explanation evolved as a domain-specific capacity (e.g., to make sense of conspecifics' behaviors) and then generalized to other domains (Ostrom 1984)? Consistent with this claim (though certainly not uniquely supporting it), studies on the early emergence of verbal explanations in development point to mental state explanations of behavior as probably the very first explanations children express (Bartsch and Welman 1995; Hood and Bloom 1979; McCabe and Peterson 1988). Gopnik (2000) argues, by contrast, that the function of explanations is quite generally to reward and advance the "theory formation system"—a postulated domain-general mechanism of the mind that creates increasingly abstract models of the world.

A final question is the degree of cross-cultural variation in explanatory processes, or more specifically in behavior explanations. It may be helpful to pose this question for each of the three layers of theory—conceptual, process, and linguistic. The assumptions and concepts of mind and behavior are arguably universal, even though cultures may show differential emphasis on mental state explanations as opposed to, for example, social and relational explanations. The cognitive processes underlying behavior explanations may also be universals, but their conditions of use may not. For example, humans in all cultures will likely be capable of simulating and inferring mental states, but there could be differences in the need to use inference as a corrective for straightforward simulation. The more similar the members of a given culture are, the more reliable such straightforward simulation should be. Finally, we can expect the greatest cultural variation at the linguistic level, where languages will differ in how or even whether they express various forms and functions of explanation.

9.5   Research Applications

Attribution research has enjoyed a broad range of applications, including clinical, medical, legal, and organizational. If the folk-conceptual theory of explanation is an improvement over traditional attribution theory (at least in the domain of intentional behavior), then we should see a variety of fruitful applications of the folk-conceptual theory in the near future.

9.5.1   Psychopathology and Medicine

There is a sizable literature on the explanatory style and the causal uncertainty of depressed individuals (e.g., Seligman et al. 1979; Silverman and Peterson 1993; Weary and Edwards 1994). But the models of attribution that underlie this research have been limited to cause explanations and trait inferences. To the extent that depressed people see the social world in a biased way, they might also give different explanations for intentional behaviors, in which case the folk-conceptual theory would offer more detailed conceptual tools to study this question—distinguishing, for example, between reasons and causal histories, different types of reasons, and so on. In addition, examining the different cognitive processes that underlie these explanatory modes and types may shed some light on the actual psychological mechanisms that mediate a depressive explanatory style.

An interesting new direction is the study of explanations in paranoia and paranoid personality disorder (Harrington et al. in press; cf. Kramer 1994). One can expect that if paranoid patients believe that others are out to get them, they will be biased toward considering most events as intentional (i.e., purposefully designed by those who conspire against them) and explaining them by reasons, particularly desire reasons.

At the opposite end of the spectrum we may suspect individuals diagnosed with disorganized schizophrenia. Their neologisms and loose associations are often quite incomprehensible to others, but it would be intriguing to explore whether their explanations in general, and behavior explanations in particular, are equally incomprehensible such that other people cannot understand, even after further inquiry, the connection between the event and the explanation given by the patient. These results would be particularly telling if schizophrenia indeed entails a theory of mind deficit (e.g., Frith and Corcoran 1996; Sarfati 2000), and they would provide a test case, just as explanations by autistic children (see 9.4), for the question of whether explanatory capacities are domain general or domain specific.

Another fascinating domain in which explanations play an important role is that of medicine and healing. With the introduction of "complementary and alternative" medicine into Western societies, new theories and postulated processes of illness and healing have rapidly proliferated (Whorton 2002), and with them come different explanations of why an illness occurred (Lynch 2003). Different cultures and medical traditions rely on different causal mechanisms to account for illness, and those mechanisms have significant consequences for the kinds of treatments proposed. For example, the assumption of a chemical imbalance suggests a pharmacological treatment, the assumption of an emotional imbalance a psycho-social treatment, and the assumption of an energy imbalance an energy-healing treatment. These treatment models also account for the healer's behavior in different ways and assign distinct roles to the patient—for example, as a more passive recipient of causal interventions (surgery, in the most extreme case) or an active agent who helps eliminate the illness (e.g., by forming healing intentions). It seems likely that the complexity of explanations in this domain (for both actions and outcomes) will not be captured by a model of person–situation attributions. Rather, it calls for an approach that takes a keen interest in the conceptual and causal assumptions the involved parties make and the consequences of these assumptions both for their explanatory behavior and their actions in pursuit of treatment and healing.

9.5.2 Social Relationships and Conflicts

Attribution concepts have had a considerable impact on the study of relationships, especially the study of conflict and satisfaction in marriage (e.g., Bradbury and Fincham 1990; Fincham, Bradbury, and Grych 1990). This literature has shown some uneasiness with the narrow concepts of traditional attribution theory, but lacking a substantially different theory of explanation, researchers tended to merely incorporate more and more "attribution dimensions," ranging from locus, stability, and globality to intentionality and responsibility (e.g., Fincham, Beach, and Nelson 1987). In addition, much of this research has been conducted with measures that ask participants to rate preselected behaviors (e.g., Fincham and Bradbury 1992; Fincham, Beach, and Baucom 1987), probably because of the "enormous difficulties [we] encountered in trying to code attributions from actual dyadic (marital) interaction using standard attribution dimensions" (Brad-bury personal communication). An alternative approach based on the folk-conceptual theory of explanations would begin by examining naturally occurring behavior explanations people give for their own behavior, their partner's behavior, and other people's behavior. Separately within unin-tentional and intentional behaviors, the variety of explanation modes and features could then be assessed and in turn be related to other variables of interest, such as frequency and intensity of conflicts, relationship sat-isfaction, communication patterns, and the like. Following the example of impression management research, the folk-conceptual theory may even pre-dict specific explanatory strategies that interactants would use depending on their pragmatic goals and (motivationally biased) judgments of behavior features. To the extent that the folk-conceptual theory of explanation sheds light on phenomena like relationship dynamics and conflict resolution, it would duly reflect Heider's (1958) timeless goal of providing a *Psychology of Interpersonal Relations*.

One of the fundamental interpersonal activities enabled by a theory of mind is teaching young children. Parents and their children have to make inferences about each other's mental states and explain each other's be-haviors to make a teaching episode successful and lasting. For example, to effectively adjust their communicative behavior of demonstrating or in-structing, parents will have to determine to what extent the child is atten-tive, interested, and understands. Also, to effectively discipline their child, parents may try to explain to the child their own behavior of disciplining. Research at our department has begun to look in detail at the folk explana-tions parents give for their children's "difficult" behaviors and the rela-tionship these explanations have with a variety of other psychological and developmental variables.

In the domain of decision making, there is considerable evidence that people want to have "good reasons" when making decisions (Shafir, Si-monson, and Tversky 1993). The question is whether such a tendency is a function of people's striving for meaning or of their attempt to manage au-diences' (including experimenters') impressions. A moderating factor may be whether the decision maker has time to actively deliberate, for in that case the very process of reasoning will tend toward explanatory coherence and meaning, even without audience demands. If audience demands are present, the justification process may diverge from the actual deliberation process or perhaps even replace it.

The political domain is ripe with examples of interpretations and explanations of collective actions that provide powerful input to political decisions and are strongly influenced by audience design and motivational biases (Jervis 1976). Systematic research on explanations in this domain is quite infrequent, however, and the folk-conceptual theory of explanation may provide a rich framework to study several of its aspects. Of interest are, for example, the linguistic strategies of explaining actions performed by the enemy and one's own group (e.g., Dimdins 2003), the cognitive processes that underlie the perception and classification of collective behaviors as unintentional or intentional events, and the political consequences of explaining behavior in different ways. Jervis (1976) sees the default perspective of international politics as quite paranoid, citing the famous remark by nineteenth-century Fürst Metternich, who said, upon hearing that the Russian ambassador had died, "I wonder why he did that." It might be valuable to compare the explanation styles we find in international politics with those of individuals who suffer from paranoid psychopathology—or, perhaps more fittingly for the current political era, with explanations given by people who suffer from narcissistic personality disorder.

9.6   Conclusions

This chapter reviewed the major themes of this book and tried to highlight what progress we have made in accounting for the mind's capacity to explain behavior. One theme was the dual nature of behavior explanations—that people use explanations as cognitive tools to find meaning and as social tools to manage interactions. This integrative approach offers a unifying framework for the various theoretical models in explanation research, ranging from logical, inferential, and conceptual models to linguistic, conversational, and rhetorical models.

The folk theory of mind ties the cognitive and social facets of explanation together, and it represents the second major theme of this book. This folk theory's evolutionary and developmental history provides the background to the mind's ability to explain behavior, a background that illustrates both the integration of cognitive and social life and the complexity of the resulting explanatory capacities. By recognizing explanations as embedded in the folk-conceptual framework we also ensure that what researchers of behavior explanation investigate is in fact the phenomenon of interest and not a faded replica, barely recognizable by ordinary people themselves.

The embedding of explanatory concepts in the human theory of mind and careful analyses of naturally occurring explanations have led to a new theory of behavior explanations labeled the *folk-conceptual theory* because it is based on the study of folk concepts of mind and behavior. It is not, however, ordinary people's own theory of explanation (they probably don't have one), but rather a genuine scientific theory. Explicating this theory has been the third theme of this book. The folk-conceptual theory has three distinct layers: First, it identifies the concepts and distinctions that deliver the tools people use when explaining behavior, including the distinct modes of explanation (reasons, causes, etc.) and their particular types (e.g., belief reasons, trait causes). Second, it identifies the psychological principles that determine choices among explanatory tools and the cognitive processes that underlie the construction of specific explanations. And third, it presents the linguistic apparatus within which explanations are expressed for communicative and social purposes.

Any new theory is measured by the facts it describes, explains, and predicts, especially compared to extant theories of the same phenomenon. Therefore, comparisons of the folk-conceptual theory with traditional models of attribution has been the fourth theme of this book. Alongside chapters 6 through 8, which featured applications of the folk-conceptual theory in classic and novel domains of attribution research, chapter 9 pointed to a variety of research directions that could profit from applying the folk-conceptual theory. To further illustrate progress achieved by the new theory I also offered specific comparisons to traditional models, regarding the conceptual assumptions of explanation (4.3), the role of covariation analysis (5.3), the communicative power of explanations (6.3), and the measurement of behavior explanations (4.2.5, 7.7). Open issues remain, of course, and they include the exact cognitive process of constructing explanations, cross-cultural variations, and the relationship between behavior explanations and other (e.g., physical) explanations.

Beginning with Fritz Heider, the tradition of attribution research has been one of the most celebrated in social psychology. It dictated major themes of research such as the contribution of cognition to social behavior and the asymmetries in thinking about self and other. But the specific theoretical models within this tradition have not changed significantly since the 1960s, despite mounting doubts, questions, and criticism. This book, and the theory it proposes, will not ease all the doubts, answer all the questions, or be immune to criticism. I hope, however, that it will serve as a starting point for another era of research into attribution and social cognition, an era that honors the classic questions but tries to answer them with modern theoretical tools.

Appendix
F.Ex: A Coding Scheme for Folk Explanations of Behavior, Version 4.2

Behavior explanations are typically extracted from texts, conversations, or experimental protocols by identifying statements that introduced by linguistic explanation markers such as *because, so . . . (that)* or *(in order) to* or that directly answered a why-question.

Before the F.Ex coding scheme is applied, candidate statements are first classified as *behavior explanations*. This step excludes, for example, statements that are explanations *how* rather than *why* or that explain physical events (e.g., "my watch stopped because . . ."). Also excluded are explanations of social events that are not behavioral events but rather unfolding processes (e.g., "their marriage dissolved because . . ."). It also excludes claim backings, that is, statements that provide evidence for a claim. For example, in the statement "It seemed like he was doing alright, 'cause the teacher didn't say anything to him," the clause beginning with *'cause* backs up an inference ("It seemed . . .") and does not explain why he was doing alright.

The F.Ex scheme assigns a three-digit code to each distinct explanation, with the first digit representing the mode of explanation (cause = 1, causal history of reason = 2, reason = 3 or 4, enabling factor = 6) and the remaining digits representing specific types within each mode.

Cause Explanations [1_ _]

Rule
If the explained behavior is unintentional, the explanation is a cause explanation. Such explanations mention the factors that caused the unintentional behavior. For example: "Anne was yawning during the lecture because she hadn't gotten enough sleep."

Further Comments

• Whether the behavior is unintentional or not must be decided from the perspective of the *explainer.* If the coder would judge a given behavior as intentional but the explainer's utterance and/or the context suggest that the explainer considered the behavior unintentional, the explanation is a cause explanation.

• Cause explanations are "mechanical" explanations, following straightforward physical or psychological regularities (e.g., stimuli cause sensations, other people cause emotions, traits influence behavior). A mechanical cause brings about the behavior without intervention of the agent's intention or will (and sometimes against the agent's will).

• Cause explanations never indicate the *purpose* of a behavior; in fact, cause explanations imply that the behavior had no particular purpose—it happened unintentionally, brought about by certain causes. Therefore it does not make sense to ask "What for?" to elicit a cause explanation (e.g., "Anne was in a great mood this morning."—"What for?")

• In the case of cause explanations, the actor need not be aware of the cause relation between the cause and the behavior. For example, "Anne is in a great mood today. Why? Because the sun is shining." Anne may not know that her good mood was caused by the sunny weather.

• In general, the actor need not even be aware of the explained behavior itself. Somebody might observe Anne grinding her teeth and say: "She is probably doing that because she is nervous," but Anne herself might not even be aware that she has been grinding her teeth.

Codes

The particular types of causes that explain an agent's behavior or experience can be classified into further subcategories.

Agent causes operate from within the agent and are represented by a second digit of 1 [11_]. They have further subforms, represented in the third digit, namely, *behaviors* [111] (including accomplishments and lack thereof, e.g., "losing a game"), *internal states* [112] (including emotions, physiological states, bodily sensations), *perceptions* [113] (including attention, imagination, and memory), *propositional states* [114] (including beliefs, desires, thoughts, hopes, fears), *traits* [115] (including both personality traits and physical traits, such as chronic illness, addiction), *passive behaviors* [116] (e.g., receiving, becoming, dying), *stable propositional states* [117] (including habitual beliefs, desires, and attitudes), *category memberships* [118] (including club memberships, high school grade, social categories, such as gender, race), and *character propositional states* [119] (those 117 that can be considered part of the agent's character or personality, e.g., "cannot seem to be alone," "no sense of responsibility").

Note: If a specific behavior has been performed a few times, use 111; if the behavior is performed as a habit, and if that habit seems to be a "characteristic" of the agent, use 115.

Situation causes operate from outside the agent but are impersonal, such as the weather or a difficult exam. They are represented by the three-digit code of 120, and no third digit is recorded.

Note: If a cited cause clearly refers to a future or counterfactual situation that the agent knows about, the code is not a 120 (because that situation could not have been causally efficacious) but a 114—referring to the agent's belief about that hypothetical situation, as in "She is sad because he won't come back."

Agent+Situation interactions are processes that involve both Agent causes and Situation causes. Their code is therefore 13_ , the addition of the 11_ and the 120 codes. For example, "fulfilling a requirement" [131] is an interaction because it involves both facts about the person, such as abilities or past behaviors, and facts about the situation, such as the particular content of the requirements. The third digit of these interactions captures the specific agent cause that was involved in the interaction—which is often a behavior [131], though other codes can occur as well. A special code of 136 applies when the explanation puts the agent in a passive position and the force impinging on the agent is in the situation (e.g., "she was thrown over by the wind").

OtherPerson causes [14_] operate from outside the agent but are another person's (or persons') states or attributes, namely, somebody's *behavior* [141], *internal state* [142], *perception* [143], *propositional states* [144], *trait* [145], *stable propositional states* [147], *category membership* [148], or *character propositional states* [149].

Agent+OtherPerson interactions are processes that involve both agent causes and OtherPerson causes, and their code is therefore 15_ , a combination of 11_ and 14_ . For example, "(I was sad because) we got into a fight" [151]. The third digit captures the agent cause that was involved in the interaction. 151 is used as the default for relationships (e.g., "she has known him for a long time"; "they are on good terms").

Note: A special code of 156 applies when the explanation puts the agent in a passive position and the force impinging on the agent is another person (e.g., being told to leave; being fired; being brought up strictly).

OtherPerson+Situation interactions are processes that involve both OtherPerson and Situation causes, hence their code is 160. For example, "(He was happy because) she was back in Cleveland." Typically no third digit is recorded.

Agent+OtherPerson+Situation interactions are processes that involve both Agent, OtherPerson, and Situation causes, hence their code is 17_ . For example, "(I was up all night because) my family and I had a neighborhood party" [171]. The third digit captures the agent cause involved in the interaction.

Examples

Code	Category	[Behavior] Explanation
111	Agent behavior	[Anne is sweating] because she just ran five miles.
112	Agent internal state	[Anne is grinding her teeth] because she is nervous.
113	Agent perception	[Anne drove above the speed limit] because she didn't look at her speedometer.
114	Agent propos. state	[Anne was worrying] because she was afraid she failed the test.
115	Agent trait	[Anne is feeling bad] because she has low self-esteem.
117	Agent stable propos. state	[Ben had a craving for cherries] because he loves them.
118	Agent category membership	[Anne liked the movie] because she is just a high school student.
119	Agent propos. state in character	[I hypnotized myself] because I have an innate fear of letting myself be controlled.
120	Situation	[Anne is in a great mood] because it's sunny outside.
131	Agent+Situation	[Anne was admitted to Princeton] because she fulfilled the requirements.
135	Agent+Situation trait	[She smiled] because she thrives in dire straits.
141	OthPers behavior	[Anne is yawning] because the teacher is giving a boring lecture.

Code	Category	[Behavior] Explanation
142	OthPers internal state	[Anne empathizes with Ben] because he is in a lot of pain.
143	OthPers perception	[Anne is disappointed] because Ben didn't notice her new haircut.
144	OthPers propos. state	[Anne is happy] because Ben wants to go to the party with her.
145	OthPers trait	[Anne likes Ben] because he is very kind and perceptive.
146	OthPers passive behavior	[I was nervous] because she was getting back the results from a health test.
147	OthPers stable propos.	[Anne is infatuated with Ben] because he has very liberal attitudes.
148	OthPers categ. memb.	[Ben envies Jeff] because Jeff is in a fraternity.
149	OthPers propos. state in character	[I was sad] because they don't share my religious convictions.
151	Agent+OthPers	[Anne is annoyed at John] because they can't agree on anything.
155	Agent+OthPers trait	[He feels guilty] because he is in control of what time he spends with whom.
156	Agent+OthPers passive beh.	[I was in a good mood] because I received a call from home.
160	Sit+OthPers	[She is really afraid] because her brother is in a bad neighborhood.
171	Agent+Sit+OthPers	[I was in a good mood] because my friends and I were returning to school.

Reason Explanations [3_ _ , 4_ _]

Rule

Reason explanations explain intentional actions by citing the kinds of things the agent considered when forming an intention to act—the reasons *for which* the agent performed the action. These reasons are subjective mental states (desires, beliefs, valuings) that the agent had at the time of deciding to act. For example, "Anne ignored Greg's arguments because she knew she was right" or "Why did Jarron give in?"—"He wanted to end the argument."

Further Comments

▪ The presence of an intention can be verified by testing the meaningfulness of a reformulation of the explained behavior in the following format: ". . . [explanation], and *that was her reason for choosing to* [behavior] . . ." For example, "Anne ignored Greg's argument because she knew she was right," would be reformulated as "She knew she was right, and that was her reason for choosing to ignore his argument." Such a reformulation need not sound elegant, but it must sound acceptable. "She had a stomach ache because she ate too many cherries" is not a reason explanation because the reformulation, "She ate too many cherries and that was her reason for choosing to have a stomach ache," makes little sense.

▪ Because the actor behaves for the reason given, he or she must be (at least dimly) *aware* of those reasons at the time of acting (subjectivity rule). If "Anne applauded the musicians" is explained by "because other people did so," then Anne must have been aware that she applauded for that reason. If she wasn't, then other people's applauding *caused* her to applaud (she did it "automatically"), which would suggest a cause explanation code. (We thus classify unconscious "reasons" as cause explanations.)

▪ The agent also must have regarded the cited reasons as suitable or reasonable grounds for acting (rationality rule). For example, "Ben interrupted his mother because he was thinking about other things" is not a reason explanation because his thinking about other things did not seem to provide reasonable grounds for interrupting her. However, "Ben interrupted his mother because he was thinking about leaving and wanted to let her know" is a reason explanation because we can assume that Ben perceived the cited information as reasonable grounds for acting.

Codes

Mental state markers.   Reasons can be linguistically marked as mental states by an appropriate mental state verb ("Anne watered her new plants because she *wanted* the plants to survive"), or they can be unmarked ("Anne watered her new plants to save the plants"). Typical mental state markers are *want, need, fear, hope, think, realize, like, believe, know.* If a mental state marker is used, the first digit in the coding number is 3, if no marker is used, the first digit is 4.

Reason type. Reasons are always mental states of the agent. They can come in three types: *desires, beliefs,* or *valuings.* This distinction is coded in the third digit: 1 stands for desires, 2 for beliefs, 3 for valuings.

Desires are mental states that can be *fulfilled.* The content of these states (e.g., what I wish or want) refers to objects or events that the agent would like to see realized. For example, "Anne interrupted her mother because she wanted to tell her something" [311]. When the reason explanation contains a mental state marker, it is easy to recognize desires—they are marked by "to want to," "to need to," "to feel like," and so on. When no mental state marker is mentioned, the coder must try to "mark" the content: "Why did you go back into the house?"—"To get my wallet." → "[Because I wanted] to get my wallet."

Beliefs can be true or false. The content of these states (what I believe) refers to events that may or may not exist but that the agent presumes to be factual. "He started a diet because he thought he had gained too much weight" [312]. If mental state markers are used, beliefs are easily recognizable—they are marked by "He thinks," "I believed," "She knew," and so on. Many beliefs are unmarked, however. In that case, only the content of the belief (the fact or circumstance believed to be true) is mentioned: "I applauded because the show was good" [422]; "I interrupted her because I got a call on the other line" [412]; "I invited her for lunch because she had helped me out" [442]. A rule of thumb for deciding whether a given explanation is a belief reason is to ask whether the content of the explanation was likely in the agent's thoughts at the time of deciding to act. For example, when deciding to interrupt his mother, Ben was thinking, "I have a call on the other line."

Valuings include appreciations, attitudes, likings, and so on—e.g., "I liked the music," "I enjoy skiing," "I wasn't enthralled with the offer." These states are neither desires (they are not something that can be "fulfilled") nor beliefs (they cannot be true or false). Valuings are relatively easy to recognize because they are almost always marked with particular verbs—"to love," "to dislike," "to enjoy," "to be excited about," "to be unimpressed by." Under the valuing code we also classify missing or trusting someone, being interested in something, being upset with someone, and getting fed up with something.

Reason content.   Whether marked or unmarked, reasons always have a *content*—what is desired is the content of a desire, what is believed is the content of a belief, what is valued is the content of a valuing. The content of a reason is coded in the second digit after 3 or 4. This content can be coded in various ways. One such way is to classify it into the traditional person–situation categories, refined by distinctions made earlier. That is, a reason can be about *the Agent* [31_ /41_], about *the Situation* [32_ /42_], about an *Agent+Situation interaction* [33_ /43_], about *an Other Person* [34_ /44_], about an *Agent+OtherPerson interaction* [35_ /45_], about an *OtherPerson+ Situation interaction* [36_ /46_], or about an *Agent+OtherPerson+Situation interaction* [37_ /47_].

For example, "Anne thought she is going to be late" has as its content "she is going to be late," and this content refers to the actor's being late, so it is coded as *Agent* content [31_]. In the statement "Anne didn't want the plants to die," the content is "that the plants die," so it is coded as *Situation* content [32_]. In "Anne didn't bring the gift because she thought Ben would bring it," the content is "that Ben would bring it" and is therefore coded as *OtherPerson* content [34_].

Possible modification: Rather than using the second digit for fine distinctions between different situations and interactions, it could also be used for coding the more classic combination of person–situation and stable–unstable or for coding the social desirability of the reason content.

Examples

Marked Reasons

Desires

311	Agent content	[Anne asked Mike out for dinner] because she wanted to get to know him.
321	Situation	[Anne watered the plants] because she wanted them to thrive.
331	Agent+Sit	[Ben flew to Spain] because he wanted to be somewhere warm.
341	OthPer	[Anne didn't call Ben] because she wanted him to call first.
351	Agent+OthPer	[Ben called Anne] because he hoped they would make up again.
361	OthPer+Sit	[My father puts pressure on me] because he wants many doors to be open to me.

371   Agent+Sit+Oth   [She took a hotel room] because she didn't want to stay in the same room with my brothers.

Beliefs

312   Agent content   [Anne ignored Greg's arguments] because She knew she was right.

322   Situation   [Anne applauded] because she thought the performance was excellent.

332   Agent+Sit   [Anne applied] because she thought she fit the job requirements.

342   OthPer   [Anne didn't bring the gift] because she thought Ben would bring it.

352   Agent+OthP   [Anne didn't call Mike] because she felt they didn't click.

362   OthPer+Sit   [Anne won't go to the party] because she knows her ex is gonna be there.

Unmarked Reasons

Desires

411   Agent content   [Anne drove way above the speed limit] to be on time.

421   Situation   [Anne watered the plants] so they grow faster.

431   Agent+Sit   [Anne called the office] so the meeting wouldn't start without her.

441   OthPer   [Anne teased Ben] so he would show some reaction.

451   Agent+OthP   [Anne invited Cathy over] so they could study together.

461   OthPer+Sit   [I took him there] so he could be at his favorite restaurant one more time.

Beliefs

412   Agent content   [Anne refused the salesman's offer] because she didn't have any money.

422   Situation   [Anne refused the salesman's offer] because it was too high.

432   Agent+Sit   [Anne drove way above the speed limit] because her presentation was starting soon.

442   OthPer   [Anne moved in with Cathy] because Cathy offered her the room.

452   Agent+OthP   [Anne invited Cathy on a trip] because they were getting along very well.

462   OthPer+Sit   [She stopped by] because it was his birthday.

472   Ag+OthP+Sit   [He couldn't quit his job] 'cause that's where our money was coming from.

Valuings are rarely unmarked. The few cases we have encountered involve the phrases "It's fun to . . . ," "It's easier," or "It's a thrill."

Special Coding Cases and Conventions

Explanations that involve *liking* may seem ambiguous. In "I plan to invite her because I would like to get to know her better," the phrase *would like to* is synonymous with *want to* [311]. A contrasting case is "Anne applauded the musicians because she liked how they played." In this case, *she liked* is coded as a valuing [343].

Fears can be either beliefs or valuings. To fear or be afraid *that* something happens usually denotes a belief. For example, "(Ben didn't tell her the truth because) he feared that she would get mad [342]." To fear or be afraid *of* something usually denotes a (de-)valuing. For example, "(She didn't go to the welcome party because) she was afraid of all the new people there."

The verb *need* is by default coded as a desire (e.g., "I went back because I needed another loaf of bread" [321]) unless there is evidence in the context that it refers to a normative assessment, in which case it is coded as an unmarked belief about one's obligation (e.g., "I stayed home because I needed to finish the tax report" [412]; cf. "I have to finish my paper" [412]).

Desires and beliefs can play two different roles in explanations. First, desires/beliefs can be mere causes for unintentional behaviors, as in "Anne was worrying about the test results because she wanted to do well" [114]. Here, the desire is not Anne's reason for worrying but rather its cause (because she didn't choose to worry). Second, desires/beliefs can be reasons for intentional actions, as in "Anne watered the plants because she wanted them to grow" [321]. Here, Anne did act for the reason given in the explanation.

"I drove above the speed limit because *I was in a hurry*" is best coded as [411], an unmarked desire to get somewhere quickly (see dictionary definition). By contrast, "I drove above the speed limit because *I was late*" is best coded as [412], an unmarked belief about being late. Pain as a reason is coded as an unmarked valuing: "I called the nurse because it hurt so bad" [413].

"I don't have any money" is either a 412 (when it means I was broke, as in explaining why the agent decided not to buy a new car) or a 432 (when it means I didn't have any money on me, at this place and time, as in explaining why the agent turned back home when arriving at the movie theater).

Belief or knowledge states that are not themselves the propositional reasons for which the agent acted are coded as the content of unmarked beliefs: "I didn't say anything because I didn't know the answer" [412]. In its marked form, this explanation would be, "I realized I didn't know the answer." By contrast, "I kissed him good-bye because I didn't know whether he would make it" should be coded as [342] because the agent's reason is roughly "I thought he might not make it."

Bodily states can also be the reason for acting, as in "She decided to go to sleep because she wasn't feeling well" [412]. The (unmarked) realization that she wasn't feeling well was directly her reason for going to sleep.

To disagree with someone can be coded as a belief that one thinks the other is wrong [342].

Causal Histories of Reasons [2_ _]

Rule

Causal history of reason explanations also explain intentional behavior, but they cite factors that *preceded* (and caused) the agent's reasons. These factors literally lie in the causal history of the actor's reasons but are not themselves reasons. For example, "Why did Jarron give in?"—"He is good natured." Here, Jarron wasn't actually thinking, "I am good natured; therefore, I should give in." In fact, he may not even be aware that he is good natured. Rather, the explainer presents Jarron's good-natured character as an objective fact that brought about his specific reasons (e.g., his desire to end the argument).

Further Comments

• Contrary to reasons, causal history factors are not considered by agents when forming an intention to act. Agents may not be aware of the causal history of their reasons, at least at the time they form their intention. Thus, when coders encounter an intentional behavior and need to decide whether it is explained by a causal history or a reason explanation, they should follow this rule: An explanatory content of which the agent was not aware *cannot* be the reason for which she acted; it is likely a causal history of her reasons.

• If the explanation contains a factor of which the agent *was* aware, then it likely functioned as a reason: "Anne applauded the musicians. Why? because she enjoyed their performance [443] and she wanted to show that [311]." However, sometimes agents are generally aware of causal history factors, even if they did not actively consider them when they formed their intention. For example, "Anne invited Ben for lunch. Why? Because they are good friends [251]." Anne is generally aware of the fact that she and Ben are good friends. However, when deciding to invite him for lunch, she probably did not think, "We are good friends; therefore I should invite him to lunch."

• When we code something as a causal history factor, there must be some reason on which the action is based (whether it is mentioned in the explanation or not). If the explainer's utterance suggests that there was no reason for which the agent performed the behavior—that is, the behavior was unintentional— then we have a cause explanation, not a causal history of reason explanation.

• Sometimes causal histories of reasons co-occur with reasons. For example "Anne invited Ben for lunch. Why?—Because she is outgoing, and she wanted to talk to Ben." In addition to a particular reason why Anne invited Ben for lunch (she wanted to talk to him [311]), the explainer also cites a fact that preceded both Anne's reason and her action—her trait of being outgoing [215].

Codes

Causal histories (2_ _) and cause explanations (1_ _) have the same possible codes in their second and third digits. The crucial difference between cause explanations and causal histories is that causal histories apply to intentional behaviors whereas cause explanations apply to unintentional behaviors.

Examples

211	Agent behavior	[Anne asked Mike out for dinner] because she has done it before.
212	Agent internal state	[Anne refused the salesman's offer] because she was in a bad mood.
213	Agent perception	[Anne stole a pound of peaches] because she saw them on display.
214	Agent propos. state	[Anne slept until ten] because she didn't realize the exam was in the morning.

215	Agent trait	[Anne invited Mike to dinner] because she is friendly.
217	Agent stable prop.	[She pushes people away] because she doesn't want to look vulnerable.
218	Agent category memb.	[I hurt my sister] because I was an adolescent boy.
220	Situation	[Anne invited Sue to have lunch with her] because it was sunny.
231	Agent+Situation	[Ben greeted his aunt emphatically] because he was having a great day.
241	OthPers behavior	[Anne went to the party after all] because Mike had pressured her a bit.
242	OthPers internal state	—[1]
245	OthPers trait	[Anne didn't say hello to him] because he is the kind of person nobody likes.
248	OthPers cat. memb.	[I was going out with a guy at South] 'cause Jennie was at South.
251	Agent+OthPers	[Anne invited Sue to lunch] just because they always hang out together.
256	Agent passive	[Anne was very polite to the guests] because she was taught to.
260	Sit+OthPers	[Her parents visited her] because she was away at school.
271	Agent+Sit+OthPers	[Why did you stay up so late?] Because our whole dorm was having a party.

[1] We are currently unable to list examples for the causal history codes 242, 243, 244, and 247. Even though these explanations exist theoretically, they are extremely rare because internal states, perceptions, and beliefs/desires of another person rarely cause an agent's reasons directly; rather, the agent realizes the presence of these factors, so they become reasons rather than causal histories.

Special Coding Cases and Conventions

The explanation ". . . because she was hungry" is ambiguous. If it is used to explain, say, Anne's inviting Ben for lunch, then it is merely a causal history [212] of whatever reason Anne had to invite Ben for lunch. The hunger typically fails to explain why she asked the person out for lunch. In contrast, the same explanation ". . . because she was hungry" may be used to explain why Anne stole a pound of peaches. In that case, the statement probably refers to Anne's desire to reduce her hunger [411]. This desire can be considered a reason Anne had for acting that way.

"Nothing (better) to do" can be a reason [432] if the agent took that fact into account when deciding to act (e.g., "He took a train to Philly because there was nothing to do in their little town"); more often, however, it is a CHR [231], as in "They vandalized the gym because they had nothing better to do."

Raw emotions ("He was scared" or "She was angry") are coded as 212 when they triggered whatever reason the agent had for acting. If the emotions are formulated as propositional states, however, they are typically reasons ("He was scared she would hurt him" [342] or "She was angry at him" [343]). Being bored can also be either a 212 or a 412, depending on the specific context. For example, "She went to the movies because she was bored" [412] is best coded as a reason because the person seemed to have actually considered her boredom and then chose a way of combating it. By contrast, "Why did that man start talking with you?"—"He was probably just bored" [212] is better coded as a CHR, because the explainer seems to consider his boredom more like the occasion for talking to someone and not his specific reason for talking.

Unconscious desires, beliefs, or tryings are coded as 214 or 217. "Why was this man broadcasting God's news in the amphitheater?"—"Probably a psycho-Christian [215] who feels he needs to spread his zeal to others" [217]. The explainer's specific formulation often provides a clue as to whether the desire/belief is a psychoanalytic ascription or the actual reason that the agent had on his or her mind (e.g., the man would never think "I need to spread my zeal to others").

To like or love someone is often a 217, unless the agent likely considered that fact when deciding to act.

"He couldn't control himself" (when explaining an intentional action such as eating up all the chocolate) is coded as a 212.

"I was lazy, irresponsible, selfish, greedy" are all motivational states (214) that are less than conscious and certainly not rational grounds for acting. They can be 215s if the context allows the inference that the person is assumed to be lazy, greedy, and so forth, in general.

Enabling Factor Explanations [6_ _]

Rule

Enabling factor explanations cite factors that clarify *how it was possible* that an agent completed an intended action. Enabling factor explanations take it for granted that the agent had an intention to act as well as reasons to form that intention. They do not explain why the intention and reasons came about (as reason explanations or CHRs do) but rather cite factors that enabled the agent to turn the intention into a successful action. For example, if asked "How come Phoebe got all her work done?," one might say, "Because she had a lot of coffee." Phoebe's act of drinking coffee does not explain why she was trying to get her work done. Rather, given that she was trying to get it done, the coffee enabled her to succeed.

Further Comments

• This mode of explanation does not really answer "Why?" questions, as all the other modes do, but rather "How was this possible?" questions. For example, "Jarron finished the assignment because he worked all night." That he worked all night is not his reason for finishing, nor did it bring about his reason for finishing; rather, it explains how it was possible that he finished his assignment (given that he intended to do so).

• Enabling factors include the agent's skill, opportunities, and other facilitating forces.

• Enabling factor explanations only explain the action's occurrence—they cannot be used to explain why the agent formed the intention in the first place (which is what reason explanations do).

Codes

Enabling factors (6_ _) have the same codes in their second and third digit as do cause explanations (1_ _) and causal history of reason explanations (2_ _).

Examples

The following table is incomplete because this explanation is rare and certain cause types are unlikely to be enabling factors.

611	Agent behavior	[Mary bought a new car] because she borrowed money.
612	Agent internal state	[Bob finished the assignment] because he had energy.
613	Agent perception	[Anne figured out the answer] because she paid attention.
614	Agent propos. state	[Jack finished his homework] because he knew the material.

615	Agent trait	[Bob finished a difficult class assignment] because he is smart.
617	Agent stable propos. state	[She made it through the crisis] because she believes things will always turn out for the best.
618	Agent category membership	[She finished the paper] because she is a senior.
620	Situation	[Bob finished the assignment] because it was not difficult.
631	Agent+Situation	[She won the game] because things went her way.
641	OthPers behavior	[Mary bought a new car] because her brother gave her money.
651	Agent+OthPers	[Jack wrote a great paper] because he talked with the teacher.
656	Agent+OthPers passive beh.	[Mary, who is poor, bought a new car] because she was given a loan.

Notes

Chapter 1

1. Philosophically, this theory may leave much to be desired, but psychologically it was a remarkable model that successfully combined constructivism with causal realism.

2. For example: "Heider began by assuming that just as objects have enduring qualities that determine their appearances, so people have stable psychological characteristics that determine their behavior" (D. T. Gilbert 1998, p. 94).

3. To illustrate: "How do we search for the causal structure of interpersonal events? According to Heider, we do so by reliance upon attributions to the environment (external factors) or to something about the other person (internal factors)." (Weary, Edwards, and Riley 1994, p. 292). "Central to Heider's entire theoretical position is the proposition that man perceives behavior as being caused, and that the causal locus can be either in the perceiver or in the environment" (Hastorf, Schneider, and Polefka 1970, p. 63). "Heider suggested that environmental and personal factors are two general classes of force that enter into the production of action" (Ross and Fletcher 1985, p. 75). "Heider had emphasized the distinction between personal and situational causes of behavior" (Gilbert 1998, p. 101).

4. This picture could be expanded by examining people's explanations for failures, for which one might be tempted to postulate a class of "disabling factor explanations." However, such a postulate is unnecessary because failures are explained no differently from other unintentional events, namely, by straightforward cause explanations (see chapter 4).

5. Throughout this book, I use female pronouns for the *agent*—the person whose behavior is explained—and male pronouns for the *explainer*.

6. Interestingly, the theory of correspondent inferences was restricted to intentional actions: "[T]he attribution of intentions is a necessary step in the assignment of more stable characteristics to the actor" (p. 222). This assumption was not further explicated or ever tested empirically, and as a general statement it is almost certainly false,

as noted by Ross and Fletcher (1985, p. 77). A number of traits are inferred from unintentional behaviors, such as tripping and dropping things ($\rightarrow$ clumsiness) or sweating and stuttering in group settings ($\rightarrow$ shyness).

7. More specifically, "experiment-like variations of conditions [that are] a naïve version of J. S. Mill's method of difference" (p. 194).

8. In one section (pp. 213–219), Kelley offers an attributional analysis of participant responses in dissonance experiments, which sometimes concern intentional actions. But in this section, the internal–external distinction suddenly takes on a new meaning. It now refers, not to causes of events, but to the perceived voluntariness (intentionality) of an action: "[V]olition means that the behavior is attributed to the self rather than to external forces" (p. 217). However, this altered meaning of the external–internal distinction is deeply problematic. If "external" refers to "unintentional," we cannot distinguish between enjoyment caused by the quality of the movie and enjoyment caused by the viewer's low standards. And if "internal" refers to "intentional," then we cannot distinguish between an action explanation that refers to the agent ("I did it because I wanted to help out the experimenter") and an action explanation that refers to the situation ("I did it because the task wasn't so boring after all"). Because of these problems, the meaning of the person–situation distinction must remain causal (not blended with intentionality), and Kelley's analysis can only apply to unintentional events.

9. On closer inspection, Kelley's model did not fit the data all too well. Subsequent model improvements (e.g., Cheng and Novick 1990; Försterling 1989; Hewstone and Jaspars 1987) seriously had to expand the range of information provided to participants in order to make judgments conform to the model. In Försterling's (2001) words (that were not meant ironically): "[W]hen experimental participants are provided with "complete" information, and when all the potential causes (i.e., person, entity, and time), the three two-way (i.e., person × entity, person × time, entity × time) and the three-way interaction (person × entity × time) are presented to the subjects, attributions are remarkably consistent with the ANOVA model's predictions" (p. 65).

10. The examples in this book typically are original explanations that participants in our studies provided and, except for minor copyedits, are presented verbatim. Unless otherwise specified, the explanations were spontaneous statements in conversation or free-response answers to an experimenter's why-question (see e.g., Malle et al. 2000, study 5; Malle, Knobe, and Nelson 2004, passim; O'Laughlin and Malle 2002). The rare cases of constructed examples will be indicated with an asterisk after the example number, e.g., (1-8)*.

The classification of all explanations followed the F.Ex coding scheme, which yields agreements of around 90 percent ($\kappa \approx .80$) among trained coders. For details of the coding scheme, see the appendix and http://darkwing.uoregon.edu/~bfmalle/fex.html.

Chapter 2

1. Kant (1998/1787) postulated a number of categories (among them space, time, causality, and substance) that the human mind applies to the perception of objects. These categories, Kant argued, are not just arbitrary frames but the very conditions of the possibility of perception. By analogy, the concepts of a theory of mind would then be the conditions of the possibility of social cognition. But this should not be taken as a logical claim (i.e., that to posit social cognition without a theory of mind would be a formal contradiction); rather, we may say that this framework provides the concepts in terms of which social cognition and interpretation has proven most effective for dealing with other human beings.

2. Wellman (1990, chap. 4) is somewhat of an exception in that he sketches out a network of interconnected concepts that operate like filters in the cognition of human behavior. As a committed "theory" theorist, however, Wellman insists that the network develops like a scientific theory or "research programme" (Wellman 1993, p. 18) and that people use this network as a set of laws and abstract principles that aid in action explanation and mental state ascription.

3. The addressee's mind state must involve the recognition of the speaker's communicative intention or else it is not a communication but merely an act causing some mind state in the addressee (e.g., intending to frighten or confuse another person). Communication, according to Grice (1957), Sperber and Wilson (1986), Gibbs (1998), and many others, requires that there is some sort of mutual recognition of the act *as* a communicative act.

4. This report and subsequent quotes are extracted from a fascinating discussion of autistic adults who have read the theory of mind literature and try to make sense of their own views of social life.

5. This is not to say that there aren't autistic persons with more severe deficits even at the level of information input or processing. My point here is merely that, even when information input is largely intact, the relevant information cannot be interpreted (cf. Baron-Cohen 1992).

6. This distinction has been expanded in philosophy and all of science to a general dichotomy between measurable, observable appearance and unobservable, underlying reality (e.g., of mathematical relationships, subatomic forces, and the like)—a dichotomy that we take for granted when characterizing good science (Moravcsik 1998).

7. To reinstate confidence in Cummins's dominance theory we would need to demonstrate that the degree of rivalry between siblings, and especially the degree of dominance exerted by the older sibling, differentially predict precocious theory of mind performance.

8. Even this interpretation may be too strong. Evidence for a cheater detection sensitivity has relied on the comparison of a logical reasoning task (Wason 1968) with a deontic reasoning task (Cosmides and Tooby 1992). For example, participants read one of the following statements:

(L) "When I ride my bike I always wear a helmet."

or

(D) "When you ride your bike you must wear a helmet."

   People then need to select, from several options, which pieces of evidence are critical for testing the truth of this statement. (Critical are: When riding the bike, does the person wear a helmet? When not wearing a helmet, does the person ride a bike?) Across ages and cultures, people are better at identifying both critical pieces for the (D) statement than for the (L) statement, which has been taken as evidence for a cognitive adaptation to detecting rule violations. A potential problem with this interpretation, however, is that the two tasks do not seem to be logically parallel. Fodor (2000) argued that (L) must be written as a logical implication *when riding bike → wearing helmet* but that (D) means *given riding bike,* REQUIRED *(wearing helmet).* In other words, (D) describes a restricted obligation: for a certain class of cases (when riding your bike), it is required that you wear a helmet. The truth test is therefore more transparent, because you obviously have to check *both* for the restriction and the required event. Proposition (L), however, is a true implication, and one needs to know something about implications to test them correctly. Fodor therefore concludes that (D) is simply an easier problem and therefore solved more readily. A cheater detection mechanism would not be necessary to account for this pattern of data.

9. Recently, the role of executive control (especially inhibitory control) has been brought into play as a potential precursor or element of theory of mind (e.g., Hughes 1998; Carlson and Moses 2001). However, executive control is usually defined as the capacity to monitor and control one's own thoughts and intentions, thus requiring both concepts of mental state and introspective abilities. For example, inhibitory control can be described as identifying and holding back one intention to act and identifying and fostering an alternative intention to act. In essence, executive control is self-awareness and self-regulation of mental states, and I therefore consider self-awareness a better candidate as a precursor than executive control.

10. *Apes* include orangutans, gorillas, bonobos, and chimpanzees. Together with humans, apes form the family of *hominids.*

Chapter 3

1. After we published our 1997 paper, I discovered an analysis of why-questions by Sylvain Bromberger (1992) that shares at least two conditions in common with ours

(awareness and relevance). His analysis is more of a logical nature, but the overlap is still noteworthy.

2. A variety of controls in these studies ruled out alternative interpretations. For example, we showed that actors and observer did not merely report what they thought the experimenter most expected from their roles, and they did not just construct memories after the interaction according to an implicit theory.

Chapter 4

1. Citing mental states thus *functions as* citing reasons when the explainer makes the assumptions of rationality and subjectivity, but mental states can also be used as mere causes (see example 4-1) or causal history factors.

2. The term *valuing* should not to be confused with *values,* which are deeply held preferences, norms, or abstract ideals that, in behavior explanations, typically serve as causal history factors.

3. Asking participants to identify "causal history of reason explanations" would make no sense, because they don't use this technical label. The situation is comparable to that of speaking grammatically. People make grammatical distinctions for which they have no labels unless they are explicitly taught these labels by grammarians. The *reason* concept, by contrast, is a folk concept for which people have an intuitive understanding.

4. These explanations for why the chicken crossed the road have been circulating on the internet for quite a while. They can be found, for example, at eserver.org/philosophy/chicken.txt.

5. These numbers are computed from the five studies reported in Malle, Knobe, and Nelson (2004), averaged across actor and observer explanations. Fewer than 1 percent of explanations referred to enabling factors.

6. What can we say about difficult actions that *failed?* Because failure is not intentional, people account for failure with simple cause explanations (discussed next). The causes cited for failure might be called preventing or disabling factors, but they are really no different from other causes and don't compete with any other explanation modes. Enabling factor explanations are unique in this respect because they compete with reasons and CHRs for the explanation of intentional actions.

Chapter 5

1. This is the one time when I deviate from my self-imposed rule and actually make the explainer female because it makes for better balance with the male bachelor.

2. Dan Adams pointed out to me that sometimes a social perceiver is faced with a be-havior whose intentionality has yet to be determined, and consideration of possible explanations (especially possible belief and desire reasons for the behavior) may aid in determining the intentionality. This would imply some bidirectional paths or feed-back loops in figure 5.1, complications that I am not addressing here.

3. When referring to *choices,* I am not implying that explainers necessarily make con-scious choices. Sometimes they may well do so, but most of the time consciousness is directed at the mental *content* of cognition relevant to the explanations, leaving the construction of the actual *form* of explanations to well-practiced unconscious opera-tions.

4. For the purpose of this illustration, I ignore other forces besides knowledge that can encourage the explainer to use causal history rather than reason explanations, such as audience design or impression management.

5. For those unfamiliar with regression, here is a brief introduction. Regression equa-tions relate an "outcome variable" (on the left in table 5.1) to one or more "predictor variables" (on the right). In essence, the value of the outcome variable (in our case, the probability of making a certain explanatory choice) is the weighted sum of the chosen predictor variables. Each predictor variable has a "regression weight" ($b1$, $b2$, etc.), which is a number that both puts the predictor on the appropriate scale (so that the summing procedure yields a meaningful score for the outcome variable) and indicates how strongly weighted the predictor is in the summing procedure. The so-called intercept, $b0$, further adjusts the summing such that it yields a meaning-ful outcome score. (The specific values of regression weights are typically found empirically.)

6. Some of these theories did not explicitly deal with the construction of *specific* causes. For example, Kelley's (1967) questions about consensus, distinctiveness, and consistency, are designed to single out only whether the cause is more likely to be "in the person" or "in the situation."

7. The meaning of *projection* here is decidedly not psychodynamic. What is meant is that when perceivers do not know another person's mental states, they will some-times assume (consciously or unconsciously) that the other person sees, thinks, knows, or wants the same as they themselves do (Dawes 1990; Gordon 1992; Krueger and Clement 1997; Ross, Greene, and House 1977).

8. The sample explanations were culled from our actor–observer project (Malle, Knobe, and Nelson 2004). The sampling obeyed three criteria. (1) Entries had to come from a variety of contexts (e.g., spontaneous explanations in conversation; answers to experimenter's why-questions about a stranger's behavior or about one's own be-havior). (2) The explanations had to be fairly concise and understandable even with-out context. (3) Entries with topic content similar to already selected entries were skipped.

9. Interestingly, in example 5-19, an actor offers a desire and a valuing even though actors predominantly offer beliefs as their reasons (see chapter 7). A possible hypothesis is that movements (i.e., changes of location or activity), are often explained by reference to desires (and sometimes valuings), even by actors. Consider "I had gone outside **to get the mail**" or "I went back and I put a lock on our storage **so he** [estranged husband] **couldn't get into it.**"

Chapter 6

1. A challenge comes from the set of verbs that have been called stimulus–experiencer (S–E) verbs (e.g., A amazed/amused/bored/disappointed B), because their causal structure is ambiguous. In one study examining ten such S–E verbs previously used in the literature, I found that on average 30% of people considered such a verb to depict the first person's behavior (A's act of amazing B), 48% considered it to depict the second person's experience (B's state of being amazed), and 16% considered it to depict the entire transaction (a category that was not even offered but that participants spontaneously invented). These verbs, however, are not only ambiguous; they are also very rarely used in their interpersonal form—the form studied in the literature. In a count of *amaze* and *amuse,* forms such as "this amused me" or "she was amazed" were most common; A amused/amazed B occurred in only 10% of cases (Malle 2002c).

2. To be precise, the agent does not sort through beliefs and desires *qua* mental states but through their contents—what she considers facts, prospects, goals, and outcomes. Likewise, the agent forms her intention not literally in light of beliefs and desires but in light of the facts, prospects, goals, and outcomes *represented* by her beliefs and desires.

3. It just wouldn't be a felicitous reason explanation to say "She is taking an umbrella because it's going to rain, but she is not aware that it's going to rain." An unmarked belief reason is still a well-groomed *belief* reason, even though it doesn't carry its mental state type on its sleeve (see Malle et al. 2000).

4. The following results were not reported in the original publication.

Chapter 7

1. There might be one exception. Explainers can offer a vague trait generalization with (limited) explanatory function that does not commit to a judgment of whether the behavior in question was intentional or not. For example, "Why is she late for this important meeting?"—"She always is; she is just very unreliable."

2. Enabling factors are an infrequent third option when the action performed was exceptionally difficult or obstructed (McClure and Hilton 1997, 1998), which is rarely the case with social behaviors. In fact, across more than four thousand explanations examined for actor–observer asymmetries, we found no more than a handful of

enabling factors (Malle, Knobe, and Nelson 2004). This scarcity may appear to be a result of the type of question ("Why?") that we use to elicit explanations (McClure et al. 2001), but we had shown earlier that question format has little effect unless the action is actually difficult (Malle et al. 2000).

3. Judgments of behavior attributes are unlikely to influence actor–observer asymmetries here. As argued in 7.1, there is no clear evidence for an asymmetry in judged intentionality, nor is there any indication of an asymmetry in judgments of behavior trends.

4. Valuings are fairly rare, amounting to 10–15% of all reasons. Because they combine features from both desires and beliefs it is difficult to make predictions about factors that increase or decrease their use. If there is a trend detectable in the data, then it is that valuings look a bit more like desires than beliefs. On the whole, however, we have found hardly any systematic variation of valuing rates as a function of psychological variables, such as perspective (actor versus observer) or self-presentation (e.g., portraying oneself as rational).

5. There is an ongoing debate in the literature over the question whether children's early desire concept is "nonrepresentational" and perhaps even nonmentalistic. Children may initially conceptualize desires not as subjective mental states but as an action's directedness toward an outcome, or perhaps merely as an agent-action-outcome link (Goldman 2001; Perner 1991; Povinelli 2001; Russell 1996; Wellman and Phillips 2001). Exactly what *directedness* may mean is an open question, but if there is such an early behaviorist concept of desire, it might continue on into adulthood as a low-effort heuristic for explaining intentional actions. Using this heuristic, explainers would not try to infer the agent's actual mental states but instead point to a desirable outcome to which the action appears directed.

6. We also analyzed the data such that even moderately stable states were included in the trait category, but the results remained the same as when using a more stringent trait definition.

7. These rates use person causes and person causal histories as the denominator. The rates of traits mentioned among the total number of explanations are less than half the size.

8. Jones and Nisbett (1972) also argued that this fear of losing their freedom motivates actors to cite *situation* causes. However, this part of the claim appears to be contradicted by our data (fewer than a fourth of actors' causes or causal histories are of the situation type) is it entirely convincing, because being "controlled" by the situation is perhaps even more freedom constraining than being controlled by one's own dispositions (Knobe and Malle 2002).

9. To maximize statistical power in this analysis, we included not only person versus situation factors in causes explanations and causal history explanations but also per-

son versus situation *contents* in reason explanations. Breaking the analyses down into these subpatterns made no difference.

Chapter 8

1. Most writers use Campbell's original term *entitativity*. Robert Abelson (cf. Abelson et al. 1998) rightfully pointed out that this term contains one too many syllables, and he suggested replacing it with *entitivity*. For whatever reason, this suggestion has not been heeded, though I stubbornly cling to the hope that it will, in the end, prevail.

2. Cf. Tönnies's (2001/1887) concept of *Gemeinschaft* (community), which has considerable similarity with the notion of jointly acting groups (Knowles 1982). The same is true for Lewin's (1947) description of *dynamic groups*.

3. Some authors have suggested that aggregate groups are not really groups. For example, Hamilton, Sherman, and Rodgers (in press) maintain that "100 persons, carrying briefcases, hurriedly moving through Grand Central Station from train to street, would not usually be considered a group." I agree with the spirit of this suggestion, and not much is riding on the issue of whether the term *group* can only mean *jointly acting group* (as Hamilton and colleagues prefer) or can also subsume aggregates. Far more important is the fact that, in language and cognition, people represent and explain plural actions—whether performed by an aggregate or a group agent—and we have to account for all of these representations, not just the ones directed at jointly acting groups.

4. As discussed in more detail in section 5.2.3, explainers who cannot even recruit such general information may resort to generic explanations such as "They wanted to," and "Because it's fun" (O'Laughlin and Malle 2002, study 3).

5. I want to make clear that my use of these examples from the Nürnberg indictment in no way implies a critique of either its content or of the war tribunal's goals as a whole. I merely want to persuade the reader that these linguistic and conceptual devices are universal and not just used by propagandists, liars, and fascists.

6. "Regular readers of THE NEW AMERICAN know that [the CFR] has worked for decades to submerge the United States in a one-world government ruled by (you guessed it!) the elite" (Bonta 2000). See also McManus (1994) and many related documents at http://jbs.org/student/focus/conspiracy.

Chapter 9

1. Among the exceptions to this trend we find a small literature following Buss's (1978, 1979) call for research on reason explanations (e.g., Hinkle and Schmidt 1984; Schoeneman and Rubanowitz 1985) and of course the literature on goal-based explanations (McClure 2002), which did not, however, expand the specific goal concept

into the broader reason concept. Other exceptions exist, but in those reasons were studied not as explanations but as influential cognitive activity in the agent (e.g., Hodges and Wilson 1993; Wilson et al. 1989; Shafir, Simonson, and Tversky 1993).

2. Al Mele pointed out that one could also answer the why-question with a belief reason. For example, "Meteorologists put them there because they thought this would be a good way to collect rain." Linguistically, this is indeed a belief reason, but one whose explanatory power comes chiefly from the agent's desire or purpose *to collect rain.* The explanation would have no explanatory power (though still be a belief reason) if it said ". . . because they thought it would be a good way to fulfill their goals." It is a fact of many languages that a desire reason *can* be reformulated as a belief reason, but the content of such a reformulation is at heart still citing the agent's desire content. Because such reformulations are wordy and awkward, they rarely occur in naturalistic explanations.

References

Abelson, R. P., Dasgupta, N., Park, J., and Banaji, M. R. (1998). Perceptions of the collective other. *Personality and Social Psychology Review* 2: 243–250.

Abelson, R. P., and Lalljee, M. (1988). Knowledge structures and causal explanations. In D. J. Hilton (ed.), *Contemporary Science and Natural Explanation: Commonsense Conceptions of Causality* (pp. 175–203). Brighton: Harvester.

Abramson, L. Y., Seligman, M. E. P., and Teasdale, J. D. (1978). Learned helplessness in humans: Critique and reformulation. *Journal of Abnormal Psychology* 87: 49–74.

Acheson, D. (1951). Presentation as part of hearings before the Committee on Appropriations, U.S. Senate, 81st Congress, 2nd session, *Supplemental appropriations for 1951.*

Adams, D. (1982). *Life, the Universe, and Everything.* New York: Harmony Books.

Adler, J. E. (2002). *Belief's Own Ethics.* Cambridge, Mass.: The MIT Press.

Ahn, W., and Kalish, C. W. (2000). The role of mechanism beliefs in causal reasoning. In F. Keil and R. A. Wilson (eds.), *Explanation and Cognition* (pp. 199–226). Cambridge, Mass.: The MIT Press.

Ahn, W.-K., and Bailenson, J. (1996). Causal attribution as a search for underlying mechanisms: An explanation of the conjunction fallacy and the discounting principle. *Cognitive Psychology* 31: 82–123.

Ahn, W.-K., Kalish, C. W., Medin, D. L., and Gelman, S. A. (1995). The role of covariation versus mechanism information in causal attribution. *Cognition* 54: 299–352.

Allport, F. H. (1924). *Social Psychology.* Boston, Mass.: Houghton Mifflin.

Ames, D. R. (in press). Inside the mind-reader's toolkit: Projection and stereotyping in mental state inference. *Journal of Personality and Social Psychology.*

Ames, D. R., Knowles, E. D., Morris, M. W., Kalish, C. W., Rosati, A. D., and Gopnik, A. (2001). The social folk theorist: Insights from social and cultural psychology on the contents and contexts of folk theorizing. In B. F. Malle, L. J. Moses, and D. A. Baldwin (eds.), *Intentions and Intentionality: Foundations of Social Cognition* (pp. 307–330). Cambridge, Mass.: The MIT Press.

Anderson, C. A., Krull, D. S., and Weiner, B. (1996). Explanations: Processes and consequences. In E. T. Higgins and A. W. Kruglanski (eds.), *Social Psychology: Handbook of Basic Principles* (pp. 271–296). New York: Guilford Press.

Andrews, K. (2002). Knowing mental states: The asymmetry of psychological prediction and explanation. In Q. Smith and A. Jokic (eds.), *Consciousness: New Philosophical Essays*. New York: Oxford University Press.

Antaki, C. (1988). *Analyzing Everyday Explanation: A Casebook of Methods*. London: Sage.

Antaki, C. (1994). *Explaining and Arguing: The Social Organization of Accounts*. Thousand Oaks, Calif.: Sage.

Antaki, C., and Leudar, I. (1992). Explaining in conversation: Towards an argument model. *European Journal of Social Psychology* 22: 181–194.

Armstrong, D. M. (1973). *Belief, Truth, and Knowledge*. London: Cambridge University Press.

Arranz, E., Artamendi, J., Olabarrieta, F., and Martin, J. (2002). Family context and theory of mind development. *Early Child Development and Care* 172: 9–22.

Asch, S. E. (1952). *Social Psychology*. Englewood Cliffs, N.J.: Prentice-Hall.

Ashmore, R. D., and Del Boca, F. L. (1981). Conceptual approaches to stereotypes and stereotyping. In D. L. Hamilton (ed.), *Cognitive Processes in Stereotyping and Intergroup Behavior* (pp. 1–35). Hillsdale, N.J.: Lawrence Erlbaum.

Astington, J. W. (1988). Promises: Words or deeds? *First Language* 8: 259–270.

Astington, J. W. (2001). The paradox of intention: Assessing children's metarepresentational understanding. In B. F. Malle, L. J. Moses, and D. A. Baldwin (eds.), *Intentions and Intentionality: Foundations of Social Cognition* (pp. 85–104). Cambridge, Mass.: The MIT Press.

Augoustinos, M., Tuffin, K., and Sale, L. (1999). Race talk. *Australian Journal of Psychology* 51: 90–97.

Augoustinos, M., and Walker, I. (1995). *Social Cognition: An Integrated Introduction*. London: Sage.

Baird, J. A., and Baldwin, D. A. (2001). Making sense of human behavior: Action parsing and intentional inference. In B. F. Malle, L. J. Moses, and D. A. Baldwin (eds.), *Intentions and Intentionality: Foundations of Social Cognition* (pp. 193–206). Cambridge, Mass.: The MIT Press.

Baldwin, D. A., Baird, J. A., Saylor, M. M., and Clark, M. A. (2001). Infants parse dynamic action. *Child Development* 72: 708–717.

Baron, A. (2003). *Baron's Guide to "Gay" Sex: A Primer for Children and Young People.* Retrieved April 20, 2003 from <www.geocities.com/CapitolHill/Embassy/2634/barons_guide_1.html>.

Baron-Cohen, S. (1992). The girl who shouted in the church. In R. Campbell (ed.), *Mental Lives: Case Studies in Cognition* (pp. 11–23). Oxford: Blackwell.

Baron-Cohen, S. (1995). *Mindblindness: An Essay on Autism and Theory of Mind.* Cambridge, Mass.: The MIT Press.

Baron-Cohen, S. (1999). The evolution of a theory of mind. In M. C. Corballis and S. E. G. Lea (eds.), *The Descent of Mind: Psychological Perspectives on Hominid Evolution* (pp. 261–277). New York: Oxford University Press.

Baron-Cohen, S. (2000). Theory of mind and autism: A fifteen year review. In S. Baron-Cohen, H. Tager-Flusberg, and D. Cohen (eds.), *Understanding Other Minds: Perspectives from Developmental Cognitive Neuroscience* (pp. 3–20). New York: Oxford University Press.

Baron-Cohen, S., Leslie, A. M., and Frith, U. (1985). Mechanical, behavioral, and intentional understanding of picture stories in autistic children. *British Journal of Developmental Psychology* 4: 113–125.

Barresi, J. (2000). Intentional relations and divergent perspectives in social understanding. In S. Gallagher and S. Watson (eds.), *Ipseity and Alterity.* Special Issue of Arob@se: *Journal des lettres et sciences humaines* 4: 74–99.

Barresi, J., and Moore, C. (1996). Intentional relations and social understanding. *Behavioral and Brain Sciences* 19: 107–154.

Barrett, H. (1986). *Maintaining the Self in Communication.* Medford, Ore.: Alpha and Omega.

Bartsch, K., and Wellman, H. (1989). Young children's attribution of action to beliefs and desires. *Child Development* 60: 946–964.

Bartsch, K., and Wellman, H. M. (1995). *Children Talk about the Mind.* New York: Oxford University Press.

Baumböck, K. (1942). *Juden machen Weltpolitik.* (The Jews in world politics.) Berlin: Propaganda-Verlag Paul Hochmuth.

Belmore, S. M. (1987). Determinants of attention during impression formation. *Journal of Experimental Psychology: Learning, Memory, and Cognition* 13: 480–489.

Bertenthal, B. I. (1993). Infants' perception of biomechanical motions: Intrinsic image and knowledge-based constraints. In C. Granrud (ed.), *Visual Perception and Cognition in Infancy* (pp. 175–214). Hillsdale, N.J.: Lawrence Erlbaum.

Binford, L. (1981). *Bones: Ancient Men and Modern Myths.* San Diego, Calif.: Academic Press.

Blackburn, J., Gottschewski, K., George, E., and L—, N. (2000). *A Discussion about Theory of Mind: From an Autistic Perspective.* From Autism Europe's 6th International Congress, Glasgow, May 19–21, 2000. Retrieved on April 10, 2003, from <http://www.autistics.org/library/AE2000-ToM.html>.

Blakemore, S., and Decety, J. (2001). From the perception of action to the understanding of intention. *Nature Reviews Neuroscience* 2: 561–567.

Blumstein, P. W. (1974). The honoring of accounts. *American Sociological Review* 39: 551–566.

Boesch, C. (1991). Teaching among wild chimpanzees. *Animal Behavior* 41: 530–532.

Boesch, C. (1993). Aspects of transmission of tool use in wild chimpanzees. In K. G. Gibson and T. Ingold (eds.), *Tools, Language and Cognition in Human Evolution* (pp. 171–183). Cambridge: Cambridge University Press.

Bogdan, R. (2000). *Minding Minds: Evolving a Reflexive Mind by Interpreting Others.* Cambridge, Mass.: The MIT Press.

Bohner, G., Bless, H., Schwarz, N., and Strack, F. (1988). What triggers causal attributions? The impact of valence and subjective probability. *European Journal of Social Psychology* 18: 335–345.

Bonta, S. (2000). The power elite and George W. *New American* 16 (15), July 17, 2000. Retrieved on April 20, 2003, from <www.thenewamerican.com/tna/2000/07-17-2000/vol16no15_bush.htm>.

Boucher, J., and Osgood, E. E. (1969). The pollyanna hypothesis. *Journal of Verbal Learning and Verbal Behavior* 8: 1–8.

Bradbury, T. M., and Fincham, F. D. (1990). Attributions in marriage: Review and critique. *Psychological Bulletin* 107: 3–33.

Bradley, G. W. (1978). Self-serving biases in the attribution process: A reexamination of the fact or fiction question. *Journal of Personality and Social Psychology* 36: 56–71.

Braginsky, B. M., Braginsky, D. D., and Ring, K. (1969). *Methods of Madness: The Mental Hospital as a Last Resort.* New York: Holt, Rinehart, and Winston.

Braginsky, D. D., and Braginsky, B. M. (1971). *Hansels and Gretels: Studies of Children in Institutions for the Mentally Retarded.* New York: Holt, Rinehart, and Winston.

Bratman, M. E. (1993). Shared intention. *Ethics* 104: 97–113.

Brewer, M. B. and Harasty, A. S. (1996). Seeing groups as entities: The role of perceiver motivation. In R. M. Sorrentino and E. T. Higgins (eds.), *The Handbook of Motivation and Cognition*, volume 3: *The Interpersonal Context* (pp. 347–370). New York: Guilford Press.

Brewer, M. B., Weber, J. G., and Carini, B. (1995). Person memory in intergroup contexts: Categorization versus individuation. *Journal of Personality and Social Psychology* 69: 29–40.

Brewer, W. F. (1994). Autobiographical memory and survey research. In N. Schwarz and S. Sudman (eds.), *Autobiographical Memory and the Validity of Retrospective Reports* (pp. 11–20). New York: Springer.

Bromberger, S. (1965). An approach to explanation. In R. Butler (ed.), *Analytical Philosophy* (second series, pp. 72–105). Oxford: Basil Blackwell.

Bromberger, S. (1992). What we don't know when we don't know why. In *On What We Know We Don't Know* (pp. 145–169). Chicago, Ill.: The University of Chicago Press.

Brown, R. (1973). *A First Language: The Early Stages*. Cambridge, Mass.: Harvard University Press.

Brown, R., and Fish, D. (1983). The psychological causality implicit in language. *Cognition* 14: 237–273.

Brown, R., and Van Kleeck, M. H. (1989). Enough said: Three principles of explanation. *Journal of Personality and Social Psychology* 57: 590–604.

Bruner, J. S. (1990). *Acts of Meaning*. Cambridge, Mass.: Harvard University Press.

Bruner, J., and Feldman, C. (1994). Theories of mind and the problem of autism. In S. Baron-Cohen and H. Tager-Flusberg (eds.), *Understanding Other Minds: Perspectives from Autism* (pp. 267–291). New York: Oxford University Press.

Burke, K. (1945). *A Grammar of Motives*. New York: Prentice-Hall.

Buss, A. R. (1978). Causes and reasons in attribution theory: A conceptual critique. *Journal of Personality and Social Psychology* 36: 1311–1321.

Buss, A. R. (1979). On the relationship between reasons and causes. *Journal of Personality and Social Psychology* 37: 1458–1461.

Butterworth, G. (1991). The ontogeny and phylogeny of joint visual attention. In A. Whiten (ed.), *Natural Theories of Mind* (pp. 223–232). Oxford: Blackwell.

Byrne, R. W., and Whiten, A. (1988). *Machiavellian Intelligence: Social Expertise and the Evolution of Intellect in Monkeys, Apes, and Humans*. New York: Oxford University Press.

Call, J., and Tomasello, M. (1996). The effect of humans on the cognitive development of apes. In A. E. Russon, K. A. Bard, and S. T. Parker (eds.), *Reaching into Thought* (pp. 371–403). Cambridge: Cambridge University Press.

Calvin, W. H. (1996). *How Brains Think: Evolving Intelligence, Then and Now.* New York: Basic Books.

Campbell, D. T. (1958). Common fate, similarity, and other indices of the status of aggregates of persons as social entities. *Behavioral Science* 3: 14–25.

Carlson, S. M., and Moses, L. J. (2001). Individual differences in inhibitory control and children's theory of mind. *Child Development* 72: 1032–1053.

Carlston, D. E., and Skowronski, J. J. (1994). Savings in the relearning of trait information as evidence for spontaneous inference generation. *Journal of Personality and Social Psychology* 66: 840–856.

Carpenter, M., Akhtar, N., and Tomasello, M. (1998). Fourteen- through 18-month-old infants differentially imitate intentional and accidental actions. *Infant Behavior and Development* 21: 315–330.

Carpenter, M., and Tomasello, M. (2000). Joint attention, cultural learning, and language acquisition: Implications for children with autism. In A. M. Wetherby and B. M. Prizant (eds.), *Autism Spectrum Disorders: A Transactional Developmental Perspective* (pp. 31–54). Baltimore, Md.: P. H. Brookes.

Carruthers, P., and Smith, P. K. (eds.) (1996). *Theories of Theories of Mind.* New York: Cambridge University Press.

Cavalli-Sforza, L. L. (2000). *Genes, People, and Languages.* M. Seielstad, trans. New York: North Point Press.

CBS (2002). A rare glimpse inside Bush's cabinet. Nov. 17, 2002. Retrieved on April 20, 2003, from <www.cbsnews.com/stories/2002/11/17/60minutes/main529657.shtml>.

Charpa, U. (2001). *Wissen und Handeln: Grundzüge einer Forschungstheorie.* Stuttgart/ Weimar: Metzler.

Cheney, D. L., and Seyfarth, R. M. (1990). Attending to behaviour versus attending to knowledge: Examining monkeys attribution of mental states. *Animal Behaviour* 40: 742–753.

Cheng, P. W. (2000). Causality in the mind: Estimating contextual and conjunctive power. In F. C. Keil and R. A. Wilson (eds.), *Explanation and Cognition* (pp. 227–253). Cambridge, Mass.: The MIT Press.

Cheng, P. W., and Novick, L. R. (1990). A probabilistic contrast model of causal induction. *Journal of Personality and Social Psychology* 58: 545–567.

Cheng, P. W., and Novick, L. R. (1992). Covariation in natural causal induction. *Psychological Review* 99: 365–382.

Choi, I., Dalal, R., Kim-Prieto, C., and Park, H. (2003). Culture and judgement of causal relevance. *Journal of Personality and Social Psychology* 84: 46–59.

Churchland, P. M. (1981). Eliminative materialism and the propositional attitudes. *Journal of Philosophy* 78: 67–90.

Churchland, P. M. (1991). Folk psychology and the explanation of human behavior. In J. D. Greenwood (ed.), *The Future of Folk Psychology: Intentionality and Cognitive Science* (pp. 51–69). Cambridge: Cambridge University Press.

Clark, A. G. (1994). Beliefs and desires incorporated. *Journal of Philosophy* 91: 404–425.

Clark, H. H. (1996). *Using Language*. New York: Cambridge University Press.

Clark, H. H., and Brennan, S. E. (1991). Grounding in communication. In L. B. Resnick, J. M. Levine, and S. D. Teasley (eds.), *Socially Shared Cognition* (pp. 127–149). Washington, D.C.: American Psychological Association.

Clary, E. G., and Tesser, A. (1983). Reactions to unexpected events: The naïve scientist and interpretive activity. *Personality and Social Psychology Bulletin* 9: 609–620.

Coltheart, M., and Langdon, R. (1998). Autism, modularity, and levels of explanation in cognitive science. *Mind and Language* 13: 138–152.

Comrie, N., and Polinsky, M. (eds.) (1993). *Causatives and Transitivity*. Amsterdam: John Benjamins.

Cook, K. (2002). *Critical Eye on Nanking*. Retrieved on April 20, 2003, from <www.stanford.edu/~kcook/perspectives.html>.

Corkum, V., and Moore, C. (1995). Development of joint visual attention in infants. In C. Moore and P. Dunham (eds.), *Joint Attention: Its Origins and Role in Development* (pp. 61–83). Hillsdale, N.J.: Lawrence Erlbaum.

Corkum, V., and Moore, C. (1998). The origins of joint visual attention in infants. *Developmental Psychology* 34: 28–38.

Cosmides, L., and Tooby, J. (1992). Cognitive adaptations for social exchange. In J. H. Barkow, L. Cosmides, and J. Tooby (eds.), *The Adapted Mind: Evolutionary Psychology and the Generation of Culture* (pp. 163–228). New York: Oxford University Press.

Cowan, N. (1995). *Attention and Memory: An Integrated Framework*. New York: Oxford University Press.

Craik, K. J. W. (1943). *The Nature of Explanation*. Cambridge: Cambridge University Press.

Cruz, J. L. H. (1998). Mindreading: Mental state ascription and cognitive architecture. *Mind and Language* 13: 323–340.

Cummins, D. D. (1998). Social norms and other minds: The evolutionary roots of higher cognition. In D. D. Cummins and C. Allen (eds.), *The Evolution of Mind* (pp. 30–50). New York: Oxford University Press.

D'Andrade, R. (1987). A folk model of the mind. In D. Holland and N. Quinn (eds.), *Cultural Models in Language and Thought* (pp. 112–148). New York: Cambridge University Press.

Davidson, D. (1963). Actions, reasons, and causes. *Journal of Philosophy* 60: 685–700.

Davidson, D. (1982). Rational animals. *Dialectica* 36: 317–327.

Davies, M., and Stone, T. (eds.) (1995). *Mental Simulation: Evaluations and Applications.* Cambridge, Mass.: Blackwell.

Dawes, R. M. (1990). The potential nonfalsity of the false consensus effect. In R. M. Hogarth (ed.), *Insights in Decision Making: A Tribute to Hillel J. Einhorn* (pp. 179–199). Chicago, Ill.: University of Chicago Press.

Dawson, G., Webb, A., Schellenberg, G. D., Dager, S., Friedman, S., Aylward, E., and Richards, T. (2002). Defining the broader phenotype of autism: Genetic, brain, and behavioral perspectives. *Development and Psychopathology* 14: 581–611.

Day, S. X. (2004). *Theory and Design in Counseling and Psychotherapy.* Boston, Mass.: Lahaska Press, Houghton Mifflin.

Deaux, K., and Lewis, L. L. (1984). Structure of gender stereotypes: Interrelationships among components and gender labels. *Journal of Personality and Social Psychology* 46: 991–1004.

Decety, J. (2002). Is there such a thing as functional equivalence between imagined, observed, and executed action? In A. N. Meltzoff and W. Prinz (eds.), *The Imitative Mind: Development, Evolution, and Brain Bases* (pp. 291–310). New York: Cambridge University Press.

Dennett, D. C. (1987). *The Intentional Stance.* Cambridge, Mass.: The MIT Press.

Dershowitz, A. M. (1994). *The Abuse Excuse: And Other Cop-Outs, Sob Stories, and Evasions of Responsibility.* Boston, Mass.: Little, Brown.

Deuser, W. E., and Anderson, C. A. (1995). Controllability attributions and learned helplessness: Some methodological and conceptual problems. *Basic and Applied Social Psychology* 16: 297–318.

Devine, P. (1989). Stereotypes and prejudice: Their automatic and controlled components. *Journal of Personality and Social Psychology* 56: 5–18.

Devlin, K. J. (2000). *The Math Gene: How Mathematical Thinking Evolved and Why Numbers Are Like Gossip.* New York: Basic Books.

Dimdins, G. (2003). Shared reality and false polarization in intergroup perception. Doctoral dissertation, Department of Psychology, Stockholm University, Sweden.

Dirven, R. (1995). The construal of cause: The case of cause prepositions. In J. R. Taylor and R. E. MacLaury (eds.), *Language and the Cognitive Construal of the World* (pp. 95–118). New York: Mouton de Gruyter.

Dittrich, W. J., and Lea, S. E. G. (1994). Visual perception of intentional motion. *Perception* 23: 253–268.

Dixon, T. (1905). *The Clansman: An Historical Romance of the Ku Klux Klan.* New York: Doubleday, Page. Retrieved on April 15, 2003, from <http://docsouth.unc.edu/dixonclan/dixon.html>.

Donald, M. (1991). *Origins of the Modern Mind: Three Stages in the Evolution of Culture and Cognition.* Cambridge, Mass.: Harvard University Press.

Donellan, K. S. (1967). Reasons and causes. In B. Edwards (ed.), *Encyclopedia of Philosophy* (volume 7, pp. 85–88). New York: Macmillan.

Dretske, F. (1988). *Explaining Behavior: Reasons in a World of Causes.* Cambridge, Mass.: The MIT Press.

Dunbar, R. I. M. (1993). Coevolution of neocortical size, group size, and language in humans. *Behavioral and Brain Sciences* 16: 681–735.

Dunbar, R. I. M. (1996). *Grooming, Gossip, and the Evolution of Language.* Cambridge, Mass.: Harvard University Press.

Dunn, J., Brown, J., and Beardsall, L. (1991). Family talk about feeling states and children's later understanding of others' emotions. *Developmental Psychology* 27: 448–455.

Edwards, D., and Potter, J. (1993). Language and causation: A discursive action model of description and attribution. *Psychological Review* 100: 23–41.

Egan, F. (1995). Folk psychology and cognitive architecture. *Philosophy of Science* 62: 179–196.

Fein, S. (1996). Effects of suspicion on attributional thinking and the correspondence bias. *Journal of Personality and Social Psychology* 70: 1164–1184.

Fein, S. (2001). Beyond the fundamental attribution era? *Psychological Inquiry* 12: 16–21.

Festinger, L. (1957). *A Theory of Cognitive Dissonance.* Stanford, Calif.: Stanford University Press.

Fiedler, K., Walther, E., and Nickel, S. (1999). Covariation-based attribution: On the ability to assess multiple covariates of an effect. *Personality and Social Psychology Bulletin* 25: 607–622.

Fincham, F. D., and Bradbury, T. N. (1992). Assessing attributions in marriage: The relationship attribution measure. *Journal of Personality and Social Psychology* 62: 457–468.

Fincham, F. D., Beach, S. R., and Baucom, D. H. (1987). Attribution processes in distressed and nondistressed couples: 4. Self-partner attribution differences. *Journal of Personality and Social Psychology* 52: 739–748.

Fincham, F. D., Beach, S. R., and Nelson, G. (1987). Attribution processes in distressed and nondistressed couples: 3. Causal and responsibility attributions for spouse behavior. *Cognitive Therapy and Research* 11: 71–86.

Fincham, F. D., Bradbury, T. N., and Grych, J. H. (1990). Conflict in close relationships: The role of intrapersonal phenomena. In S. Graham and V. S. Folkes (eds.), *Attribution Theory: Applications to Achievement, Mental Health, and Interpersonal Conflict* (pp. 161–184). Hillsdale, N.J.: Lawrence Erlbaum.

Fiske, S. T., and Taylor, S. E. (1991). *Social Cognition,* second edition. New York: McGraw-Hill.

Flavell, J. H. (1999). Cognitive development: Children's knowledge about the mind. *Annual Review of Psychology* 50: 21–45.

Fletcher, P. C., Happé, F., Frith, U., Baker, S. C., Dolan, R. J., Frackowiak, R. S. J., and Frith, C. D. (1995). Other minds in the brain: A functional imaging study of "theory of mind" in story comprehension. *Cognition* 57: 109–128.

Fodor, J. (1992). A theory of the child's theory of mind. *Cognition* 44: 283–296.

Fodor, J. A. (2000). *The Mind Doesn't Work That Way: The Scope and Limits of Computational Psychology.* Cambridge, Mass.: The MIT Press.

Føllesdal, D. (1982). The status of rationality assumptions in interpretation and in the explanation of action. *Dialectica* 36: 301–316.

Fontana, A. F. (1971). Machiavellianism and manipualtion in the mental patient role. *Journal of Personality* 39: 1021–1029.

Forguson, L. (1989). *Common Sense.* London, New York: Routledge.

Försterling, F. (1989). Models of covariation and attribution: How do they relate to the analogy of analysis of variance? *Journal of Personality and Social Psychology* 57: 615–625.

Försterling, F. (1992). The Kelley model as an analysis of variance analogy: How far can it be taken? *Journal of Experimental Social Psychology* 28: 475–490.

Försterling, F. (2001). *Attribution: An Introduction to Theories, Research, and Applications.* Philadelphia, Penn.: Psychology Press.

Forsyth, D. R. (1980). The functions of attributions. *Social Psychology Quarterly* 43: 184–189.

Foster, G. M. (1976). Disease etiologies in non-Western medical systems. *American Anthropologist* 78: 773–782.

Frank, J. D., and Frank, J. B. (1991). *Persuasion and Healing: A Comparative Study of Psychotherapy,* third ed. Baltimore, Maryland: Johns Hopkins University Press.

Frankl, V. E. (1962). *Man's Search for Meaning: An Introduction to Logotherapy.* Ilse Lasch, trans. Boston, Mass.: Beacon Press.

Frawley, W. (1992). Events. In W. Frawley, *Linguistic Semantics* (chap. 4, pp. 140–196). Hillsdale, N.J.: Lawrence Erlbaum.

Frith, C. D., and Corcoran, R. (1996). Exploring "theory of mind" in people with schizophrenia. *Psychological Medicine* 26: 521–530.

Frith, U. (2000). Cognitive explanations of autism. In K. Lee (ed.), *Childhood Cognitive Development: The Essential Readings* (pp. 324–337). Malden, Mass.: Blackwell.

Frith, U., and Happé, F. (1999). Theory of mind and self-consciousness: What is it like to be autistic? *Mind and Language* 14: 1–22.

Fugelsang, J. A., and Thompson, V. A. (2000). Strategy selection in causal reasoning: When beliefs and covariation collide. *Canadian Journal of Experimental Psychology* 54: 15–32.

Fussell, S. R., and Krauss, R. M. (1992). Coordination of knowledge in communication: Effects of speakers' assumptions about what others know. *Journal of Personality and Social Psychology* 62: 378–391.

Gaffie, B., Marchand, P., and Cassagne, J.-M. (1997). Effect of political position on group perception. *European Journal of Social Psychology* 27: 177–187.

Gallese, V., and Goldman, A. (1998). Mirror neurons and the simulation theory of mind-reading. *Trends in Cognitive Sciences* 2: 493–501.

Garfinkel, H. (1967). *Studies in Ethnomethodology.* Englewood Cliffs, N.J.: Prentice-Hall.

Garvey, C., and Caramazza, A. (1974). Implicit causality in verbs. *Linguistic Inquiry* 5: 459–464.

Gelman, S. A., and Wellman, H. M. (1991). Insides and essences: Early understandings of the non-obvious. *Cognition* 28: 213–244.

Gergely, G., Nádasdy, Z., Csibra, G., and Bíró, S. (1995). Taking the intentional stance at 12 months of age. *Cognition* 56: 165–193.

Gibbs, R. W., Jr. (1998). The varieties of intentions in interpersonal communication. In S. R. Fussell and R. J. Kreuz (eds.), *Social and Cognitive Approaches to Interpersonal Communication* (pp. 19–37). Mahwah, N.J.: Lawrence Erlbaum.

Gilbert, D. T. (1989). Thinking lightly about others: Automatic components of the social inference process. In J. S. Uleman and J. A. Bargh (eds.), *Unintended Thought: Limits of Awareness, Intention, and Control* (pp. 189–211). New York: Guilford.

Gilbert, D. T. (1995). Attribution and interpersonal perception. In A. Tesser (ed.), *Advanced Social Psychology* (pp. 99–147). New York: McGraw-Hill.

Gilbert, D. T. (1998). Ordinary personology. In D. T. Gilbert, S. T., Fiske, and G. Lindzey (eds.), *The Handbook of Social Psychology,* fourth edition (pp. 89–150). New York: McGraw Hill.

Gilbert, D. T., and Hixon, J. G. (1991). The trouble of thinking: Activation and application of stereotypic beliefs. *Journal of Personality and Social Psychology* 60: 509–517.

Gilbert, D. T., and Malone, P. S. (1995). The correspondence bias. *Psychological Bulletin* 117: 21–38.

Gilbert, D. T., Pelham, B. W., and Krull, D. S. (1988). On cognitive busyness: When person perceivers meet persons perceived. *Journal of Personality and Social Psychology* 54: 733–740.

Gilbert, M. (1989). *On Social Facts*. New York: Routledge.

Gil-White, F. J. (2001). Are ethnic groups biological "species" to the human brain? *Current Anthropology* 42: 515–536.

Givón, T. (1975). Cause and control: On the semantics of interpersonal manipulation. *Syntax and Semantics* 4: 59–89.

Givón, T. (ed.) (1997). *Conversation: Cognitive, Communicative, and Social Perspectives* (Typological Studies in Language, vol. 34). Amsterdam: John Benjamins.

Givón, T., and Malle, B. F. (eds.) (2002). *The Evolution of Language Out of Pre-language.* Amsterdam: Benjamins.

Givón, T., and Young, P. (1994). Trust and cooperation in the society of intimates. Paper presented at Conference on Trust, Institute of Cognitive and Decision Sciences, University of Oregon, November 4–5, 1994.

Glymour, C. (2000). Bayes nets as psychological models. In F. C. Keil and R. A. Wilson (eds.), *Explanation and Cognition* (pp. 169–197). Cambridge, Mass.: The MIT Press.

Goffman, E. (1959). *The Presentation of Self in Everyday Life*. New York: Doubleday.

Goffman, E. (1967). On face-work. In E. Goffman, *Interaction Ritual: Essays in Face-to-face Behavior*. Garden City, N.Y.: Anchor.

Goldman, A. I. (1989). Interpretation psychologized. *Mind and Language* 4: 161–185.

Goldman, A. I. (2001). Desire, intention, and the simulation theory. In B. F. Malle, L. J. Moses, and D. A. Baldwin (eds.), *Intentions and Intentionality: Foundations of Social Cognition* (pp. 207–225). Cambridge, Mass.: The MIT Press.

Gollwitzer, P. M. (1996). The volitional benefits of planning. In P. M. Gollwitzer and J. A. Bargh (eds.), *The Psychology of Action: Linking Cognition and Motivation to Behaviour* (pp. 287–312). New York: Guilford.

Gómez, J. C. (1996). Non-human primate theories of (non-human primate) minds: Some issues concerning the origins of mind-reading. In P. Carruthers and P. K. Smith (eds.), *Theories of Theories of Mind* (pp. 330–343). Cambridge: Cambridge University Press.

Goody, E. N. (Ed.) (1995). *Social Intelligence and Interaction: Expressions and Implications of the Social Bias in Human Intelligence*. Cambridge: Cambridge University Press.

Gopnik, A. (1993). How we know our minds: The illusion of first-person knowledge of intentionality. *Behavioral and Brain Sciences* 16: 1–14.

Gopnik, A. (2000). Explanation as orgasm and the drive for causal knowledge: The function, evolution, and phenomenology of the theory formation system. In F. C. Keil and R. A. Wilson (eds.), *Explanation and Cognition* (pp. 299–323). Cambridge, Mass.: The MIT Press.

Gopnik, A., and Meltzoff, A. N. (1997). *Words, Thoughts, and Theories*. Cambridge, Mass.: The MIT Press.

Gopnik, A., and Wellman, H. M. (1992). Why the child's theory of mind really *is* a theory. *Mind and Language* 7: 145–171.

Gopnik, A., and Wellman, H. M. (1994). The theory theory. In L. A. Hirschfeld and S. A. Gelman (eds.), *Mapping the Mind: Domain Specificity in Cognition and Culture* (pp. 257–293). New York: Cambridge University Press.

Gordon, R. M. (1986). Folk psychology as simulation. *Mind and Language* 1: 158–171.

Gordon, R. M. (1992). The simulation theory: Objections and misconceptions. *Mind and Language* 7: 11–34.

Gordon, R. M. (2001). Simulation and reason explanation: The radical view. *Philosophical Topics* 29: 175–192.

Gosling, S. D., John, O. P., Craik, K. H., and Robins, R. W. (1998). Do people know how they behave? Self-reported act frequencies compared with on-line codings by observers. *Journal of Personality and Social Psychology* 74: 1337–1349.

Graesser, A. C., Millis, K. K., and Zwaan, R. A. (1997). Discourse comprehension. *Annual Review of Psychology* 48: 163–189.

Grandin, T. (1995). *Thinking in Pictures: And Other Reports from My Life with Autism.* New York: Doubleday.

Grèzes, J., and Decety, J. (2001). Functional anatomy of execution, mental simulation, observation, and verb generation of actions: A meta-analysis. *Human Brain Mapping* 12: 1–19.

Grice, H. P. (1957). Meaning. *Philosophical Review* 64: 377–388.

Grice, H. P. (1975). Logic and conversation. In P. Cole and J. L. Morgan (eds.), *Syntax and Semantics 3: Speech Acts* (pp. 41–58). New York: Academic Press.

Grigg, W. N. (1996). An internationalist primer. *New American Magazine* 12 (19), September 16, 1996. Retrieved on March 12, 2003, from <www.thenewamerican.com/tna/1996/vo12no19/vo12no19_cfr.htm>.

Hale, M. (2003). FACTS! That the government and the media don't want you to know. Retrieved on February 16, 2004, from <www.epatriot.org/facts>.

Hamilton, D. L. (1998). Dispositional and attributional inferences in person perception. In J. M. Darley and J. Cooper (eds.), *Attribution and Social Interaction: The Legacy of Edward E. Jones* (pp. 99–114). Washington, D.C.: American Psychological Association.

Hamilton, D. L., and Sherman, S. J. (1996). Perceiving persons and groups. *Psychological Review* 103: 336–355.

Hamilton, D. L, Sherman, S. J., and Lickel, B. (1998). Perceiving social groups: The importance of the entitativity continuum. In C. Sedikides and J. Schopler (eds.), *Intergroup Cognition and Intergroup Behavior* (pp. 47–74). Mahwah, N.J.: Erlbaum.

Hamilton, D. L., Sherman, S. J., and Rodgers, J. S. (in press). Perceiving the groupness of groups: Entitativity, essentialism, and stereotypes. In V. Yzerbyt, C. M. Judd, and O. Corneille (eds.), *The Psychology of Group Perception: A Contribution to the Study of Perceived Variability, Entitaitivity, and Essentialism*. Philadelphia, Penn.: Psychology Press.

Hamilton, D. L., Sherman, S. J., and Sack, J. D. (2001). [Commentary on Gil-White (2001).] *Current Anthropology* 42: 540–541.

Hamilton, V. L. (1978). Who is responsible? Towards a *social* psychology of responsibility attribution. *Social Psychology* 41: 316–328.

Hampson, S. E. (1983). Trait ascription and depth of acquaintance: The preference for traits in personality descriptions and its relation to target familiarity. *Journal of Research in Personality* 17: 398–411.

Harrington, L., Langdon, R., Siegert, R., and McClure, J. (in press). Schizophrenia, theory of mind and persecutory delusions. *Cognitive Neuropsychiatry*.

Harris, P. (1992). From simulation to folk psychology: The case for development. *Mind and Language* 7: 120–144.

Harris, P. (1996). Desires, beliefs, and language. In P. Carruthers and P. K. Smith (eds.), *Theories of Theories of Mind* (pp. 200–220). Cambridge: Cambridge University Press.

Harvey, J. H., Ickes, W., and Kidd, R. F. (1978). A conversation with Edward E. Jones and Harold H. Kelley. In J. H. Harvey, W. Ickes, and R. F. Kidd (eds.), *New Directions in Attribution Research* (volume 2, pp. 371–388). Hillsdale, N.J.: Lawrence Erlbaum.

Harvey, J. H., Orbuch, T. L., and Weber, A. L. (1990). *Interpersonal Accounts*. Oxford: Blackwell.

Harvey, J. H., Orbuch, T. L., and Weber, A. L. (1992). *Attributions, Accounts, and Close Relationships*. New York: Springer.

Harvey, J. H., and Tucker, J. A. (1979). On problems with the cause–reason distinction in attribution theory. *Journal of Personality and Social Psychology* 37: 1441–1446.

Haslam, N., and Fiske, A. P. (forthcoming). Social expertise: Theory of mind or theory of relationships? In N. Haslam (ed.), *Relational Models Theory*. Hillsdale, N.J.: Lawrence Erlbaum.

Haslam, N., and Giosan, C. (2002). The lay concept of "mental disorder" among American undergraduates. *Journal of Clinical Psychology* 58: 479–485.

Haslam, N., Rothschild, L., and Ernst, D. (2000). Essentialist beliefs about social categories. *British Journal of Social Psychology* 39: 113–127.

Hastie, R. (1984). Causes and effects of causal attribution. *Journal of Personality and Social Psychology* 46: 44–56.

Hastorf, A. H., Schneider, D. J., and Polefka, J. (1970). *Person Perception*. Reading, Mass.: Addison-Wesley.

Hauser, M. (1996). *The Evolution of Communication*. Cambridge, Mass.: The MIT Press.

Heal, J. (1996). Simulation, theory, and content. In P. Carruthers and P. K. Smith (eds.), *Theories of Theories of Mind* (pp. 75–89). Cambridge: Cambridge University Press.

Heider, F. (1920). *Zur Subjektivität der Sinnesqualitäten*. (On the subjectivity of sense qualities.) Unpublished doctoral dissertation. University of Graz, Austria.

Heider, F. (1925). Ding und Medium. *Symposium* 1: 109–157.

Heider, F. (1958). *The Psychology of Interpersonal Relations*. New York: Wiley.

Heider, F. (1959). Thing and medium. In F. Heider (1959), On perception, event-structure and psychological environment: Selected papers (pp. 1–34). *Psychological Issues* 1: 1–123.

Herbsleb, J. D. (1999, February). Metaphorical representation in collaborative software engineering. In *Proceedings of the International Joint Conference on Work Activities, Coordination, and Collaboration* (pp. 117–125). San Francisco, Calif.

Hernandez-Cruz, J. L. (1998). Mindreading: Mental state ascription and cognitive architecture. *Mind and Language* 13: 323–340.

Hesslow, G. (1988). The problem of causal selection. In D. J. Hilton (ed.), *Contemporary Science and Natural Explanation: Commonsense Conceptions of Causality* (pp. 11–32). New York: New York University Press.

Hewstone, M. (1990). The "ultimate attribution error"? A review of the literature on intergroup causal attribution. *European Journal of Social Psychology* 20: 311–335.

Hewstone, M., and Jaspars, J. (1987). Covariation and causal attribution: A logical model of the intuitive analysis of variance. *Journal of Personality and Social Psychology* 53: 663–672.

Higgins, E. T. (1992). Achieving "shared reality" in the communication game: A social action that creates meaning. *Journal of Language and Social Psychology* 11: 107–131.

Hilton, D. J. (1990). Conversational processes and causal explanation. *Psychological Bulletin* 107: 65–81.

Hilton, D. J., and Knibbs, C. S. (1988). The knowledge-structure and inductivist strategies in causal attribution: A direct comparison. *European Journal of Social Psychology* 18: 79–92.

Hilton, D. J., and Slugoski, B. R. (1986). Knowledge-based causal attribution: The abnormal conditions focus model. *Psychological Review* 93: 75–88.

Hilton, D. J., Smith, R. H., and Kin, S. H. (1995). Processes of causal explanation and dispositional attribution. *Journal of Personality and Social Psychology* 68: 377–387.

Hinkle, S., and Schmidt, D. F. (1984). The Buss cause/reason hypotheses: An empirical investigation. *Social Psychology Quarterly* 47: 358–364.

Hirschberg, N. (1978). A correct treatment of traits. In H. London (ed.), *Personality: A New Look at Metatheories* (pp. 45–68). New York: Wiley.

Hirschfeld, L. A. (1994). The child's representation of human groups. In D. L. Medin (ed.), *The Psychology of Learning and Motivation: Advances in Research and Theory* (volume 31, pp. 133–185). San Diego, Calif.: Academic Press.

Hobson, R. P., and Lee, A. (1999). Imitation and identification in autism. *Journal of Child Psychology and Psychiatry and Allied Disciplines* 40: 649–659.

Hodges, S. D., and Wilson, T. D. (1993). Effects of analyzing reasons on attitude change: The moderating role of attitude accessibility. *Social Cognition* 11: 353–366.

Honecker, E. (1984, June). Party and revolutionary young guard firmly allied. *Neues Deutschland* 9/10: 1–3.

Hong, Y., Levy, S. R., and Chiu, C. (2001). The contribution of the lay theories approach to the study of groups. *Personality and Social Psychology Review* 5: 98–106.

Hood, L. and Bloom, L. (1979). What, when, and how about why: A longitudinal study of early expressions of causality. *Monographs of the Society for Research in Child Development* 44: 1–47.

Horton, W. S., and Gerrig, R. J. (2002). Speakers' experiences and audience design: Knowing when and knowing how to adjust utterances to addresses. *Journal of Memory and Language* 47: 589–606.

Horwitz, A. V. (2002). *Creating Mental Illness.* Chicago, Ill.: University of Chicago Press.

Hughes, C. (1998). Executive function in preschoolers: Links with theory of mind and verbal ability. *British Journal of Developmental Psychology* 16: 233–253.

Hughes, C., and Dunn, J. (1998). Understanding mind and emotion: Longitudinal associations with mental-state talk between young friends. *Developmental Psychology* 34: 1026–1037.

Huhns, M. N., and Singh, M. P. (1998). Agents on the web: Cognitive agents. *IEEE Internet Computing* 2(6): 87.

Humphrey, N. K. (1976). The social function of intellect. In P. P. G. Bateson and R. Hinde (eds.), *Growing Points in Ethology.* New York: Cambridge University Press.

Ickes, W. (1976). A conversation with Fritz Heider. In J. H. Harvey, W. Ickes, and R. F. Kidd (eds.), *New Directions in Attribution Research* (volume 1, pp. 3–18). Hillsdale, N.J.: Lawrence Erlbaum.

Ickes, W. (ed.). (1997). *Empathic Accuracy.* New York: Guilford.

Insko, C. A., Schopler, J., and Sedikides, C. (1998). Personal control, entitativity, and evolution. In C. Sedikides, J. Schopler, and C. A. Insko (eds.), *Intergroup Cognition and Intergroup Behavior* (pp. 109–120). Mahwah, N.J.: Lawrence Erlbaum.

International Military Tribunal (1947). *Trial of the Major War Criminals Before the International Military Tribunal* (volume 1). Nuremberg: International Military Tribunal.

Islam, M. R., and Hewstone, M. (1993). Intergroup attributions and affective consequences in majority and minority groups. *Journal of Personality and Social Psychology* 64: 936–950.

Janoff-Bulman, R. (1992). *Shattered Assumptions: Towards a New Psychology of Trauma.* New York: Free Press.

Jenkins, J. M., and Astington, J. W. (1996). Cognitive factors and family structure associated with theory of mind development in young children. *Developmental Psychology* 32: 70–78.

Jervis, R. (1976). *Perception and Misperception in International Politics.* Princeton, N.J.: Princeton University Press.

Johnson, J. T., Boyd, K. R., and Magnani, P. S. (1994). Causal reasoning in the attribution of rare and common events. *Journal of Personality and Social Psychology* 66: 229–242.

Johnson, J. T., Long, D. L., and Robinson, M. D. (2001). Is a cause conceptualized as a generative force? Evidence from a recognition memory paradigm. *Journal of Experimental Social Psychology* 37: 398–412.

Johnson, S., Slaughter, V., and Carey, S. (1998). Whose gaze will infants follow? The elicitation of gaze-following in 12-month-olds. *Developmental Science* 1: 233–238.

Jones, E. E., and Davis, K. E. (1965). From acts to dispositions: The attribution process in person perception. In L. Berkowitz (ed.), *Advances in Experimental Social Psychology* (volume 2, pp. 219–266). New York: Academic Press.

Jones, E. E., and Harris, V. A. (1967). The attribution of attitudes. *Journal of Experimental Social Psychology* 3: 1–24.

Jones, E. E., Kanouse, D., Kelley, H. H., Nisbett, R. E., Valins, S., and Weiner, B. (1972). (eds.), *Attribution: Perceiving the Causes of Behavior.* Morristown, N.J.: General Learning Press.

Jones, E. E., and Nisbett, R. E. (1972). The actor and the observer: Divergent perceptions of the causes of behavior. In E. E. Jones, D. Kanouse, H. H. Kelley, R. E. Nisbett, S. Valins, and B. Weiner (eds.), *Attribution: Perceiving the Causes of Behavior* (pp. 79–94). Morristown, N.J.: General Learning Press.

Jones, E. E., and Thibaut, J. W. (1958). Interaction goals as bases of inference in interpersonal perception. In R. Tagiuri and L. Petrullo (eds.), *Person Perception and Interpersonal Behavior* (pp. 151–178). Stanford, Calif.: Stanford University Press.

Judd, C. M., Ryan, C. S., and Park, B. (1991). Accuracy in the judgment of in-group and out-group variability. *Journal of Personality and Social Psychology* 61: 366–379.

Kahneman, D., and Miller, D. T. (1986). Norm theory: Comparing reality to its alternatives. *Psychological Review* 93: 136–153.

Kalish, C. (1998). Reasons and causes: Children's understanding of conformity to social rules and physical laws. *Child Development* 69: 706–720.

Kammrath, L. K., Mendoza–Denton, R., and Mischel, W. (2003). Lay dispositional theories of person × situation (if . . . then . . .) relations. Paper presented at the Third Annual convention of the Society of Personality and Social Psychology, Universal City, California.

Kant, I. (1998/1787). *Critique of Pure Reason.* Translated and edited by Paul Guyer, Allen W. Wood. New York: Cambridge University Press. (Originally published 1787.)

Kasari, C., Sigman, M., Mundy, P., and Yirmiya, N. (1990). Affective sharing in the context of joint attention interactions of normal, autistic, and mentally retarded children. *Journal of Autism and Developmental Disorders* 20: 87–100.

Keil, F. C. and Wilson, R. A. (eds). (2000). *Explanation and Cognition.* Cambridge, Mass.: The MIT Press.

Kelley, H. H. (1960). The analysis of common sense. A review of "The psychology of interpersonal relations" by Fritz Heider. *Contemporary Psychology* 5: 1–3.

Kelley, H. H. (1967). Attribution theory in social psychology. In D. Levine (ed.), *Nebraska Symposium on Motivation* (volume 15, pp. 129–238). Lincoln, Nebr.: University of Nebraska Press.

Kelley, H. H., and Michela, J. L. (1980). Attribution theory and research. *Annual Review of Psychology* 31: 457–501.

Kelly, G. A. (1955). *The Psychology of Personal Constructs.* New York: Norton.

Kerber, K. W., and Singleton, R. (1984). Trait and situational attributions in a naturalistic setting: Familiarity, liking, and attribution validity. *Journal of Personality* 52: 205–219.

Kidd, R. F., and Amabile, T. M. (1981). Causal explanations in social interaction: Some dialogues on dialogue. In J. H. Harvey, W. J. Ickes, and R. F. Kidd (eds.), *New Directions in Attribution Research* (volume 3, pp. 307–328). Hillsdale, N.J.: Lawrence Erlbaum.

Klin, A., Jones, W., Schultz, R., Volkmar, F., and Cohen, D. (2002). Defining and quantifying the social phenotype in autism. *American Journal of Psychiatry* 159: 895–908.

Knobe, J. (2003a). Intentional action and side effects in ordinary language. *Analysis* 63: 190–194.

Knobe, J. (2003b). Intentional action in folk psychology: An experimental investigation. *Philosophical Psychology* 16: 309–324.

Knobe, J., and Malle, B. F. (2002). Self and other in the explanation of behavior: 30 years later. *Psychologica Belgica* (special issue on self-other asymmetries) 42: 113–130.

Knowles, E. S. (1982). From individuals to group members: A dialectic for the social sciences. In W. Ickes and E. S. Knowles (eds.), *Personality, Roles, and Social Behavior* (pp. 1–32). New York: Springer.

Knowles, E. S, and Bassett, R. L. (1976). Groups and crowds as social entities: Effects of activity, size, and member similarity on nonmembers. *Journal of Personality and Social Psychology* 34: 837–845.

Koehler, D. J. (1991). Explanation, imagination, and confidence in judgment. *Psychological Bulletin* 110: 499–519.

Kramer, R. M. (1994). The sinister attribution error: Paranoid cognition and collective distrust in organizations. *Motivation and Emotion* 18: 199–230.

Krauss, R. M., and Fussell, S. R. (1991). Constructing shared communicative environments. In L. B. Resnick, J. M. Levine, and S. D. Teasley (eds.), *Perspectives on Socially Shared Cognition* (pp. 172–200). Washington, D.C.: American Psychological Association.

Krebs, J. R., and Dawkins, R. (1984). Animal signals: Mind-reading and manipulation. In J. R. Krebs and N. B. Davies (eds.), *Behavioural Ecology: An Evolutionary Approach* (pp. 380–402). Oxford: Blackwell.

Krim, S. (1968). *Views of a Nearsighted Cannoneer.* New York: Dutton.

Krueger, J., and Clement, R. W. (1997). Estimates of social consensus by majorities and minorities: The case for social projection. *Personality and Social Psychology Review* 1: 299–313.

Krueger, J., and Rothbart, M. (1990). Contrast and accentuation effects in category learning. *Journal of Personality and Social Psychology* 59: 651–663.

Kruglanski, A. W. (1975). The endogenous–exogenous partition in attribution theory. *Psychological Review* 82: 387–406.

Kruglanski, A. W. (1979). Causal explanation, teleological explanation: On radical particularism in attribution theory. *Journal of Personality and Social Psychology* 37: 1447–1457.

Kruglanski, A. W. (1989). *Lay Epistemics and Human Knowledge.* New York: Plenum.

Kugelmass, S., and Breznitz, S. (1968). Intentionality in moral judgment: Adolescent development. *Child Development* 39: 249–256.

Kuhl, J. (1987). Action control: The maintenance of motivational states. In F. Halisch and J. Kuhl (eds.), *Motivation, Intention, and Volition* (pp. 279–291). Berlin: Springer.

Kunda, Z. (1999). *Social Cognition*. Cambridge, Mass.: The MIT Press.

Kunda, Z., and Oleson, K. C. (1997). When exceptions prove the rule: How extremity of deviance determines the impact of deviant examples on stereotypes. *Journal of Personality and Social Psychology* 72: 965–979.

Lalljee, M., and Abelson, R. P. (1983). The organization of explanations. In M. Hewstone (ed.), *Attribution Theory: Social and Functional Extensions* (pp. 65–80). Oxford: Basil Blackwell.

Lalljee, M., Lamb, R., Furnham, A. F., and Jaspars, J. (1984). Explanations and information search: Inductive and hypothesis-testing approaches to arriving at an explanation. *British Journal of Social Psychology* 23: 201–212.

Langer, E. J. (1975). The illusion of control. *Journal of Personality and Social Psychology* 32: 311–328.

Langer, E. J., Blank, A., and Chanowitz, B. (1978). The mindlessness of ostensibly thoughtful action: The role of "placebic" information in interpersonal interaction. *Journal of Personality and Social Psychology* 36: 635–642.

Lazare, B. (1995/1894). *Antisemitism: Its History and Causes* (abridged American version). Lincoln, Neb.: University of Nebraska Press. (Originally published in French in 1894.) Retrieved April 20, 2003 from <http://aaargh-international.org/engl/Blantisem$.html>, whereby the $ sign must be replaced by the number of the specific chapter desired.

Leakey, R. E. (1994). *The Origin of Humankind*. New York: Basic Books.

Leary, M. R. (1995). *Self-presentation: Impression Management and Interpersonal Behavior*. Boulder, Colo.: Westview.

Leddo, J., and Abelson, R. P. (1986). The nature of explanations. In J. Galambos, R. P. Abelson, and J. B. Black (eds.), *Knowledge Structures* (pp. 103–122). Hillsdale, N.J.: Lawrence Erlbaum.

Legerstee, M. (1991). The role of person and object in eliciting early imitation. *Journal of Experimental Child Psychology* 51: 423–433.

Lehrer, J. (2002a). *The NewsHour with Jim Lehrer*. Thursday, February 21, 2002. Retrieved from Lexis-Nexis electronic database, transcript no. 7272.

Lehrer, J. (2002b). *The NewsHour with Jim Lehrer*. Friday, October 4, 2002. Retrieved from Lexis-Nexis electronic database, transcript no. 7470.

Lehrer, J. (2002c). *The NewsHour with Jim Lehrer*. Thursday, December 12, 2002. Retrieved from Lexis-Nexis electronic database, transcript no. 7519.

Lehrer, J. (2003). *The NewsHour with Jim Lehrer.* Friday, February 28, 2003. Retrieved from Lexis-Nexis electronic database, transcript no. 7575.

Lennon, K. (1990). *Explaining Human Action.* La Salle, Ill.: Open Court.

Leslie, A. M. (1987). Pretense and representation: The origins of "theory of mind." *Psychological Review* 94: 412–426.

Leslie, A. M. (1992). Autism and the "theory of mind" module. *Current Directions in Psychological Science* 1: 18–21.

Leslie, A. M. (1994). ToMM, ToBy, and Agency: Core architecture and domain specificity. In L. A. Hirschfeld, S. A. Gelman, et al. (eds.), *Mapping the Mind: Domain Specificity in Cognition and Culture* (pp. 119–148). New York: Cambridge University Press.

Levenson, R. W., and Ruef, A. M. (1997). Physiological aspects of emotional knowledge and rapport. In W. Ickes (ed.), *Empathic Accuracy* (pp. 44–72). New York: Guilford.

Lewin, K. (1947). *Frontiers in Group Dynamics: Concept, Method, and Reality in Social Science, Social Equilibria, and Social Change.* Indianapolis, Ind.: Bobbs-Merrill.

Lewis, C., Freeman, N. H., Kyriakidou, C., and Maridaki–Kassotaki, K. (1996). Social influences on false belief access: Specific sibling influences or general apprenticeship? *Child Development* 67: 2930–2947.

Lewis, D. (1972). Psychophysical and theoretical identifications. *Australasian Journal of Philosophy* 50: 249–258.

Lickel, B., Hamilton, D. L., and Sherman, S. J. (2001). Elements of a lay theory of groups: Types of groups, relationship styles, and the perception of group entitativity. *Personality and Social Psychology Review* 5: 129–140.

Lickel, B., Hamilton, D. L, Wieczorkowska, G. Lewis, A., Sherman, S. J., and Uhles, A. N. (2000). Varieties of groups and the perception of group entitativity. *Journal of Personality and Social Psychology* 78: 223–246.

Lillard, A. (1998). Ethnopsychologies: Cultural variations in theories of mind. *Psychological Bulletin* 123: 3–32.

Liu, T. J., and Steele, C. M. (1986). Attributional analysis of self-affirmation. *Journal of Personality and Social Psychology* 51: 531–540.

Locke, D., and Pennington, D. (1982). Reasons and other causes: Their role in attribution processes. *Journal of Personality and Social Psychology* 42: 212–223.

Lopes, L. L. (1982). Doing the impossible: A note on induction and the experience of randomness. *Journal of Experimental Psychology: Learning, Memory, and Cognition* 8: 626–636.

Lynch, E. B. (2003). Group differences in causal models of illness: The second spear. Unpublished manuscript, Northwestern University.

Lyon, T. D. (1993). Young children's understanding of desire and knowledge. Unpublished doctoral dissertation, Stanford University, Stanford, Calif.

Maass, A. (1999). Linguistic intergroup bias: Stereotype perpetuation through language. *Advances in Experimental Social Psychology* 31: 79–121.

MacWhinney, B. (2002). The gradual evolution of language. In T. Givón and B. F. Malle (eds.), *The Evolution of Language Out of Pre-Language* (pp. 233–263). Amsterdam: Benjamins.

Malle, B. F. (1994). Intentionality and explanation: A study in the folk theory of behavior. Unpublished doctoral dissertation, Stanford University, Stanford, Calif.

Malle, B. F. (1998). F.Ex: Coding scheme for people's folk explanations of behavior. Retrieved April 20, 2003, from <http://darkwing.uoregon.edu/~bfmalle/fex.html>. Reprinted with minor revisions in the appendix of this volume.

Malle, B. F. (1999). How people explain behavior: A new theoretical framework. *Personality and Social Psychology Review* 3: 23–48.

Malle, B. F. (2001a). Attribution processes. In N. J. Smelser and P. B. Baltes (eds.), *International Encyclopedia of the Social and Behavioral Sciences* (volume 14, Developmental, social, personality, and motivational psychology; section editor N. Eisenberg, pp. 913–917). Amsterdam: Pergamon/Elsevier.

Malle, B. F. (2001b). Folk explanations of intentional action. In B. F. Malle, L. J. Moses, and D. A. Baldwin (eds.), *Intentions and Intentionality: Foundations of Social Cognition* (pp. 265–286). Cambridge, Mass.: The MIT Press.

Malle, B. F. (2002a). The relation between language and theory of mind in development and evolution. In T. Givón and B. F. Malle (eds.), *The Evolution of Language Out of Pre-Language* (pp. 265–284). Amsterdam: Benjamins.

Malle, B. F. (2002b). The social self and the social other. Actor–observer asymmetries in making sense of behavior. In J. P. Forgas and K. D. Williams (eds.), *The Social Self: Cognitive, Interpersonal, and Intergroup Perspectives* (pp. 189–204). Philadelphia, Penn.: Psychology Press.

Malle, B. F. (2002c). Verbs of interpersonal causality and the folk theory of mind and behavior. In M. Shibatani (ed.), *The Grammar of Causation and Interpersonal Manipulation* (pp. 57–83). Amsterdam: Benjamins.

Malle, B. F. (in press). Folk theory of mind: Conceptual foundations of human social cognition. In R. Hassin, J. S. Uleman, and J. A. Bargh (eds.), *The New Unconscious*. New York: Oxford University Press.

Malle, B. F., and Ickes, W. (2000). Fritz Heider: Philosopher and psychologist. In G. A. Kimble and M. Wertheimer (eds.), *Portraits of Pioneers in Psychology* (volume 4, pp. 193–214*)*. Washington, D.C. and Mahwah, N.J.: American Psychological Association and Lawrence Erlbaum.

Malle, B. F., and Knobe, J. (1997a). The folk concept of intentionality. *Journal of Experimental Social Psychology* 33: 101–121.

Malle, B. F., and Knobe, J. (1997b). Which behaviors do people explain? A basic actor–observer asymmetry. *Journal of Personality and Social Psychology* 72: 288–304.

Malle, B. F., and Knobe, J. (2001). The distinction between desire and intention: A folk-conceptual analysis. In B. F. Malle, L. J. Moses, and D. A. Baldwin (eds.), *Intentions and Intentionality: Foundations of Social Cognition* (pp. 45–67). Cambridge, Mass.: The MIT Press.

Malle, B. F., Knobe, J., and Nelson, S. (2004). *Actor–observer Asymmetries in Folk Explanations of Behavior: New Answers to an Old Question.* Manuscript under revision.

Malle, B. F., Knobe, J., O'Laughlin, M., Pearce, G. E., and Nelson, S. E. (2000). Conceptual structure and social functions of behavior explanations: Beyond person–situation attributions. *Journal of Personality and Social Psychology* 79: 309–326.

Malle, B. F., Moses, L. J., and Baldwin, D. A. (2001a). The significance of intentionality. In B. F. Malle, L. J. Moses, and D. A. Baldwin (eds.), *Intentions and Intentionality: Foundations of Social Cognition* (pp. 1–24). Cambridge, Mass.: The MIT Press.

Malle, B. F., Moses, L. J., and Baldwin, D. A. (eds.). (2001b). *Intentions and Intentionality: Foundations of Social Cognition.* Cambridge, Mass.: The MIT Press.

Malle, B. F., and Nelson, S. E. (2003). Judging *mens rea:* The tension between folk concepts and legal concepts of intentionality. *Behavioral Sciences and the Law* 21: 1–18.

Malle, B. F., and Pearce, G. E. (2001). Attention to behavioral events during social interaction: Two actor–observer gaps and three attempts to close them. *Journal of Personality and Social Psychology* 81: 278–294.

Malone, B. E., and DePaulo, B. M. (2001). Measuring sensitivity to deception. In J. A. Hall and F. J. Bernieri (eds.), *Interpersonal Sensitivity: Theory and Measurement* (pp. 103–124). Mahwah, N.J.: Lawrence Erlbaum.

Mameli, M. (2001). Mindreading, mindshaping, and evolution. *Biology and Philosophy* 16: 567–628.

Margolis, J. (1991). The autonomy of folk psychology. In J. D. Greenwood (ed.), *The Future of Folk Psychology: Intentionality and Cognitive Science* (pp. 242–262). Cambridge: Cambridge University Press.

McArthur, L. Z. (1972). The how and what of why: Some determinants and consequences of causal attribution. *Journal of Personality and Social Psychology* 22: 171–193.

McArthur, L. Z., and Post, D. L. (1977). Figural emphasis and person perception. *Journal of Experimental Social Psychology* 13: 520–535.

McCabe, A., and Peterson, C. (1988). A comparison of adults' versus children's spontaneous use of *because* and *so*. *Journal of Genetic Psychology* 149: 257–268.

McClelland, D. C. (1987). *Human Motivation*. New York: Cambridge University Press.

McClure, J. (2002). Goal-based explanations of actions and outcomes. In W. Stroebe and M. Hewstone (eds.), *European Review of Social Psychology* (volume 12, pp. 201–235). New York: Wiley.

McClure, J., and Hilton, D. (1997). For you can't always get what you want: When preconditions are better explanations than goals. *British Journal of Social Psychology* 36: 223–240.

McClure, J., and Hilton, D. (1998). Are goals or preconditions better explanations? It depends on the question. *European Journal of Social Psychology* 28: 897–911.

McClure, J., Hilton, D. J., Cowan, J., Ishida, L., and Wilson, M. (2001). When people explain difficult actions, is the causal question how or why? *Journal of Language and Social Psychology* 20: 339–357.

McClure, J., Lalljee, M., and Jaspars, J. (1991). Explanations of extreme and moderate events. *Journal of Research in Personality* 25: 146–166.

McClymont, K. (2002). The end of a tampon affair. *Sydney Morning Herald,* March 2, p. 24.

McConnell, A. R., Sherman, S. J., and Hamilton, D. L. (1994). On-line and memory-based aspects of individual and group target judgments. *Journal of Personality and Social Psychology* 67: 173–185.

McConnell, A. R., Sherman, S. J., and Hamilton, D. L. (1997). Target entitativity: Implications for information processing about individual and group targets. *Journal of Personality and Social Psychology* 72: 750–762.

McGill, A. L. (1989). Context effects in judgments of causation. *Journal of Personality and Social Psychology* 57: 189–200.

McGill, A. L., and Klein, J. G. (1993). Contrastive and counterfactual reasoning in causal judgment. *Journal of Personality and Social Psychology* 64: 897–905.

McGill, A. L., and Klein, J. G. (1995). Counterfactual and contrastive reasoning in explanations for performance: Implications for gender bias. In N. J. Roese and J. M. Olson (eds.), *What Might Have Been: The Social Psychology of Counterfactual Thinking* (pp. 333–351). Mahwah, N.J.: Lawrence Erlbaum.

McManus, J. F. (1994). *Americans Have a Right to Know about the Council on Foreign Relations.* Retrieved on April 19, 2003, from <http://jbs.org/student/focus/conspiracy/righttoknow_cfr.htm>.

Medin, D. L., and Ortony, A. (1989). Psychological essentialism. In S. Vosniadou and A. Ortony (eds.), *Similarity and Analogical Reasoning* (pp. 179–195). New York: Cambridge University Press.

Mele, A. R. (1992). *Springs of Action: Understanding Intentional Behavior.* New York: Oxford University Press.

Mele, A. R. (2001). Acting intentionally: Probing folk notions. In B. F. Malle, L. J. Moses, and D. A. Baldwin (eds.), *Intentions and Intentionality: Foundations of Social Cognition* (pp. 27–44). Cambridge, Mass.: The MIT Press.

Meltzoff, A. N. (1995). Understanding the intentions of others: Re-enactment of intended acts by 18-month-old children. *Developmental Psychology* 31: 838–850.

Meltzoff, A. N., and Brooks, R. (2001). "Like me" as a building block for understanding other minds: Bodily acts, attention, and intention. In B. F. Malle, L. J. Moses, and D. A. Baldwin (eds.), *Intentions and Intentionality: Foundations of Social Cognition* (pp. 171–191). Cambridge, Mass.: The MIT Press.

Meltzoff, A. N., and Moore, M. K. (1977). Imitation of facial and manual gestures by human neonates. *Science* 198: 75–78.

Meltzoff, A. N., and Moore, M. K. (1989). Imitation in newborn infants: Exploring the range of gestures imitated and the underlying mechanisms. *Developmental Psychology* 25: 954–962.

Menon, T., Morris, M. W., Chiu, C.-Y., and Hong, Y.-Y. (1999). Culture and the construal of agency: Attribution to individual versus group dispositions. *Journal of Personality and Social Psychology* 76: 701–717.

Miller, D. T., and Ross, M. (1975). Self-serving biases in the attribution of causality: Fact or fiction? *Psychological Bulletin* 82: 213–225.

Milligan, D. (1980). *Reasoning and the Explanation of Actions.* Sussex: Harvester Press.

Mills, C. W. (1940). Situated actions and vocabularies of motive. *American Sociological Review* 5: 904–913.

Mills, D. L., Coffey-Corina, S. A., and Neville, H. J. (1994). Variability in cerebral organization during primary language acquisition. In G. Dawson and K. W. Fischer (eds.), *Human Behavior and the Developing Brain* (pp. 427–455). New York: Guilford Press.

Mischel, W., Ebbesen, E. B., and Raskoff–Zeiss, A. (1972). Cognitive and attentional mechanisms in delay of gratification. *Journal of Personality and Social Psychology* 21: 204–218.

Mitchell, P. (1997). *Introduction to Theory of Mind: Children, Autism, and Apes.* New York: St. Martin's Press.

Mithen, S. (1996). *The Prehistory of the Mind.* London: Thames and Hudson.

Moerman, D. E. (2002). *Meaning, Medicine, and the "Placebo Effect."* New York: Cambridge University Press.

Monson, T. C., and Snyder, M. (1976). Actors, observers, and the attribution process: Toward a reconceptualization. *Journal of Experimental Social Psychology* 13: 89–111.

Moravcsik, J. M. E. (1998). *Meaning, Creativity, and the Partial Inscrutability of the Human Mind.* Stanford, Calif.: CSLI Publications.

Morris, M. W., Menon, T., and Ames, D. R. (2001). Culturally conferred conceptions of agency: A key to social perception of persons, groups, and other actors. *Personality and Social Psychology Review* 5: 169–182.

Morris, M. W., and Peng, K. (1994). Culture and cause: American and Chinese attributions for social and physical events. *Journal of Personality and Social Psychology* 67: 949–971.

Moscovici, S. (2001). *Social Representations: Explorations in Social Psychology.* New York: New York University Press.

Moses, L. J. (2001). Some thoughts on ascribing complex intentional concepts to young children. In B. F. Malle, L. J. Moses, and D. A. Baldwin (eds.), *Intentions and Intentionality: Foundations of Social Cognition* (pp. 69–83). Cambridge, Mass.: The MIT Press.

Moses, L. J., and Chandler, M. (1992). Traveler's guide to children's theories of mind. *Psychological Inquiry* 3: 286–301.

Mullen, B., and Riordan, C. A. (1988). Self-serving attributions for performance in naturalistic settings: A meta-analytic review. *Journal of Applied Social Psychology* 18: 3–22.

Mundy, P., and Neal, A. R. (2001). Neural plasticity, joint attention, and a transactional social-orienting model of autism. In L. M. Glidden (ed.), *International Review of Research in Mental Retardation: Autism* (volume 23, pp. 139–168). San Diego, Calif.: Academic Press.

Mundy, P., and Sigman, M. (1989). The theoretical implications of joint-attention deficits in autism. *Development and Psychopathology* 1: 173–183.

Mundy, P., Sigman, M., and Kasari, C. (1990). A longitudinal study of joint attention and language development in autistic children. *Journal of Autism and Developmental Disorders* 20: 115–128.

Nelson, S. E. (2003). Setting the story straight: A study of discrepant accounts of conflict and their convergence. Unpublished doctoral dissertation, University of Oregon.

Nelson, S., and Malle, B. F. (2004). *Self-serving Biases in Explanations of Intentional behavior.* Manuscript in preparation, University of Oregon.

Nelson-LeGall, S. A. (1985). Motive–outcome matching and outcome foreseeability: Effects on attribution of intentionality and moral judgments. *Developmental Psychology* 21: 323–337.

Newman, L. S., and Uleman, J. S. (1989). Spontaneous trait inference. In J. S. Uleman, and J. A. Bargh (eds.), *Unintended Thought* (pp. 155–188). New York: Guilford.

Nickerson, R. S. (1999). How we know—and sometimes misjudge—what others know: Imputing one's own knowledge to others. *Psychological Bulletin* 125: 737–759.

Nisbett, R. E. (1980). The trait construct in lay and professional psychology. In L. Festinger (ed.), *Retrospections on Social Psychology* (pp. 109–113). New York: Oxford University Press.

Nisbett, R. E., Caputo, C., Legant, P., and Marecek, J. (1973). Behavior as seen by the actor and as seen by the observer. *Journal of Personality and Social Psychology* 27: 154.

Nisbett, R. E., and Ross, L. D. (1980). *Human Inference: Strategies and Shortcomings of Social Judgment.* Englewood Cliffs, N.J.: Prentice-Hall.

Norem, J. K. (2001). *The Positive Power of Negative Thinking: Using Defensive Pessimism to Manage Anxiety and Perform at Your Peak.* New York: Basic Books.

O'Laughlin, M. J., and Malle, B. F. (2002). How people explain actions performed by groups and individuals. *Journal of Personality and Social Psychology* 82: 33–48.

Orbell, J. M., Morikawa, T., Hartwig, J., Hanley, J., and Allen, N. (in press). "Machiavellian" intelligence as a basis for the evolution of cooperative dispositions. *American Political Science Review.*

Orbuch, T. L. (1997). People's accounts count: The sociology of accounts. *Annual Review of Sociology* 23: 455–478.

Orbuch, T. L., Harvey, J., Davis, S., and Merbach, N. (1994). Account-making and confiding as acts of meaning in response to sexual assault. *Journal of Family Violence* 9: 249–264.

Origgi, G., and Sperber, D. (2000). Evolution, communication, and the proper function of language. In P. Carruthers and A. Chamberlain (eds.), *Evolution and the Human*

Mind: Modularity, Language, and Meta-Cognition (pp. 140–169). New York: Cambridge University Press.

Ostrom, T. (1984). The sovereignty of social cognition. In R. S. Wyer, Jr., and T. K. Srull (eds.), *Handbook of Social Cognition* (pp. 1–38). Hillsdale, N.J.: Lawrence Erlbaum.

Pandey, J., Sinha, Y., Prakash, A., and Tripathi, R. C. (1982). Right–Left political ideologies and attribution of the causes of poverty. *European Journal of Social Psychology* 12: 327–331.

Perner, J. (1991). *Understanding the Representational Mind*. Cambridge, Mass.: The MIT Press.

Peterson, C. (1991). The meaning and measurement of explanatory style. *Psychological Inquiry* 2: 1–10.

Peterson, C. C. (2001). Influence of siblings' perspectives on theory of mind. *Cognitive Development* 15: 435–455.

Peterson, C., Schulman, P., Castellon, C., and Seligman, M. E. P. (1991). The explanatory style scoring manual. In C. P. Smith (ed.), *Thematic Content Analysis for Motivation and Personality Research* (pp. 383–392). New York: Cambridge University Press.

Peterson, C. C., and Siegal, M. (2000). Insights into theory of mind from deafness and autism. *Mind and Language* 15: 123–145.

Pettigrew, T. F. (1979). The ultimate attribution error: Extending Allport's cognitive analysis of prejudice. *Personality and Social Psychology Bulletin* 5: 461–476.

Phillips, A. T., Wellman, H. M., and Spelke, E. S. (2002). Infants' ability to connect gaze and emotional expression to intentional action. *Cognition* 85: 53–78.

Piaget, J. (1965). *The Moral Judgment of the Child*. M. Gabain, trans. New York: Free Press. (Original work published 1932.)

Plous, S. (1993). *The Psychology of Judgment and Decision Making*. New York: McGraw-Hill.

Povinelli, D. J. (1996). Chimpanzee theory of mind: The long road to strong inference. In P. Carruthers and P. K. Smith (eds.), *Theories of Theories of Mind* (pp. 243–329). Cambridge: Cambridge University Press.

Povinelli, D. J. (2000). *Folk Physics for Apes: The Chimpanzee's Theory of How the World Works*. New York: Oxford University Press.

Povinelli, D. J. (2001). On the possibilities of detecting intentions prior to understanding them. In B. F. Malle, L. J. Moses, and D. A. Baldwin (eds.), *Intentions and Intentionality: Foundations of Social Cognition* (pp. 225–248). Cambridge, Mass.: The MIT Press.

Povinelli, D. J., and Eddy, T. J. (1996a). What young chimpanzees know about seeing. *Monographs of the Society for Research in Child Development* 61 (2): 247.

Povinelli, D. J., and Eddy, T. J. (1996b). Chimpanzees: Joint visual attention. *Psychological Science* 7: 129–135.

Povinelli, D. J., Nelson, K. E., and Boysen, S. T. (1990). Inferences about guessing and knowing in chimpanzees (*Pan troglodytes*). *Journal of Comparative Psychology* 104: 203–210.

Povinelli, D. J., Nelson, K. E., and Boysen, S. T. (1992). Comprehension of role reversal in chimpanzees: evidence of empathy? *Animal Behaviour* 43: 633–640.

Pratto, F., and John, O. P. (1991). Automatic vigilance: The attention-grabbing power of negative social information. *Journal of Personality and Social Psychology* 61: 380–391.

Premack, D. (1988). "Does the chimpanzee have a theory of mind?" revisited. In R. W. Byrne and A. Whiten (eds.), *Machiavellian Intelligence. Social Expertise and the Evolution of Intellect in Monkeys, Apes, and Humans* (pp. 160–179). New York: Oxford University Press.

Premack, D. (1990). The infant's theory of self-propelled objects. *Cognition* 36: 1–16.

Premack, D., and Premack, A. J. (1995). Intention as psychological cause. In D. Sperber, D. Premack, and A. J. Premack (eds.), *Causal Cognition: A Multidisciplinary Debate* (pp. 185–199). New York: Clarendon.

Premack, D., and Woodruff, G. (1978). Does the chimpanzee have a theory of mind? *Behavioral and Brain Sciences* 1: 515–526.

Propaganda (2002). *Examples. John Birch Society.* Retrieved February 16, 2004, from <http://www.propagandacritic.com/articles/examples.birch.html>.

Pyszczynski, T. A., and Greenberg, J. (1981). Role of disconfirmed expectancies in the instigation of attributional processing. *Journal of Personality and Social Psychology* 40: 31–38.

Quattrone, G. A. (1982). Overattribution and unit formation: When behavior engulfs the person. *Journal of Personality and Social Psychology* 42: 593–607.

Quattrone, G. A. (1985). On the congruity between internal states and action. *Psychological Bulletin* 98: 3–40.

Raffman, D. (1999). What autism may tell us about self-awareness: A commentary on Frith and Happé. *Mind and Language* 14: 23–31.

Ramsey, F. P. (1931). *The Foundations of Mathematics and Other Logical Essays.* New York: Harcourt, Brace.

Read, S. J. (1987). Constructing causal scenarios: A knowledge structure approach to causal reasoning. *Journal of Personality and Social Psychology* 52: 288–302.

Read, S. J., Druian, P. R., and Miller, L. C. (1989). The role of causal sequence in the meaning of actions. *British Journal of Social Psychology* 28: 341–351.

Read, S. J., Jones, D. K., and Miller, L. C. (1990). Traits as goal-based categories: The importance of goals in the coherence of dispositional categories. *Journal of Personality and Social Psychology* 58: 1048–1061.

Read, S. J., and Miller, L. C. (1998). On the dynamic construction of meaning: An interactive activation and competition model of social perception. In S. J. Read and L. C. Miller (eds.), *Connectionist Models of Social Reasoning and Social Behavior* (pp. 27–68). Mahwah, N.J.: Lawrence Erlbaum.

Reeder, G. D., Kumar, S., Hesson–McInnis, M. S., and Trafimow, D. (2002). Inferences about the morality of an aggressor: The role of perceived motive. *Journal of Personality and Social Psychology* 83: 789–803.

Reicher, S. D., Hopkins, N., and Condor, S. (1997). Stereotype construction as a strategy of influence. In R. Spears, P. J. Oakes, N. Ellemers, and S. A. Haslam (eds.), *The Social Psychology of Stereotyping and Group Life* (pp. 94–118). Oxford: Blackwell.

Rizzolatti, G., Fadiga, L., Fogassi, L., and Gallese, V. (2002). From mirror neurons to imitation: Facts and speculations. In A. N. Meltzoff and W. Prinz (eds.), *The Imitative Mind: Development, Evolution, and Brain Bases* (pp. 247–266). New York, N.Y.: Cambridge University Press.

Rizzolatti, G., Fadiga, L., Gallese, V., and Fogassi, L. (1996). Premotor cortex and the recognition of motor actions. *Cognitive Brain Research* 3: 131–141.

Robins, R. W., Spranca, M. D., and Mendelsohn, G. A. (1996). The actor–observer effect revisited: Effects of individual differences and repeated social interactions on actor and observer attributions. *Journal of Personality and Social Psychology* 71: 375–389.

Rogers, S. (1999). An examination of the imitation deficit in autism. In J. Nadel and G. Butterworth (eds.), *Imitation in Infancy* (pp. 255–283). Cambridge: Cambridge University Press.

Rogoff, B., Paradise, R., Mejía Arauz, R., Correa–Chávez, M., and Angelillo, C. (2003). Firsthand learning through intent participation. *Annual Review of Psychology* 54: 175–203.

Rosenthal, D. M. (forthcoming). *Consciousness and Mind.* Oxford: Clarendon Press.

Ross, L. (1977). The intuitive psychologist and his shortcomings: Distortions in the attribution process. In L. Berkowitz (ed.), *Advances in Experimental Social Psychology* (volume 10, pp. 174–221). New York: Academic Press.

Ross, L. D., Amabile, T. M., and Steinmetz, J. L. (1977). Social roles, social control, and biases in social perception processes. *Journal of Personality and Social Psychology* 35: 485–494.

Ross, L., Greene, D., and House, P. (1977). The "false-consensus effect": An egocentric bias in social perception and attribution processes. *Journal of Experimental Social Psychology* 13: 279–301.

Ross, M., and Fletcher, G. J. O. (1985). Attribution and social perception. In G. Lindsey and E. Aronson (eds.), *The Handbook of Social Psychology* (volume 2, pp. 73–114). New York: Random House.

Rothbart, M., and John, O. P. (1985). Social categorization and behavioral episodes: A cognitive analysis of the effects of intergroup contact. *Journal of Social Issues* 41: 81–104.

Rothbart, M., and Park, B. (in press). The mental representation of social categories: Category boundaries, entitativity, and stereotype change. In V. Yzerbyt, C. M. Judd, and O. Corneille (eds.), *The Psychology of Group Perception: Contributions to the Study of Homogeneity, Entitativity, and Essentialism.* Philadelphia, Penn.: Psychology Press.

Rothbart, M., and Taylor, M. (1992). Category labels and social reality: Do we view social categories as natural kinds? In G. R. Semin and K. Fiedler (eds.), *Language, Interaction and Social Cognition* (pp. 11–36). London: Sage.

Rudolph, U., and Försterling, F. (1997). The psychological causality implicit in verbs: A review. *Psychological Bulletin* 121: 192–218.

Ruffman, T., Perner, J., Naito, M., Parkin, L., and Clements, W. A. (1998). Older (but not younger) siblings facilitate false belief understanding. *Developmental Psychology* 34: 161–174.

Ruffman, T., Perner, J., and Parkin, L. (1999). How parenting style affects false belief understanding. *Social Development* 8: 395–411.

Russell, E. W., and D'Hollosy, M. E. (1992). Memory and attention. *Journal of Clinical Psychology* 48: 530–538.

Russell, J. (1996). *Agency: Its Role in Mental Development.* Hove: Erlbaum.

Russon, A. E. (1997). Exploiting the expertise of others. In A. Whiten and R. W. Byrne (eds.), *Machiavellian Intelligence II: Extensions and Evaluations* (pp. 174–206). New York: Cambridge University Press.

Russon, A. E., Mitchell, R. W., Lefebvre, L., and Abravanel, E. (1998). The comparative evolution of imitation. J. Langer and M. Killen (eds.), *Piaget, Evolution, and Development* (pp. 103–143). Mahwah, N.J.: Lawrence Erlbaum.

Sacks, O. (1995). An anthropologist on Mars. In O. Sacks, *An Anthropologist on Mars* (pp. 244–296). New York: Vintage Books.

Sagar, H. A., and Schofield, J. W. (1980). Racial and behavioral cues in black and white children's perceptions of ambiguously aggressive acts. *Journal of Personality and Social Psychology* 39: 590–598.

Sarfati, Y. (2000). Theory-of-mind deficit in schizophrenia: Clinical rereading and review of experimental arguments. *Canadian Journal of Psychiatry—Revue Canadienne de Psychiatrie* 45: 363–368.

Savage-Rumbaugh, E. S. (1984). *Pan paniscus and Pan troglodytes.* Contrasts in preverbal communicative competence. In R. L. Susman (ed.), *The Pygmy Chimpanzee* (pp. 131–177). New York: Plenum Press.

Savage-Rumbaugh, E. S., Murphy, J., Sevcik, R. A., Brakke, K. E., Williams, S. L., and Rumbaugh, D. M. (1993). Language comprehension in ape and child. *Monographs of the Society for Research in Child Development* 58(3–4), number 233.

Savage-Rumbaugh, S., and Lewin, R. (1994). *Kanzi: The Ape at the Brink of the Human Mind.* New York: Wiley.

Schank, R. C., and Abelson, R. P. (1977). *Scripts, Plans, Goals and Understanding: An Inquiry into Human Knowledge Structures.* Hillsdale, N.J.: Lawrence Erlbaum.

Schlenker, B. R. (1980). *Impression Management: The Self-Concept, Social Identity, and Interpersonal Relations.* Monterey, Calif.: Brooks/Cole.

Schlenker, B. R., and Weigold, M. F. (1992). Interpersonal processes involving impression regulation and management. *Annual Review of Psychology* 43: 133–168.

Schober, M. F. (1998). Different kinds of conversational perspective-taking. In S. R. Fussell and R. J. Kreuz (eds.), *Social and Cognitive Approaches to Interpersonal Communication* (pp. 145–174). Mahwah, N.J.: Lawrence Erlbaum.

Schober, M. F., and Clark, H. H. (1989). Understanding by addressees and overhearers. *Cognitive Psychology* 21: 211–232.

Schoeneman, T. J., and Rubanowitz, D. E. (1985). Attributions in the advice columns: Actors and observers, causes and reasons. *Personality and Social Psychology Bulletin* 11: 315–325.

Schueler, G. F. (1989). *The Idea of a Reason for Acting: A Philosophical Argument.* Lewiston, N.Y.: The Edwin Mellen Press.

Schueler, G. F. (2001). Action explanations: Causes and purposes. In B. F. Malle, L. J. Moses, and D. A. Baldwin (eds.), *Intentions and Intentionality: Foundations of Social Cognition* (pp. 251–264). Cambridge, Mass.: The MIT Press.

Schult, C. A., and Wellman, H. M. (1997). Explaining human movements and actions: Children's understanding of the limits of psychological explanation. *Cognition* 62: 291–324.

Schulz, E. H. and Frercks, R. (1934). *Warum Arierparagraph? Ein Beitrag zur Judenfrage.* (Why the Aryan law? On the Jewish question.) Berlin: Verlag Neues Volk.

Scott, M. B., and Lyman, S. M. (1968). Accounts. *American Sociological Review* 33: 46–62.

Scriven, M. (1962). Explanations, predictions, and laws. In H. Feigl and G. Maxwell (eds.), *Scientific Explanation, Space, and Time* (Minnesota studies in the philosophy of science, volume 3). Minneapolis, Minn.: University of Minnesota Press.

Searle, J. R. (1969). *Speech Acts: An Essay in the Philosophy of Language.* London: Cambridge University Press.

Searle, J. R. (1983). *Intentionality: An Essay in the Philosophy of Mind.* Cambridge: Cambridge University Press.

Searle, J. R. (1990). Collective intentions and actions. In P. R. Cohen, J. Morgan, and M. E. Pollock (eds.), *Intentions in Communication* (pp. 401–415). New York: The Free Press.

Searle, J. R. (1995). *The Construction of Social Reality.* New York: Free Press.

Searle, J. R. (2001). *Rationality in Action.* Cambridge, Mass.: The MIT Press.

Seligman, M. E. P., Abramson, L. Y., Semmel, A., and Von Baeyer, C. (1979). Depressive attributional style. *Journal of Abnormal Psychology* 88: 242–247.

Semin, G. R., and Manstead, A. S. R. (1983). *The Accountability of Conduct: A Social Psychological Analysis.* New York: Academic Press.

Shafir, E., Simonson, I., and Tversky, A. (1993). Reason-based choice. *Cognition* (special issue: Reasoning and decision making) 49: 11–36.

Shaver, K. G. (1975). *An Introduction to Attribution Processes.* Cambridge, Mass.: Winthrop.

Shaver, K. G. (1985). *The Attribution of Blame: Causality, Responsibility, and Blameworthiness.* New York: Springer.

Sheldon, K. M., and Johnson, J. T. (1993). Forms of social awareness: Their frequency and correlates. *Personality and Social Psychology Bulletin* 19: 320–330.

Shibatani, M. (ed.) (1976). *The Grammar of Causative Constructions* (Syntax and Semantics 6). New York: Academic Press.

Shoda, Y., and Mischel, W. (1993). Cognitive social approach to dispositional inferences: What if the perceiver is a cognitive social theorist? *Personality and Social Psychology Bulletin* 19: 574–585.

Shultz, T. R. (1980). Development of the concept of intention. In W. A. Collins (ed.), *Development of Cognition, Affects, and Social Cognition. The Minnesota Symposium on Child Psychology* (volume 13, pp. 131–164). Hillsdale, N.J.: Lawrence Erlbaum.

Shultz, T. R. (1988). Assessing intention: A computational model. In J. W. Astington, P. L. Harris, and D. R. Olson (eds.), *Developing Theories of Mind* (pp. 341–367). New York: Cambridge University Press.

Shultz, T. R., and Mendelson, R. (1975). The use of covariation as a principle of causal analysis. *Child Development* 46: 394–399.

Shultz, T. R., and Wells, D. (1985). Judging the intentionality of action-outcomes. *Developmental Psychology* 21: 83–89.

Silverman, R. J., and Peterson, C. (1993). Explanatory style of schizophrenic and depressed outpatients. *Cognitive Therapy and Research* 17: 457–470.

Simonson, I., and Nowlis, S. M. (2000). The role of explanations and need for uniqueness in consumer decision making: Unconventional choices based on reasons. *Journal of Consumer Research* 27: 49–68.

Slugoski, B. R., Lalljee, M., Lamb, R., and Ginsburg, G. P. (1993). Attribution in conversational context: Effect of mutual knowledge on explanation-giving. *European Journal of Social Psychology* 23: 219–238.

Smith, P. K. (1996). Language and the evolution of mind-reading. In P. Carruthers and P. K. Smith (eds.), *Theories of Theories of Mind* (pp. 344–354). Cambridge: Cambridge University Press.

Sommerville, J. A. (2002). Means-end reasoning: Infants' developing ability to interpret and perform intentional actions. Unpublished doctoral dissertation, The University of Chicago.

Sperber, D. (2000). Metarepresentations in an evolutionary perspective. In D. Sperber (ed.), *Metarepresentations: A Multidisciplinary Perspective*. New York: Oxford University Press.

Sperber, D., and Wilson, D. (1986). *Relevance: Communication and Cognition*. Cambridge, Mass.: Harvard University Press.

Sperber, D., and Wilson, D. (2002). Pragmatics, modularity and mind-reading. *Mind and Language* 17: 3–23.

Spitzberg, B. H. (2001). The status of attribution theory qua theory in personal relationships. In V. Manusov and J. H. Harvey (eds.), *Attribution, Communication Behavior, and Close Relationships: Advances in Personal Relations* (pp. 353–371). New York: Cambridge University Press.

Stangor, C., and Lange, J. (1994). Mental representations of social groups: Advances in understanding stereotypes and stereotyping. *Advances in Experimental Social Psychology* 26: 357–416.

Steele, C. M. (1988). The psychology of self-affirmation: Sustaining the integrity of the self. In L. Berkowitz (ed.), *Advances in Experimental Social Psychology* (volume 21, pp. 261–302). New York: Academic Press.

Stern, D. N. (1985). *The Interpersonal World of the Infant: A View from Psychoanalysis and Developmental Psychology.* New York: Basic Books.

Stich, S., and Nichols, S. (1992). Folk psychology: Simulation or tacit theory? *Mind and Language* 7: 35–71.

Stich, S., and Ravenscroft, I. (1994). What is folk psychology? *Cognition* 50: 447–468.

Stone, J. (2001). Behavioral discrepancies and the role of construal processes in cognitive dissonance. In G. B. Moskowitz (ed.), *Cognitive Social Psychology: The Princeton Symposium on the Legacy and Future of Social Cognition* (pp. 41–58). Mahwah, N.J.: Lawrence Erlbaum.

Storms, M. D. (1973). Videotape and the attribution process: Reversing actors' and observers' points of view. *Journal of Personality Social Psychology* 27: 165–175.

Stoughton, S. (1999). Cosmetic Center continues slide; Columbia-based chain seeks bankruptcy, new leadership. *Washington Post,* April 20, p. E03.

Strum, S. C., Forster, D., and Hutchins, E. (1997). Why Machiavellian intelligence may not be Machiavellian. In A. Whiten and R. W. Byrne (eds.), *Machiavellian Intelligence II: Extensions and Evaluations* (pp. 50–85). New York: Cambridge University Press.

Sugiyama, L. S., Tooby, J., and Cosmides, L. (2002). Cross-cultural evidence of cognitive adaptations for social exchange among the Shiwiar of Ecuadorian Amazonia. *Proceedings of the National Academcy of Sciences* 99: 11537–11542.

Susskind, J., Maurer, K., Thakkar, V., Hamilton, D. L., and Sherman, J. W. (1999). Perceiving individuals and groups: Expectancies, dispositional inferences, and causal attributions. *Journal of Personality and Social Psychology* 76: 181–191.

Sutton, R. M., and McClure, J. (2001). Covariational influences on goal-based explanation: An integrative model. *Journal of Personality and Social Psychology* 80: 222–236.

Szasz, T. S. (1961). *The Myth of Mental Illness.* New York: Delta.

Tajfel, H. (1969). Cognitive aspects of prejudice. *Journal of Social Issues* 25: 79–97.

Taylor, S. E. (1983). Adjustment to threatening events: A theory of cognitive adaptation. *American Psychologist* 38: 1161–1173.

Taylor, S. E. (1991). Asymmetrical effects of positive and negative events: The mobilization-minimization hypothesis. *Psychological Bulletin* 110: 67–85.

Taylor, S. E., and Fiske, S. T. (1975). Point-of-view and perceptions of causality. *Journal of Personality and Social Psychology* 32: 439–445.

Tedeschi, J. T., and Reiss, M. (1981). Verbal strategies as impression management. In C. Antaki (ed.), *The Psychology of Ordinary Social Behaviour* (pp. 271–309). London: Academic Press.

Thagard, P. (1989). Explanatory coherence. *Behavioral and Brain Sciences* 12: 435–467.

Todorov, A., Lalljee, M., and Hirst, W. (2000). Communication context, explanation, and social judgment. *European Journal of Social Psychology* 30: 199–209.

Tomasello, M. (1996). Do apes ape? In B. G. Galef, Jr., and C. M. Heyes (eds.), *Social Learning in Animals: The Roots of Culture* (pp. 319–346). New York: Academic.

Tomasello, M. (1998a). Social cognition and the evolution of culture. In J. Langer and M. Killen (eds.), *Piaget, Evolution, and Development* (pp. 221–245). Mahwah, N.J.: Lawrence Erlbaum.

Tomasello, M. (1998b). Uniquely primate, uniquely human. *Developmental Science* 1: 1–16.

Tomasello, M., and Call, J. (1997). *Primate Cognition.* New York: Oxford University Press.

Tomasello, M., Kruger, A. C., and Ratner, H. H. (1993). Cultural learning. *Behavioral and Brain Sciences* 16: 495–552.

Tönnies, F. (2001/1887). *Community and Civil Society.* J. Harris and M. Hollis, trans. New York: Cambridge University Press. (Original work in German published in 1887.)

Trabasso, T., and Magliano, J. P. (1996). Conscious understanding during comprehension. *Discourse Processes* 21: 255–287.

Trope, Y. (1986). Identification and inferential processes in dispositional attribution. *Psychological Review* 93: 239–257.

Tuomela, R. (1995). *The Importance of Us: A Philosophical Study of Basic Social Notions.* Stanford, Calif.: Stanford University Press.

Tuomela, R., and Miller, K. (1998). We-intentions. *Philosophical Studies* 53: 115–137.

Turnbull, W. (1986). Everyday explanation: The pragmatics of puzzle resolution. *Journal for the Theory of Social Behavior* 16: 141–160.

Turnbull, W., and Slugoski, B. (1988). Conversational and linguistic processes in causal attribution. In D. J. Hilton (ed.), *Contemporary Science and Natural Explanation* (pp. 66–93). Brighton, Sussex: Harvester Press.

Uleman, J. S., Miller, F. D., Henken, V., Riley, E., and Tsemberis, S. (1981). Visual perspective or social perspective? Two failures to replicate Storms' rehearsal, and support for Monson and Snyder on actor–observer divergence. *Replications in Social Psychology* 1: 54–58.

United States Chief of Counsel for Prosecution (1946). *Nazi Conspiracy and Aggression* (volume 1). Washington, D.C.: United States Government Printing Office.

van Fraassen, B. C. (1980). *The Scientific Image*. Oxford: Oxford University Press.

Van Kleeck, M. H., Hillger, L. A., and Brown, R. (1988). Pitting verbal schemas against information variables in attribution. *Social Cognition* 6: 89–106.

Van Overwalle, F. (1998). Causal explanation as constraint satisfaction: A critique and a feedforward connectionist alternative. *Journal of Personality and Social Psychology* 74: 312–328.

von Collani, G., Kauer, A., and Kauer, S. (1991). Use and activation of social knowledge in commonsense attribution, evidence for a schema-based attribution model. *Psychological Reports* 69: 728–730.

Wason, P. C. (1968). Reasoning about a rule. *Quarterly Journal of Experimental Psychology A* 20: 273–281.

Watson, J. K. (1999). Theory of mind and pretend play in family context. Unpublished dissertation, University of Michigan.

Weary, G., and Edwards, J. A. (1994). Individual differences in causal uncertainty. *Journal of Personality and Social Psychology* 67: 308–318.

Weary, G., Edwards, J. A., and Riley, S. (1994). Attribution. *Encyclopedia of Human Behavior* (volume 1, pp. 291–299).

Weary, G., Stanley, M. A., and Harvey, J. H. (1989). *Attribution*. New York: Springer-Verlag.

Wegner, D. M. (2002). *The Illusion of Conscious Will*. Cambridge, Mass.: The MIT Press.

Weiner, B. (1979). A theory of motivation for some classroom experiences. *Journal of Educational Psychology* 71: 3–25.

Weiner, B. (1985a). An attributional theory of achievement-related emotion and motivation. *Psychological Review* 29: 548–573.

Weiner, B. (1985b). "Spontaneous" causal thinking. *Psychological Bulletin* 97: 74–84.

Weiner, B. (1986). *An Attributional Theory of Motivation and Emotion*. New York: Springer.

Weiner, B. (1995). *Judgments of Responsibility: A Foundation for a Theory of Social Conduct*. New York: Guilford.

Weiner, B., Frieze, I., Kukla, A., Reed, L., Rest, S., and Rosenbaum, R. M. (1972). Perceiving the causes of success and failure. In E. E. Jones, D. Kanouse, H. H. Kelley, R. E. Nisbett, S. Valins, and B. Weiner (eds.), *Attribution: Perceiving the Causes of Behavior* (pp. 95–120). Morristown, N.J.: General Learning Press.

Weiss, R. S. (1975). *Marital Separation.* NewYork: Basic Books.

Weisz, C., and Jones, E. E. (1993). Expectancy disconfirmation and dispositional inference: Latent strength of target-based and category-based expectancies. *Personality and Social Psychology Bulletin* 19: 563–573.

Welbourne, J. L. (1999). The impact of perceived entitivity on inconsistency resolution for groups and individuals. *Journal of Experimental Social Psychology* 35: 481–508.

Wellman, H. M. (1990). *The Child's Theory of Mind.* Cambridge, Mass.: The MIT Press.

Wellman, H. M. (1998). Culture, variation, and levels of analysis in folk psychologies: Comment on Lillard (1998). *Psychological Bulletin* 123: 33–36.

Wellman, H. M. (1993). Early understanding of mind: the normal case. In S. Baron-Cohen, H. Tager-Flusberg, and D. J. Cohen (eds.), *Understanding Other Minds: Perspectives from Autism* (pp. 10–39). Oxford: Oxford University Press.

Wellman, H. M., Hickling, A. K., and Schult, C. A. (1997). Young children's psychological, physical, and biological explanations. In H. W. Wellman and K. Inagaki (eds.), *The Emergence of Core Domains of Thought: Children's Reasoning about Physical, Psychological, and Biological Phenomena* (pp. 7–25). San Francisco, Calif.: Jossey-Bass.

Wellman, H. W., and Phillips, A. T. (2001). Developing intentional understandings. In B. F. Malle, L. J. Moses, and D. A. Baldwin (eds.), *Intentions and Intentionality: Foundations of Social Cognition* (pp. 125–148). Cambridge, Mass.: The MIT Press.

Wellman, H. M., and Woolley, J. D. (1990). From simple desires to ordinary beliefs: The early development of everyday psychology. *Cognition* 35: 245–275.

Whitaker, C. (2002). Tired of excuses. *Leader-Post,* July 24, p. B10.

White, P. (1980). Limitations on verbal reports of internal events: A refutation of Nisbett and Wilson and of Bem. *Psychological Review* 87: 105–112.

White, P. A. (1991). Ambiguity in the internal/external distinction in causal attribution. *Journal of Experimental Social Psychology* 27: 259–270.

Whiten, A. (1994). Grades of mindreading. In C. Lewis and P. Mitchell (eds.), *Children's Early Understanding of Mind: Origins and Development* (pp. 47–70). Hove: Erlbaum.

Whiten, A. (1996). When does smart behaviour reading become mind-reading? In P. Carruthers and P. K. Smith (eds.), *Theories of Theories of Mind.* Cambridge: Cambridge University Press.

Whiten, A. (1999). The evolution of deep social mind in humans. In M. C. Corballis and S. E. G. Lea (eds.), *The Descent of Mind: Psychological Perspectives on Hominid Evolution* (pp. 173–193). New York: Oxford University Press.

Whiten, A., and Byrne, R. W. (eds.). (1997). *Machiavellian Intelligence II: Extensions and Evaluations.* New York: Cambridge University Press.

Whiten, A., and Ham, R. (1992). On the nature and evolution of imitation in the animal kingdom: Reappraisal of a century of research. In P. J. B. Slater, J. S. Rosenblatt, C. Beer, and M. Milinsky (eds.), *Advances in the Study of Behavior* (pp. 239–283). New York: Academic Press.

Whorton, J. C. (2002). *Nature Cures: The History of Alternative Medicine in America.* New York: Oxford University Press.

Wilder, D. A., and Simon, A. F. (1998). Categorical and dynamic groups: Implications for social perception and intergroup behavior. In C. Sedikides, J. Schopler, and C. Insko (eds.), *Intergroup Cognition and Intergroup Behavior* (pp. 27–44). Mahwah, N.J.: Lawrence Erlbaum.

Wilkerson, W. S. (2001). Simulation, theory, and the frame problem: The interpretive moment. *Philosophical Psychology* 14: 141–153.

Williams, J. H. G., Whiten, A., Suddendorf, T., and Perrett, D. I. (2001). Imitation, mirror neurons, and autism. *Neuroscience and Biobehavioral Reviews* 25: 287–295.

Wilson, J. Q. (1997). *Moral Judgment: Does the Abuse Excuse Threaten Our Legal System?* New York: HarperCollins.

Wilson, R. A. (2001). Group-level cognition. *Philosophy of Science* 68 (proceedings): S262–S273.

Wilson, T. D., Dunn, D. S., Kraft, D., and Lisle, D. J. (1989). Introspection, attitude change, and attitude-behavior consistency: The disruptive effects of explaining why we feel the way we do. In L. Berkowitz (ed.), *Advances in Experimental Social Psychology* (volume 22, pp. 287–343). New York: Academic Press.

Wimmer, H., and Perner, J. (1983). Beliefs about beliefs: Representation and constraining function of wrong beliefs in young children's understanding of deception. *Cognition* 13: 103–128.

Wittenbrink, B., Gist, P. L, and Hilton, J. L. (1997). Structural properties of stereotypic knowledge and their influences on the construal of social situations. *Journal of Personality and Social Psychology* 72: 526–543.

Wong, P. T., and Weiner, B. (1981). When people ask "why" questions, and the heuristics of attributional search. *Journal of Personality and Social Psychology* 40: 246–259.

Woodward, A. L. (1998). Infants selectively encode the goal object of an actor's reach. *Cognition* 69: 1–34.

Woodward, A. L. (1999). Infants' ability to distinguish between purposeful and nonpurposeful behaviors. *Infant Behavior and Development* 22: 145–160.

Woodward, A. L., Sommerville, J. A., and Guajardo, J. J. (2001). How infants make sense of intentional action. In B. F. Malle, L. J. Moses, and D. A. Baldwin (eds.), *Intentions and Intentionality: Foundations of Social Cognition* (pp. 149–170). Cambridge, Mass.: The MIT Press.

Wray, A. (2000). Holistic utterances in protolanguage: The link from primates to humans. In C. Knight, M. Studdert-Kennedy, and J. R. Hurford (eds.), *The Evolutionary Emergence of Language: Social Function and the Origins of Linguistic Form* (pp. 285–302). New York: Cambridge University Press.

Wu, M., and Cheng, P. W. (1999). Why causation need not follow from statistical association: Boundary conditions for the evaluation of generative and preventive causal powers. *Psychological Science* 10: 92–97.

Yzerbyt, V., Corneille, O., and Estrada, C. (2001). The interplay of subjective essentialism and entitativity in the formation of stereotypes. *Personality and Social Psychology Review* 5: 141–155.

Yzerbyt, V., Rocher, S., and Schadron, G. (1997). Stereotypes as explanations: A subjective essentialistic view of group perception. In E. Spears and P. Oakes (eds.), *The Social Psychology of Stereotyping and Group Life* (pp. 20–50). Oxford: Blackwell.

Yzerbyt, V., Rogier, A., and Fiske, S. T. (1998). Group entitativity and social attribution: On translating situational constraints into stereotypes. *Personality and Social Psychology Bulletin* 24: 1089–1103.

Zaibert, L. A. (2003). Collective intentions and collective intentionality. *American Journal of Economics and Sociology* 62: 209–232.

Zelazo, P. D., Astington, J. W., and Olson, D. R. (eds.) (1999). *Developing Theories of Intention: Social Understanding and Self-Control.* Mahwah, N.J.: Lawrence Erlbaum.

Zimbardo, P. G. (1999). Discontinuity theory: Cognitive and social searches for rationality and normality may lead to madness. In M. P. Zanna (ed), *Advances in Experimental Social Psychology* (volume 31, pp. 345–486). San Diego, Calif.: Academic Press.

Zuckerman, M. (1978). Actions and occurrences in Kelley's cube. *Journal of Personality and Social Psychology* 36: 647–656.

Index